BUILDING YOUR LIFE

BUILDING

JUDSON T. LANDIS Associate Professor in Family Sociology

MARY G. LANDIS

YOUR LIFE

● Department of Home Economics ● University of California, Berkeley

PRENTICE-HALL, INC.
New York

First Printing . . . . . . July, 1954
Second Printing . . . . January, 1955

PREFACE

This book is written for people in their early teens. Our purpose is to offer in compact, readily usable form information and viewpoints that may help young people as they strive to make a healthy growth toward maturity in all their relationships: at home, at school, and in their community. In writing *Building Your Life* we have had before us constantly such questions as: What can we present that will help the beginning high school person to understand himself and his family? What will help him toward maturing into a well-adjusted adult who can live with himself and with others effectively? How can the young person be guided toward an understanding and appreciation of the basic philosophy of our government and the rights and duties of all Americans? How can young people be helped toward developing the good mental health that is necessary if they are to live as worthy citizens in a complex society? What thinking and learning now will later help them make wise vocational choices? All of these questions and many others have been our challenge.

The book is divided into six parts. The division of topics should meet the needs of most schools; however, sufficient teaching aids, additional readings, and other materials have been suggested so the teacher may expand any one section of the book to meet her particular needs. To illustrate: Some schools do not have a freshman or sophomore course in civics, and they may wish to expand Part Three, "Obligations." By using more films, projects, and readings from the reading list, this section of the book can be made the basis for as much study of civics and citizenship as is desired. The school that wishes to give more time to "Growing up Economically," Part Six, or to "Physical and Mental Health," Part Five, can easily expand these units by making use of all the helps and supplementary materials suggested with the units.

Self-evaluation tests have been included with each chapter to help the student understand his present development. Review questions, key words and phrases, problems and activities, socio-dramas, ideas for role playing, class surveys, special talks, films, and other aids are offered at the end of each chapter. The six parts of the book include reference lists for those who wish to read further.

We acknowledge our debt to many different people who have contributed greatly to the development of this book. The following people read the manuscript and gave us valuable criticisms and suggestions: Mrs. Marjorie Cosgrove, Director of Home and Family Life Education in the school district of Highland Park, Michigan; Helen Vaznaian, Consultant in Home Economics for the public schools, Newton, Massachusetts; Florence M. Hellman, Associate Professor of Health Education, Kent State University, Ohio; and Dr. Esther Prevey, Director of Family Life Education in the public schools of Kansas City, Missouri. The teachers of personal adjustment and family living in Hayward High School, Hayward, California, also read and criticized the manuscript and took time to discuss certain parts of it with us. We gratefully acknowledge this help from: Jack Switzer, Don Lane, Elizabeth Lee, Eleanor Sekerak, Adrian Guilford, and Herman Dubowy. We appreciate also the cooperation of Aubrey D. Laws, principal of Hayward High School, and of Herman Dubowy, Herbert Brodahl, and the students and student photographers who worked to provide us with photographs for illustrating parts of the book.

We received special help from the Coronet Instructional Films Organization. They have been generous in providing film guides and in permitting use of film guide materials.

The cover photograph is by Syl Labrot of the Shostal Press Agency.

Dr. H. H. Remmers, Director of the Purdue Opinion Panel of Purdue University, has generously permitted us to use the research data from his periodic polls of high school students from all sections of the country.

We must also acknowledge the contribution our own teen-aged children and their friends have made to the thinking and writing that has gone into this book. Their candid and perceptive observations concerning our views keep us striving for added insight and for a more tempered understanding. Their capacity for meeting life's challenges with growth and objectivity gives us confidence in the worthwhileness of offering to young people such a book as we have attempted to write here.

While acknowledging the contributions of many, we take responsibility ourselves for any misinterpretations of youthful viewpoints and for other weaknesses which may appear in the book.

Judson T. Landis
Mary G. Landis

Berkeley, California

CONTENTS

Part Three

OBLIGATIONS

Part Four

YOU AND YOUR FAMILY

Part Five

PHYSICAL AND MENTAL HEALTH

Part Six

GROWING UP ECONOMICALLY

BUILDING YOUR LIFE

Part One

ABOUT YOU

STUDYING YOURSELF

1

As you study this book, you will be studying one of the most interesting subjects in the world — yourself. In history class, you study the origin and the development of our country; in English, you work at learning how to write and to speak effectively; in mathematics, you study the use of figures and the solution of problems; and in geography, you think about the surface of the earth, its climate, its plant and animal life, and its natural and economic resources. This course is about *you* and *your resources.*

As you go through this book, you will do some thinking about what you are like and what kind of a person you hope to grow to be. You will think also about your relationships with others in your family, at school, and in your community. A good understanding of yourself will help you in getting along with your friends and your family and yourself.

Perhaps you are wondering how a class can be directed toward you, individually, and yet meet the needs of all the other people in the class. Are not our needs and problems so different that it would take a different book for each of us if we are to understand ourselves? True, each person is different in many ways. Nevertheless, in many other ways we are all close together in our problems and in our feelings about life. Certain things are important to every one of us. When hundreds of high school students listed their problems and goals in life, the majority agreed that they were concerned about the following things: success in friendships; success in school work; economic independence; a vocation; future marriage; physical and mental health; contributing to the welfare of others.

If a survey were made of the members of your class most of

● **What are your main hopes for the future?**

you would probably agree on what are the chief problems at your age and what are your main hopes for the future.

There is value for you in looking at yourself now to see whether or not you are growing into the type of person you wish to be. Early in life, each person develops ways of thinking and acting which become more and more a part of his personality as he grows older. It is easier when we are young than when we are older to change undesirable ways of thinking. Certain traits contribute to success in friendships, in a vocation, in marriage, and in all of life.

What traits are important in your personality if you are to live effectively in today's world? How can you become the person you want to be and a citizen that is needed in the world? We shall look for answers to those questions throughout the rest of this book.

Studying Yourself

REVIEW QUESTIONS

1. How is this course different from other subjects that you study?
2. Do you agree with the statement that the most interesting subject to a person is himself?
3. How is it possible to direct a course toward *you* and, at the same time, meet the needs of many other people in the class?
4. What do studies show about the concerns and goals of young people?
5. Why is there value in looking at yourself thoughtfully at your present age?

KEY WORDS AND PHRASES

goals	achieve	economic
personality	resources	majority
anonymous	relationship	traits

PROBLEMS AND ACTIVITIES

1. Make a list of five things you hope to have accomplished by ten years from now.
2. Now make a list of all the things you are doing now that will help you toward the goals you have listed above.
3. Finally, make a list of the things you are doing or not doing at present that hinder you in your plans for the future.
4. Each member of the class hand in an anonymous list of his goals in life. Have a class committee summarize the lists and copy the summary on the blackboard for class discussion.
5. Give at least one illustration to show how planning for the future has made it possible for you to achieve some goal.

Studying Yourself

ADVISOR'S COLUMN

As an activity to carry out during this course, you might like to write anonymous letters about your problems to a consultant of an imaginary newspaper. Members of the class could take turns acting on an advisory panel to discuss the different problems presented in the anonymous letters.

TO THE TEACHER

We have suggested many films to be used as a part of the work in this course. They are an important aid in teaching courses in life adjustment and social guidance. Since some schools will not have access to films we have not included in the book teaching aids for the films. We have prepared a teacher's guide for, "*Building Your Life*," which will be sent free to all teachers. This guide includes discussion questions, study activities, and detailed information on how to use each film.

If you do not have a copy, write for your copy to:

Prentice-Hall, Inc.
70 Fifth Avenue
New York 11, New York

See reading list at end of Part One, page 47.

YOUR PERSONALITY

2

You and your friends often say of someone, "He has a wonderful personality," or "She has no personality at all." Just what is personality and how is it formed?

Personality is an individual person's total make-up. Your personality includes your physical build and the way you walk, dress, and talk. It includes the way you think and all your feelings, your fears, hopes, and interests. How you get along with others, the effect other people have on you, and how you affect them are also parts of your personality.

Each personality has many sides. Both boys and girls say Jane has a good personality. Jane is friendly to everyone, cooperates with others and gets along well with classmates and with teachers. This is the side of Jane's personality that is seen at school. But how she feels about her brothers and sisters and her parents, some fears and worries that she may have, and her likes and dislikes are also important parts of her personality. It is possible that Jane's parents see a side of her personality much different from the personality her friends see. Jane at home may not be the same Jane that is known at school.

Do we have more than one personality?

You know that you act differently when you are in different situations and with different people. Does that mean that you are a Dr. Jekyll and Mr. Hyde?

No, the fact that you are so different at different times is, in itself, a part of your personality. The Ancient Romans used the word *persona* to refer to the false faces which the leading actor would wear while playing different roles in a play. When the actor

5

played the villain, he would put on a *persona* (mask) of the villain. If he were to play the hero, he would change his *persona*. From that word came our word, *personality*. Each person has many different sides to his personality and few people know us well enough to understand all the *personas* that we may, at times, wear.

● Do we have more than one personality?

Others judge our personalities

Others judge our personalities by what they see of our outward behavior. You may sometimes feel that they misjudge you and fail to understand your real thoughts and intentions. People may say of Helen, "She is snobbish and high-hat; acts as if she doesn't have time for ordinary people." But Helen may be thinking to herself, "I wish I could think of things to say to people and be easy and friendly like Margaret. If only I didn't feel so self-conscious!"

Some of the girls may call Sue a flirt because she is always so quick to strike up a conversation with any boy who comes around.

Your Personality

● How would you rate this girl's personality? Do you think your impression of her would be the same if you were on the other end of the line? Do you have a pleasing personality on the phone? *(Hayward High School.)*

But Sue, who has four brothers and no sisters, may be wishing she could get along as well with the girls as with the boys. She may feel that she always manages to say and to do the wrong thing in a group of girls and she turns to the boys for company because she is used to boys at home and finds it easier to talk to them.

Others may see Peter as loud and noisy, always creating a disturbance by his talk or his actions and trying to attract attention to himself. But Peter's thoughts may be, "If only I could get seated in a classroom just once without bumping into anyone or knocking over a chair! Why does everyone watch me and make me feel so self-conscious? I can't help it if my voice is out of bounds most of the time. I just can't predict ahead of time how anything I say is going to sound."

So personality is one thing to those who can judge only by what they see in outward behavior; it may be entirely different as seen and felt by the person who lives inside and judges by his feelings and thoughts and intentions rather than by how his actions look to other people.

All of us respond to others' judgments of us. In some ways we change, according to our feelings about what others think of us. Therefore one's personality is necessarily a combination of what others think him to be and what he feels himself to be.

How personality is formed

Your personality today is what it is partly because of all the experiences you have had since you were born. Your relationships

● We want to be like others of our age.

in your family with your brothers and sisters and with your mother and father and your grandparents have contributed to your personality. The friends you have had, the part you have taken in activities at school and in church, and everything that you have done up to the present time is a part of you.

That you were born to certain parents and inherited certain traits also has something to do with how your personality has developed. The next two chapters will discuss how these different facts and experiences have influenced the growth and shaping of your personality. But first, we will look at ways in which all of us are alike.

How personalities are alike

All people are alike in that they work to satisfy certain wishes. We all want some kind of *recognition*. Bill gets recognition by being a good student, John by playing on the basketball team, and Chester by throwing chalk when the teacher is out of the room. Why each seeks recognition in the special way that he does depends upon the attitudes he has developed through his past experiences.

We all have the same wish *to be like others of our own age.* You probably feel more comfortable if you dress like your friends do. Your parents may not understand why you should wear some of the clothes that you want to wear. The fact that it is what the others wear may not seem to them to be a good reason. Your mother may object to your hair-style or the streak you bleached in your hair when that was a fad among your friends. At the same time, your mother may, herself, be careful to dress according to the styles for women of her age. And Dad would not be caught wearing a bow tie or a plaid jacket unless the other men he knows were wearing them too. Your parents are like you in that they wish to be like others of their age rather than different from them.

You see people at times who are nonconformists. They seem to enjoy being different instead of like others. Some people who work at being different from others do so as a way of getting the recognition that they have not received in more usual ways.

All people are alike in their strong need for *security.* Security is one's feeling that he can safely depend upon the love and protection of others who are close to him. Your feelings of security grow from all the relationships within your family and from the

● The feeling of being loved is as important to the personality growth of the baby as food is for physical growth. *(Luoma Photos.)*

fact that your father and mother loved you and worked to support you. If your need for security has been met, you are likely to have confidence in others, to trust them, and to see the good in them. You feel no need to gossip about other people and to point out their weaknesses.

Another wish is for *new experience or adventure.* The small child explores his body, later he explores the house and everything in it, and still later he takes the clock or his mechanical toys apart to find out what makes them run. At your age, you like to go to new places and to see and do new things.

One other great need of all of us is to *have friends.* We need the satisfaction that comes with being able to associate with others who like us and whom we enjoy being with.

● What effect do I have on other people? How can I understand my own personality? *(Hayward High School.)*

Getting acquainted with your personality

It is easier for a person to live comfortably if he understands himself well enough to have some idea of why he feels toward others as he does and how his feelings affect his behavior. Most of us have some personality traits that hinder us in making and holding friends or that cause us to have difficulty with brothers and sisters. No personality is perfect. Up to now, you have been growing out

● Why is it that some people find friendliness in other people wherever they go and others find people to be unfriendly? *(Hayward High School.)*

of your infancy and childhood. Now you are entering a different stage in life. From now on you can work to develop qualities that will help in your relationships with other people.

Steps in getting acquainted with your personality

One good way to understand yourself is to study the effect you have upon others. Are other people friendly to you? Do they seem happy to have you in a group? Do you feel welcome among others?

A woman whose husband's work forced them to move about often, complained, "We've lived in a dozen towns, and people are the same everywhere. They are never friendly or thoughtful to strangers. Wherever we go, I am alone and friendless."

Another woman under the same circumstances said, "One of the good things about having to move about so much is that I get to know so many interesting people. I have found that everywhere we go people are wonderful. They go out of their way to be friendly to a stranger. It is impossible to feel alone for long."

Is it possible that the two women had met two opposite kinds of people? Or were the differences in the women themselves?

That is what we mean when we say that you can begin to understand yourself better by studying the way others seem to behave toward you. As you figure yourself out, you can begin to form new habits in your behavior around others. At home, are you thoughtful

MY PERSONALITY

	Never	Some-times	Usually	Always
	0	4	7	10
1. I try to get recognition in ways that are approved at school.				
2. I feel comfortable with people and enjoy their company.				
3. I feel that people are friendly to me.				
4. Others seem to be happy to have me in their groups.				
5. At home I am thoughtful of the interests of others.				
6. I try to see that others have a good time.				
7. I say good things or nothing about other people.				
8. I like the community we live in.				
9. I feel I can trust those about me.				
10. I satisfy my desires for new experiences in ways that my parents approve of.				

Total each column

Total points

of the interests of your family? Do you demand attention and services from other family members? Do you *use* your friends or do you try to think of their wishes and interests?

It will help you also if you will study the effect your friends have upon others in a group. You may notice, for example, that whenever Hannah is in a group, the conversation usually drifts to gossiping and belittling others who are not present. Why do some of your friends follow her leadership in conversation? Why do others avoid her? What other traits does she have that make friends for her in spite of her faults? Does observing Hannah or Bill make you think of some of your own habits you want to break or of new ones you need to form?

It will help you also to understand yourself if you will try to look as an outsider would look, at your own parents and family. The next chapter will consider the subject of how your family, your friends and all your associates contribute to your personality growth.

REVIEW QUESTIONS

1. Could the statement be true that 'John has no personality'?
2. How do you define *personality?*
3. What is the origin of the word *personality?*
4. Why do people seem to have more than one personality?
5. How do others judge our personalities? Why do others sometimes misjudge our personalities?
6. What things contribute to making a personality?
7. In what ways are we all alike in our wishes?
8. If we all want to be like others why are some people so different?
9. What is meant by the need to feel secure?
10. Why is it important for you to understand your personality?
11. What steps can you take in order to get acquainted with your own personality?

KEY WORDS AND PHRASES

personality
behavior
self-conscious
persona

wish for recognition
wish for new experience
need for security
inherited

nonconformist
gossiping
cooperation
judgment

PROBLEMS AND ACTIVITIES

1. Ask five different students in school what they mean by *personality*.

2. Make a list of at least five desirable ways in which one may get recognition.

3. Make a list of at least five doubtful or undesirable ways in which some people get recognition.

4. List several ways in which young people show they have a desire for new experience and adventure.

5. List several ways in which boys and girls, or men and women, show that they want to be like others of their age.

FILM

Improve Your Personality — 10 minutes, sound, Coronet
See reading list at end of Part One, page 47.

YOUR ENVIRONMENT AND YOUR PERSONALITY

3

Your personality has been greatly affected by the environment you have lived in since you were born. Your environment is formed by your family, neighborhood, friends, school, church and community — all your surroundings from birth until now. Even before you were born, in the months when you were growing toward birth, your environment affected your physical growth and so contributed elements of your future personality.

Your family and your habits and ways

From the day you were born, the way your family has treated you has influenced your personality growth. As a baby, you had a strong need to be loved by your mother and others. If you were given plenty of affection, you knew you were loved and wanted, and the way your personality grew in response to this love may be compared to the way your body grew through getting proper food. But no parents can be perfect in the way they care for their babies; emotional needs are not always met. If early emotional needs are not met by the family, people may develop different types of personalities and may have some handicaps to overcome as they grow older. All of us have some handicaps that we have to work to overcome. If some of the baby's needs are not met well enough, the baby fights in different ways in order to get the response he needs and wants from those around him. He may learn to throw temper tantrums or he may refuse to eat. In such ways, he forces his parents to concentrate their attention upon him. Habits developed early may become a permanent part of the personality. You have known grown men and women who, at times, have temper tantrums, habits formed in early childhood.

15

● The environment in which you live will influence your personality. *(Chicago Housing Authority and Luoma Photos.)*

Anger. When babies fail to get what they want they can only respond by showing anger. If, even after you were no longer a baby, you found that anger worked well as a means of getting your own way about things, you may have developed the pattern of "letting yourself go" in anger whenever denied anything. You may believe that you were just born with a violent temper like your Uncle Herbert's. Even your family may support that idea and fail to realize that although anger is an emotion, to let one's self go and be controlled by the emotion of anger is a habit that can be broken.

For example: Carol often gave way to anger at home when things failed to go her way. She felt that the only way she ever really made an impression on her parents and got what she wanted was to have a violent temper tantrum. Carol's family took her hot temper for granted as a natural part of her personality. But Carol had learned by experience while she was still a very small child that people outside her family were not so impressed by her temper. She has long since stopped letting her anger control her actions when she is not at home. She knows that she gets along much better with friends if she controls herself and tries to be reasonable.

By letting Carol continue to get her own way at home through temper spells, her parents have not helped her personality growth. She has learned for herself that temper does not do her any good away from home. Perhaps as she becomes more mature, she may also figure out for herself that even at home there are much better ways of handling problems than by flying into a rage. Carol is at the age now where she must grow up mainly under her own power. It will not help her to blame her parents for bad habits she has developed, even if her parents are partly at fault. Carol must replace this socially unacceptable habit of anger with new and better ways if she wishes to have friends.

● The two-year-old uses temper to control the people around her. Do you sometimes see two-year-old behavior in people who are many years older? (Luoma Photos.)

● We get our habits and ways from our family.

Likes and dislikes, prejudices. Most of us like to think that we are independent in the things we like or do not like, that we make up our own minds on these things without anyone's influence. But that is not the case. Can you think of certain foods that you are sure you dislike, but that perhaps you have never tasted? Are you the only one in your family with that special dislike? Food dislikes are the most common example of how we learn likes and dislikes from our parents. Jerry says even the thought of eating fish is almost sickening to him. His father has an allergy to many kinds of sea food, so sea foods are never served in their home. Jerry does not have any allergy, but he dislikes all sea foods so much that he will not taste them even to be polite if they are offered to him when he eats in the home of a friend.

Unreasonable food dislikes are a small matter compared to some of the other feelings that we may absorb from our environment. Hatreds and prejudices are easily "caught" when children are small. To be prejudiced against someone is to "prejudge" them; that is, to form an opinion without having any real facts upon which to base the opinion, in the way that an unfair judge might hand down a decision against a prisoner without allowing any evidence to be presented in the prisoner's defense.

You may be prejudiced against people of certain political parties, or certain religious faiths or races, without ever, up to now, having stopped to figure out the basis for your feelings. If your father is a loyal Democrat, you may believe that the Republicans would ruin the country; or if he is a staunch Republican, you probably have, yourself, some strong feelings about Democrats.

In a later chapter, we will think further about prejudices and what you can do about them.

Cooperativeness. Do you like to help others and to cooperate in work and play activities with others? If you do, your family has helped to develop this characteristic in you. Perhaps your parents work together and when you were small, they made you a part of the family team. They encouraged you to play in games. They helped you to see the other person's point of view.

If you have difficulty playing the game in work or play, perhaps you have had things your own way too much. But, as in the case of anger, although your family may have let you grow in certain ways, the best thing you can do now is to try to work to develop in yourself the traits that you know are desirable. It does no good now to blame parents or family.

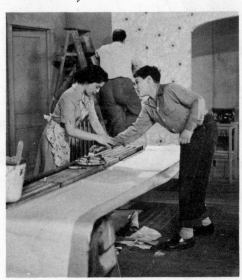

● Cooperation begins at home. Are you a cooperative person? *(Coronet Films.)*

Selfishness. A baby is entirely selfish. He is self-centered and has no thought at all for the other person. As the baby grows, he usually outgrows some of his self-centeredness and learns that others have needs too. As an adult, he will have learned not to show outwardly the self-centeredness that still remains. However, you have probably seen children and grown people who are as selfish and self-centered as small babies. Their bodies have grown, physically they look like adults; but in their emotional behavior they remain babies. A part of growing up is learning to develop at least a measure of other-centeredness, that is, thinking of the other person and his interests rather than of one's own interests only.

● A part of growing up is to overcome selfishness.

Religion. Most people receive or learn their religion from their families. It is likely, if you never go tc church, that you come from a home in which your parents are not churchgoers. If you are Catholic, you were probably born into a Catholic home, and you accept the Catholic faith as the true faith, just as you accept eating three meals a day and washing before each meal as right. If your family is of the Protestant or Jewish faith, then you just as readily accept the faith of your family as the true and right faith.

● Your religious beliefs and your interest in religion are a part of your family pattern. *(Coronet Films.)*

Attitudes about money. You are learning to value money in the same way that your parents value money. You may say, "But what do you mean? How could there be more than one way of valuing money?" People differ greatly in their attitudes about money. Sometimes two people marry and later find that they have a terrible time agreeing on how their money should be used. Each thinks of money in ways that he has learned from his parents, but the two may have learned opposite things. If your parents believe in saving money for the future, or in not buying anything until they have the cash to pay for it, you will probably grow up believing as they do. Some families cannot save money at all, no matter what their income. Others save money for the future even if they go hungry in the present.

If your family buys on the installment plan, you will probably grow up to accept this as the right way to buy things. Or their example may influence you to do the opposite. It could be that you have seen the repossession of things bought by your family on the installment plan, and you may decide that you will never buy that way when you grow up. Whether or not you do the same or the opposite from your family, you have still been influenced by your family's ideas and ways.

Manners. Up to now, you have unconsciously copied the manners of your family, and you may not change in the future. You may accept your family's manners just as you accept their politics and religion. However, you know now that what your friends think of you and of your family matters to you a great deal. You may question the table manners of your mother and father if you find that other families do things differently. We become critical of our parents, and we begin to see them as we believe our friends see them. Some people may even be oversensitive about their parents' manners or about the way their homes look. Your friends are not likely to be nearly so critical of your parents as you, yourself, may be. Whatever your feelings about your family's manners, you will be influenced by them negatively or positively.

In many other ways, your family has contributed to the growth of your personality.

Your friends and your personality

Friends, like one's family, are important to personality development. You may feel now that what your friends think of you matters far more to you than what your parents think. Your respect for the opinions of your friends helps you to work to overcome some habits you may have been allowed to develop at home — like Carol, who learned to control her temper when she realized that her friends considered temper tantrums childish. Your ideas about politics, religion, manners, and other things may be strengthened if you happen to live in a neighborhood where all other families are of the same party, religion, and economic level, and where most of your friends believe as you do. However, if your schoolmates and friends are of all religious faiths, if they hold different political and economic views, then you will begin to change in some of the attitudes you may have gained from your family.

If you have been uncooperative and selfish at home, your friends may have helped you to be less self-centered. Friends may cause us to look critically at our own manners and to begin to try to change some of our ways of acting in social situations.

What friends do, in general, for one's personality is that they tend to rub off some of the rough edges that have developed unchecked. Families may let us develop undersirable ways because they have the same ways themselves, or because they do not know how to deal with traits that they may see. But friends, playmates, and schoolmates who are not too sympathetic with weaknesses are a help at the time when most of us are willing to try to overcome our faults in order to fit into the group.

From the points discussed in this chapter, do you agree that all of your surroundings and experiences from birth until now have helped you to develop in certain directions? There has been an interplay of home, friends, and school upon your emotions, attitudes, and beliefs. Sometimes you may have felt that a pulling and hauling was going on between the influence of your friends outside your home and the influence or authority of your parents. That is often a part of growing up. Even some of that kind of conflict contributes to your personality growth.

● Friends help our personality growth if we work to overcome faults, so that we may fit into the group. *(Luoma Photos.)*

MY PERSONALITY

	Never	Some-times	Usually	Always
	0	4	7	10

1. I control my temper.

2. I like most food that is set before me.

3. I get the facts before I judge people.

4. I like to work with and help others.

5. I try to be as interested in others as in myself.

6. I have good table manners.

7. I say "please" and "thank you" when people do things for me.

8. I approve of my family.

9. I compliment people when they do things well.

10. I usually see the good in other people.

Total each column

Total points

REVIEW QUESTIONS

1. What do you understand by the terms, *environment*? *heredity*?

2. List some traits that come largely from environment.

3. Why do some children have the habit of temper tantrums?

4. How do friends sometimes help people to get over the habit of anger?

5. What is prejudice? How are prejudices formed?

6. How do children learn to be cooperative? If you have a small brother or sister tell of something the little child has done that shows he is learning to cooperate. Does he occasionally disturb the pleasure of the group by failing to cooperate?

7. What things do we learn from our families about the use of money? Are you learning to weigh various attitudes about money and to decide upon the relative importance or unimportance of money in different situations?

8. Do you think it is true that you have copied your manners from your family? Explain. Can your choice of friends influence your manners?

9. In what ways do friends support what one has been taught in one's family? In what ways may friends cause us to question things we have been taught?

10. How does the community one lives in affect one's personality development?

KEY WORDS AND PHRASES

environment	repossession	selfishness
heredity	installment plan	self-centeredness
emotional	negatively	other-centeredness
temper tantrum	fears	oversensitive
anger	prejudices	positively
handicaps	cooperativeness	

PROBLEMS AND ACTIVITIES

1. Write a short autobiography. Include ways in which you think your family has influenced you to be as you are. As you write, think of the points discussed in this chapter.

2. If you have special likes and dislikes in foods, list them. Study your list and try to figure out why you like or dislike certain foods.

3. Can you think of prejudices that you have? Where did you get these prejudices?

4. Have you ever lived in a community where all your friends believed about the same as your family believes in politics? Religion? About what is right and wrong? If you have, do you think it is better to live in this type of a community or one in which your friends might have a variety of belief? Discuss.

5. In some countries, parents are punished for wrong things their children do. What would be the reason for such a policy? What do you think of the policy?

6. If children have bad manners, is it always a reflection on the parents? Why or why not?

See reading list at end of Part One, page 47.

YOUR HEREDITY AND
YOUR PERSONALITY

4

It is not possible to know which is more important in your personality growth, your environment or the characteristics you have inherited. Physical features such as eye color, height, straight or curly hair, or your sex, are settled before birth by heredity. Many other things, such as disposition, are determined largely by the environment. However, even these are affected by one's physical inheritance. Heredity and environment cannot be separated, for they work together to produce personality.

How heredity works

For a clearer picture of what things are settled by heredity, we need to think about the way biological heredity works. If you have had a course in biology, this will be review for you. If you have not had a biology course, you may wish to get a biology book and read further on the subject of heredity. One of the films suggested at the end of the chapter will help to answer questions.

Boy or girl? To start with, how did it happen that you turned out to be a boy rather than a girl, or a girl rather than a boy? Your sex was determined once and for all the minute your life began. There have been many theories about how the sex of a baby is determined, but biologists now accept the following: In each human cell there are 24 pairs of chromosomes. In the female, all 24 pairs are alike. But in the male, one pair, the sex-bearing pair of chromosomes, is different. Biologists call this unlike pair XY and call all the like pairs XX. Women always have all the like pairs (the XX chromosomes). But men always have the one unlike (XY) pair of chromosomes. When two parent cells unite (see diagram) and the X chromosome from the male parent joins with the X from the female parent, then the baby conceived is a girl, for the union has provided 24 identical (or XX chromosomes) as in females. Nothing can change the sex from then on. On the other hand, if it happens that the Y chromosome, instead of one of the X chromosomes from the father, joins the X chromosome from the egg of the mother, then the baby is a boy, for the union has produced 23 XX chromosomes and one XY chromosome, as in males. It is all chance whether two X chromosomes unite or whether the Y unites with an X. But once the parent cells have united, the sex of the future child is settled.

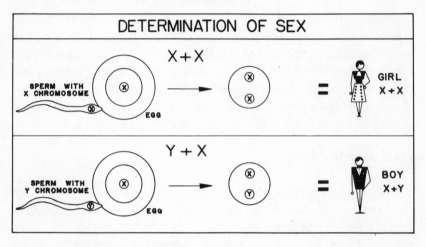

● The sex of the new baby is determined at the instant the parent cells unite to form a new individual. Nothing can be done after that to change the sex of the new person.

How we inherit traits. Why is it that your hair may be dark when you have two sisters with blond hair? Moreover, you may be tall and your sisters short and your nose may be of a different shape. How all of such physical features are inherited from parents is complicated, but such features are determined at the time of the union of the parent cells and are not later changed any more than sex is.

The heredity works something like this: We have said that you received 48 chromosomes from your parents, 24 from your mother and 24 from your father. (Your father got 24 of his chromosomes from his mother and 24 from his father, and your mother got 24 of

Your Heredity and Your Personality

her chromosomes from her father and 24 from her mother.) On each of the chromosomes are many "genes" which determine the different physical traits passed on through heredity. That is, there are several genes on each chromosome from your mother, and several genes on each chromosome from your father. Certain genes would give you dark hair. It is all chance which genes you get. Your sisters were produced by different parent cells with a different combination of genes; hence, their blond hair. Each time a new life is started by the uniting of parent cells, a different combination of genes result. In your cells, you carry chromosomes and genes from great numbers of ancestors. An endless number of combinations is possible. Biologists have estimated that almost 500,000 different combinations are possible for each person; therefore, no two brothers and sisters are ever alike in all physical features. Two brothers or two sisters are alike only if they are *identical twins* because identical twins grow from one egg and one sperm which develop into two individuals instead of one. In a way, identical twins may be said to be two of the same person. They have exactly the same combinations of genes. Twins that are not identical are produced by two different eggs and sperms and are no more alike than are other brothers and sisters.

To complicate the way heredity works, it is known that certain genes are *dominant*, while others are *recessive*. That is, when a dominant gene and a recessive gene are both present, it is the trait carried by the dominant one that will show up as a physical feature in the person. To illustrate, genes for dark eyes are dominant over genes for blue eyes; genes for curly hair are dominant over genes

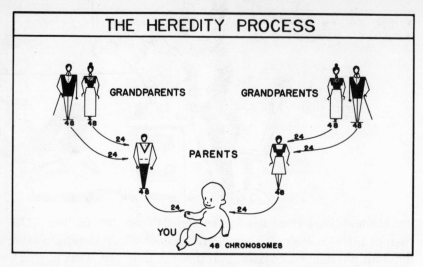

THE HEREDITY PROCESS

GRANDPARENTS   GRANDPARENTS

PARENTS

YOU

48 CHROMOSOMES

● You inherit from your ancestors everything that you are, physically. You received 24 chromosomes from your mother and 24 chromosomes from your father. Your parents, in turn, received 24 chromosomes from each of their parents. The hundreds of genes in the chromosomes determine all of your physical characteristics.

for straight hair. This means that if your father is brunette and has curly hair, and your mother is blond with straight hair, there is a good chance that you will be dark and have curly hair or wavy hair like your father. If both your parents have brown eyes, you are very likely to have brown eyes. However, both parents can have brown eyes and their child may have blue eyes. This is possible since both parents may also be carrying recessive genes for blue eyes; and if, in a particular union of parent cells, these recessive genes join without a dominant gene getting into the picture, then the new baby is blue-eyed, or shows the recessive rather than the dominant characteristic.

For our discussion here it is not necessary to go into greater detail about how heredity works. Now, how may your personality be affected by your heredity?

Inherited traits that are changed little by environment

From the previous discussion, it has become evident that environment cannot change some of the things that are settled by

Your Heredity and Your Personality

ORDER OF DOMINANCE FOR HAIR-FORM GENES

"KINKY" GENE   "CURLY" GENE   "WAVY" GENE   "STRAIGHT" GENE
    DOMINATES   DOMINATES   DOMINATES

● The dominant genes from one parent "cover over" the recessive genes from the other parent. If your father has kinky or curly hair and your mother has straight hair, you probably have curly or wavy hair, since genes for kinkiness and curliness are dominant. Name some other genes that are dominant.

heredity. Sex is fixed. Hair color, skin pigmentation, eye color, the approximate height that you will ever reach, shape of eyes, nose, ears, and some other features were all settled long before the day you were born. Some change may be brought about in your skin by exposure to the sun, and if you eat a properly balanced diet you may grow somewhat taller than if you do not have a good diet. But the sun can never make a brunette out of you if your genes made you a blonde. And the difference in your height must still remain within the limits set by your heredity, although good health may allow you to reach your greatest possible height.

Inherited traits which depend upon environment for development

People have argued over the question, are geniuses born or made? Mental ability is inherited; the raw material that makes it possible for us to learn is inherited from our parents. Many different genes are probably involved in determining various kinds of mental ability. Heredity sets a limit beyond which a brain will not develop, but most of us will never make use of our fullest possible mental development. We all are inclined to stop short of using all

Your Heredity and Your Personality   31

our abilities. The environment has something to do with how much the mental ability of each person will be developed. To illustrate: A boy may inherit mental ability at the genius level, but if he has no chance to get an education, if his community does not require school attendance, and if his friends and associates are unaware of or uninterested in any kind of mental achievement, there is a good chance that the boy with the genius possibility may live and achieve at much the same level as others in his community who have far less ability than he. On the other hand, if the same boy had been born into a home and a community that stressed and encouraged mental achievement and that provided opportunities for learning, then the same boy would be much more likely to use and to develop more of his inherited mental ability.

Musical ability. Some facts suggest that the ability to become a good musician depends upon certain inherited traits. Physical coordination, an ear for tone and pitch, and a sense of rhythm may be inherited. Heredity may set the limits on those characteristics, but environment fosters or discourages their development.

The fact that there were five generations of Bachs who were famous in music is usually taken as proof that heredity was important in this line of musicians. But we must remember that all the young Bachs were exposed to music from earliest childhood. In their environment music was all-important. Naturally, they developed whatever musical ability they had.

Physical ability. Recently, a magazine carried the story of Josephine Berosini, a tightrope walker. Her great-grandfather, Charles Blondin, was the first man to cross Niagara Falls on a wire.

His children and grandchildren have been tightrope walkers. No doubt a certain physical agility and ability to balance has been passed on through heredity, but the fact that the children lived in homes in which tightrope walking was the means of making a living had much to do with their developing this skill. By her fourth birthday, Josephine Berosini had joined the family act, walking the rope. If Josephine had been born into a family with different interests, she might have become a dancer or a skater or even an artist. Her inherited physical characteristics could have been used differently and developed in any one of several directions.

In summary, it can be said that you are *you* because of the physical features and the mental and emotional possibilities with which you were born, *plus* the surroundings in which you have lived until now. Your physical appearance has something to do with the first impression others get of you. But your own feelings about your appearance are, in the long run, more important in determining your effect on others than are your actual physical features.

Similarly, the mental ability that you inherited is important, but perhaps not so important as your interest in achieving. Your determination to find out what your abilities are and to make the most of them will be worth just as much to you as, or possibly even more than, your inherited ability. As we go through this book we shall consider many ways in which you can make the most of all you were born with and all your surroundings have given you.

REVIEW QUESTIONS

1. List some personality traits that are determined chiefly by our environment. List some that we get chiefly through heredity.

2. When is the sex of a new individual determined?

3. Explain how the XY chromosomes work in determining sex.

4. Why do brothers have different physical features when they have the same parents?

5. Why are identical twins identical, but other twins are not?

6. Explain how dominant and recessive genes work.

7. List inherited traits that cannot be changed by environment.

8. Show how heredity and environment may be related in the development of a person with special mental ability.

9. How can you explain the fact that five generations of Bachs were outstanding in music?

10. Will Josephine Berosini's skill as a tightrope walker be passed on to her children through heredity? Explain.

11. Explain why the son of a criminal can turn out to be a law-abiding person or why the son of a respected man can turn out to be a criminal.

KEY WORDS AND PHRASES

heredity	chromosomes	mental ability
environment	genes	musical ability
disposition	identical twins	physical ability
achievement	dominant genes	criminal
sperm cell	recessive genes	characteristics
egg cell	genius	physical features

PROBLEMS AND ACTIVITIES

1. Make a diagram of your family tree going back as far as you can. Give the occupations of your parents, grandparents, great-grandparents, great-great-grandparents, and further if you can. Does an occupation run in your family? If so, do you think it is due to a special inherited ability or due to the environment the children are reared in?

2. Many states have considered laws which would not permit criminals to marry and have children. Does your state have such a law? Give arguments for and against such a law.

FILM

Heredity and Environment — 10 minutes, sound, Coronet
See reading list at end of Part One, page 47.

Your Heredity and Your Personality

YOUR APPEARANCE AND
YOUR PERSONALITY

5

How do you feel about your looks? Have you always been perfectly satisfied with the shape of your mouth and chin, the size of your nose, and the color of your hair? If so, you are a person in a thousand, for almost all of us have some feature that we have wished we could change. No matter how handsome the other person may look to you, he may secretly wish he could exchange one of his features for one of yours. That seems to be human nature.

Studies show that most young people do worry about some of their physical features. On page 36 are summarized some things which bothered 580 tenth grade boys and girls in another school. Have you ever worried about some of these?

Although few people are perfectly happy about their looks, a part of satisfactory growing up is becoming able to accept one's own physical features. You look like some of your relatives on both sides of your family, and your looks help to make up your whole personality. Even the fact that you dislike some of your features and are willing to work to make the best of the features that you have is part of your personality.

Fortunately the "build" of your face or figure has very little to do with how attractive you are. Think of the most attractive and well-liked person you know. Then look at that person's actual features. Does he or she have a perfect build, exactly the *right* height and weight? Does he or she have just the right-sized nose, perfectly arranged features, hair that is naturally manageable and the beautiful eyes that are considered attractive according to our standards of good looks?

The most attractive person may have none of those physical characteristics, or he may have only a small share of them. The basis of attractiveness is not in specific physical features. Your looks and your personality go together. You have some choice in building your own personality, and you have much choice in how attractive you are in appearance.

PROBLEMS OF PHYSICAL GROWTH

I want to improve my complexion
(blackheads or pimples).

I have irregular teeth.

I don't like the shape of my nose.

My face is too long, too round.

My skin is too dry, too oily.

I don't like to wear glasses.

(Adapted from Alexander Frazier and Lorenzo K. Lisonbee, "Adolescent Concerns with Physique," *School Review*, 58:397–405 (1950).

● It is helpful to know that many people have the same worries about how they are developing.

The chart above lists some of the most common concerns of 10th grade boys and girls in one school.

How our bodies grow

An understanding of how bodies grow and change may help you to accept and do less worrying about any physical characteristics that may bother you right now.

There are two periods in life when we grow very rapidly. The first period comes before birth and for about one year after birth. After that, the average person grows fairly gradually for some years. Between the ages of nine and twelve or later, girls may again grow very fast. Rapid growth starts in boys when they are between the ages of ten and fifteen and continues for some time.

Growth during the second period may sometimes make you wonder what is happening. Bodily growth at this time is not always even. Your arms, legs, feet, and hands may seem to be out-

• How do you feel
about your looks?

growing the rest of you. Or some of your facial features may seem to be growing out of proportion. Whether you are a girl or a boy, you may wonder if you are going to be permanently fat because your weight is not evenly distributed on your frame. If you are already through this stage, you know that quite suddenly these stages pass.

During the period of rapid growth, the glands also change in their functioning. The sweat glands may seem to be out of control. With little reason, you may break out in sweat; hands and feet may perspire in an annoying way. Blackheads and pimples may become a problem and infections may develop.

If skin eruptions become a serious problem at this time, a check-up with a doctor is a good idea. He may advise some changes in your diet and living routines, or he may suggest treatment that will help. But in many cases, skin troubles do not last long. They begin to clear up as one goes into the next stage of growth.

Growth processes make problems

The second rapid stage in growth takes place in girls about two years earlier than in boys. From ages 11 to 15 many girls are taller than the boys the same age. The girl who has her spurt in growth early may, for a short time, be almost a foot taller than the other girls and boys in her class. If you are one of the fast-growing girls, you know that it makes certain problems for you.

These problems will pass within a year or two when your later-growing friends catch up with you.

Most people have their growth problems. Since people grow in an irregular way, there is likely to be a time when you feel you are too tall or too short, too fat or too thin, have a bad complexion, or cannot control your voice. Those who have a regular and fairly even growth are the exceptions, not the average.

● Boys and girls mature at different ages. These boys and girls are thirteen years old. They differ considerably from one another in physical maturity and size. Such differences are normal. (the E. C. Brown Trust.)

Of 580 tenth grade students in one high school, both the boys and girls who developed late said they felt that they had more worries than the boys and girls who had developed early. These growth problems become easier to live through if you understand about the growth process, for then you can appreciate that even a little time does a lot to remedy the problem. Many of you have already gone through the time when your body was out of proportion or when you had complexion troubles.

Janet described one of her friends whom she saw at camp each summer, this way: "Two years ago when I met Sue, she was just a little thin person with no personality. Last summer she was chubby and was always worrying about being fat. But you should see her this summer! She is slim and has a lovely complexion. Everyone is talking about how pretty she is. She's going to be *beautiful* when she gets the braces off her teeth!"

Regardless of what growth stage you may be in, you can handle your problems better if you know the rules that are followed by those who want to make the most of their appearance.

Rules that help your appearance

1. No matter what your type, tall, short, blonde, or brunette, the first essential is *cleanliness*. There is nothing that money can buy that will do so much for attractiveness as a good scrubbing with soap and water at least once a day. The clothes you wear rate far below cleanliness in what they do for the impression you make.

Many of the complexion problems that plague people clear up much faster if soap and water are used regularly. In most parts of the United States today, a boy can go almost anywhere wearing jeans or levis and a tee shirt or sport shirt *if* he is scrubbed and clean. And the girls accepted as most attractive are those whose hair is brushed and shining and who put their emphasis upon soap and water rather than upon make-up, other than the minimum of lipstick that most high school girls wear.

2. Next to cleanliness in importance is your *posture*, or *the way you carry yourself*. If you are too tall, look at it this way: Will you look better slumped over, so that your figure seems to have odd angles and curves in the wrong places, or walking as straight and tall as you naturally are, with all the natural grace that you have? Whether you are only five feet tall or six feet seven, walk as if you enjoyed every inch of your height, and you will find that other people will accept your height as an attractive part of your appearance and personality.

3. Habits of cleanliness and good posture are most important,

● Small children often run from soap and water; but when boys and girls begin to care about their appearance, they find that cleanliness is the basis of attractiveness. (Coronet Films.)

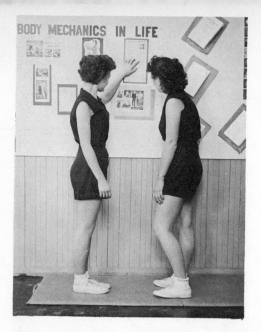

but of course the clothes you wear are also a help or a handicap. Clothes *suitable to the occasion and to your own personal type* will always do the most for you. The cost of clothes — whether you have a lot of money to spend for clothes or very little money at all — has little to do with the appearance you make.

Ann felt sorry for Margaret because Margaret had so little money for clothes, yet when the two girls went to a class dance, Margaret's good taste proved its value. Ann appeared in an expensive dress cut along lines that made her look ten years older than her classmates. She was obviously trying to copy the dress and manner of the leading lady in a recent play. Margaret wore a becoming, fresh white dress that she had made herself. The crisp cotton dress exactly suited Margaret's type and had cost so little that she could probably manage to have several new dresses for different parties during the year. Margaret made a far better and more attractive appearance than Ann did, regardless of the fact that Ann was more expensively dressed.

In choosing clothes, the best-dressed people have learned that simplicity and freedom from fussiness is almost always smartest for any type. Look at the people on the street and see if you agree. You can learn a lot about what to wear and what not to wear by looking at the appearance made by some middle-aged people who seem to have stopped caring how they look. Do you see

THE CARE OF MY BODY

	Never	Some-times	Usually	Always
	0	4	7	10

1. I take a bath or shower several times per week.

2. I brush my teeth after I eat.

3. I refrain from biting or breaking hard substances (including my fingernails) with my teeth.

4. I breathe through my nose with my mouth closed.

5. I give special attention to cleanliness and to food when my complexion is bad.

6. I keep my hands away from my face and avoid squeezing or picking at pimples.

7. I keep my fingers away from my nose.

8. I keep from poking things in my nose and ears.

9. If I find myself slouching because of fatigue, I do something about it.

10. I spend at least an hour outdoors every day.

Total each column

Total points

● What shall I wear? *(Coronet Films.)*

women who wear too many frills and only look overdone, thin
people who wear such straight tight clothes that they look far
thinner than they should, and fat people who wear loose, full,
baggy clothes that make them look far worse than necessary?
Most rules that apply to clothes types for older people apply also
for people of your age.

4. *Grooming.* In some ways, boys have the best of it because
they have less necessity for choice in clothes, and they do not have
to bother with make-up. They have to keep their hair neatly cut,
however, and now or later they have to shave their faces regularly. The boy who rates as good-looking never neglects those
essential necessities.

In the matter of cosmetics, many girls make the mistake of
overdoing it because they have not figured out the real logic of
make-up. In some families, how much lipstick the daughter can
wear becomes a point of constant argument and struggle. The
parents may not explain or may not even have figured out for
themselves why they hate to see Sue overdoing her make-up. The
truth is that many kinds of make-up are frankly designed as props
or camouflages for middle-aged or older women who want to do

MY CLOTHES AND GROOMING

	Never	Some-times	Usually	Always
	0	4	7	10
1. My clothes look right on me because I carry myself well.				
2. I keep my hair brushed.				
3. I keep my hair clean.				
4. I keep my clothes clean and neat.				
5. I wear the right clothes at the right time.				
6. I keep my nails clean and fairly short.				
7. I take pride in my clothes.				
8. My shoes are shined and in repair.				
9. I change my socks and underwear several times per week.				
10. I use deodorant and foot powders when necessary.				

Total each column

Total points

something about their fading skins. Cosmetics manufacturers have worked to create aids that help older women to hide drying complexions and other defects. But when a young girl puts on most types of make-up, she is more likely to hide the natural attractiveness of her skin than to increase her attractiveness. Thus, if your mother says, "Leave it off. You're prettier with a clean face and no make-up," she may be telling the truth, whether or not she has figured out the reason why you look better without it.

● Girls may make the mistake of overdoing it.

If you are a girl and have a tendency to concentrate too much of your grooming effort on make-up rather than cleanliness, stop and consider whether it is possible that you are letting an urge to "play grown-up" — as you did when you were a child — cramp your style!

Boy or girl, you would like to be sensationally attractive. Who wouldn't? So cleanliness, neatness — brushed hair and shined shoes and pressed clothes — and a good straight way of carrying yourself may not sound like a startling enough way to go about making an impression. But it works.

● "I dunno. I just read somewhere that it helps your posture." (Emmy Lou, by Marty Links.)

Beyond that, you can still accomplish something by studying yourself and deciding what kind of a haircut or hair style makes your square face look less square, or your long face rounder, and whether your hands are the type that look better with long sharp fingernails or nails filed to fit the ends of your fingers.

Most people want to conform in general to what friends and schoolmates accept as wearable, but if you are not afraid to be somewhat independent about sticking to what you know to be your own best style, you will find that others will be copying *you,* you will not have to copy them.

REVIEW QUESTIONS

1. Do you think that many young people are critical of their own looks?
2. Does knowing that others have a similar problem help you to accept your physical features?

3. When are the two periods in life in which we grow most rapidly?
4. What things sometimes cause people to worry about how they are growing during the second period of growth?
5. What are some causes of complexion troubles?
6. What is the first rule to follow to make the most of your appearance?
7. Why do many people fail to develop a good posture?
8. What are some important principles to follow in choosing clothes to wear?
9. What mistake do girls often make when they start using make-up?

PROBLEMS AND ACTIVITIES

1. *Class survey.* Each student without signing his name write on a piece of paper the things which he does not like about his physical features. Have a class committee summarize the information and put on the blackboard as a basis for discussion. Compare the study with the one given in this chapter.
2. What is the accepted dress for different occasions at your school? For everyday; a Friday night party; a formal dance?
3. Boys sometimes resist wearing a suit and tie when it is the proper dress for the occasion. They might go to the party in levis or slacks and no tie and feel more at home than if they had worn a coat and tie. Why is this?

SOCIO-DRAMA

A group from the class play the parts of adults who are discussing teenagers. Bring out many of the things which you consider thoughtless that are said by adults about teenagers, their growth, dress, manners, and ways of doing things.

FILMS

The Story of Human Growth — 20 minutes, sound, Association Films
Personal Hygiene for Boys — 10 minutes, sound, Coronet
Personal Hygiene for Girls — 10 minutes, sound, Coronet

MORE ABOUT YOU

BAILARD, VIRGINIA AND RUTH STRANG, *Ways to Improve Your Personality*. New York: McGraw-Hill Book Company, Inc., 1951, chs., 1–3.

BECK, LESTER F., *Human Growth*. New York: Harcourt, Brace and Company, 1949.

BILLET, ROY C. AND J. WENDELL YEO, *Growing Up*. Boston: D. C. Heath and Company, 1951, chs., 1–4.

COSGROVE, MARJORIE C. AND MARY I. JOSEY, *About You*. Chicago: Science Research Associates, Inc., 1952, chs., 1–3.

CRAWFORD, JOHN E. AND LUTHER E. WOODWARD, *Better Ways of Growing Up*. Philadelphia: The Muhlenberg Press, 1948, chs., 1–3.

HENRY, WILLIAM E., *Exploring Your Personality*. Chicago: Science Research Associates, Inc., 1952.

KELIHER, ALICE V., *Life and Growth*. New York: D. Appleton-Century Company, 1941.

LEVINE, MILTON I. AND JEAN H. SELIGMANN, *The Wonder of Life*. New York: Simon and Schuster, 1940.

NEUGARTEN, BERNICE L., *How You Grow*. Chicago: Science Research Associates, Inc., 1951.

———, *Your Heredity*. Chicago: Science Research Associates, Inc., 1951.

NOVIKOFF, ALEX, *From Head to Foot*. New York: International Publishers Company, Inc., 1946.

SHACTER, HELEN, *Understanding Ourselves*. Bloomington: McKnight & McKnight, 1945, chs., 1–8.

———, *How Personalities Grow*. Bloomington: McKnight & McKnight, 1949., chs., 1–2.

Part Two

LEARNING TO UNDERSTAND OTHERS

MAKING FRIENDS

6

If you were asked to list the two or three things most important to your happiness, it is quite sure that on your list, and perhaps first on the list, would be friends or friendships. Most of us, if we stop to think of it, appreciate our families and all that they do for us; we know that good health, food, and shelter are necessary things. But we find it easy to take those essentials for granted and to feel that life would be awfully dull if we had no friends.

Among your classmates, you can see some people who seem to have all the friends that anyone could want and others who have a hard time making or keeping any friends at all. Perhaps you yourself are one of the lucky ones with many friends. But is it "luck"?

What is it that attracts and holds friends? What lies back of real, solid popularity? If you will figure out your own success or failure in making friends or if you study the person who is very successful in friendships, you will find some important rules for success in friendships.

Interest in other people

People who make friends always have this trait: they *really like and are interested in other people.* You might answer, "But of course I like other people, or why would I want them for friends?" There is more to it than that. You may like people because you want to have a good group to go around with, or want to have it known that you are popular, or because many friends mean a kind of success that is important in any school. All those reasons are what might be called "selfish" reasons, since they arise from one's

49

own needs or wants. Even so, everyone has those reasons for wanting friends, and there is nothing wrong with those reasons. But many people have, in addition, an unselfish interest in other people. Their interest in others attracts friends to them.

● **What is it that attracts and holds friends?**

Alice and her family moved into a new town in the middle of Alice's freshman year in high school. Alice dreaded entering a new school as a stranger in midyear, but it had to be done. When she came home at the end of the first day she said, "I was feeling pretty low when I started for the lunchroom alone this noon. Everyone else was in groups with friends. Then I saw another new girl who didn't even know where the lunchroom was, and she was too shy to ask anyone. I felt so sorry for her; I went over and offered to take her in with me. During lunch, she told me that if someone hadn't helped her, she wasn't even going to stick the day out, but had thought she would leave and go home. I told her tomorrow was sure to be easier — the second day always is."

What was the difference between Alice's attitude and that of the other new girl? Which would be likely to begin making new friends sooner?

Alice's thought had been for the other person. Not "*I* need someone to go to the lunchroom with," but, "There's a person who looks

Making Friends

as if she's about to give up if someone doesn't go to her rescue."

Do you see what is meant by saying that the person who is successful in friendships has a sincere interest in and liking for other people?

The habit of friendliness

If you cultivate in yourself an interest in other people, you will find the next rule easier to follow. *Make it a habit to be friendly to everyone you meet.* Don't wait to see what the other person is going to do.

You may feel like holding back and waiting to see if someone else will speak first or smile first. But if everyone did that, no one would do any smiling or speaking at all.

The person who has the habit of being friendly toward others does not save his or her friendliness only for "those who matter," or who are desirable as friends, or for those who can help one's popularity. People are quick to notice it and remember it if you are all charm for some people and around others behave as if you did not notice that they were alive. The person who is friendly to everyone will always have a wide range of people from whom to choose friends.

A girl who had few friends said of Lynn, who was among the most popular girls in school, "I'd certainly like to have Lynn for a friend. She is always so *nice* to me when we meet anywhere. She smiles and stops a minute even if she only has time to say 'Hi.' I think Lynn really likes me, but she has so many other friends that I don't see much of her." Another girl who envied Lynn her social success said, "No wonder Lynn is popular. Look at the clothes she has! And that football hero for a big brother! Some people get all the breaks."

Do you think Lynn's good clothes and her football playing brother were the reasons for her popularity?

Habits are wonderfully useful things. You can practice a piece on the piano until playing it is so much a habit that you can do it with your eyes shut. You can practice shooting basketball goals until, from certain positions, it is almost easier to score than to miss. In the same way, you can deliberately build habits that will help you in all your dealings with people.

Cheerfulness

High on the list of important habits is *cheerfulness*. Do you wonder at our calling cheerfulness a habit? You may have thought, as some people do, that one is cheerful if things are going well and that one cannot be expected to be cheerful if things are not going well. But cheerfulness is a habit.

Cheerful people are not those who have fewer troubles or problems than other people have; they are people who have made it a habit not to wear their troubles and their problems on their faces. They know that no matter how sympathetic others may be toward troubles, people like those who are cheerful.

A five-year-old boy said it well. One day his older sister overheard him talking to himself. He was looking in a mirror, working at making pleasant faces and saying to himself, "I don't like your face, Jimmy. Your ears are too big and that hair hanging down your forehead looks ugly, so you better look awfully happy if you want other people to like your face." He achieved a pleasant, cheerful expression that satisfied him and went away from the mirror looking very pleased with himself. Even at five, he had learned that a cheerful face is more important than a handsome one.

Giving compliments

Another important habit is to *give honest compliments*. If you are really interested in other people, you will see plenty of things in them worth complimenting. Every one of us loves to hear good things about himself if he can think there is truth in the good words said. Don't stoop to flattery, which is giving a dishonest compliment or saying the thing that you think the person wants to hear when you don't honestly think it is true. Even the flattered person becomes suspicious of the flatterer; no one likes insincerity.

But look for the good things in your associates and then *say* the good words that you think of. Don't worry, they will not think you are just trying to "get around" them. If compliments are sincere, your friends will accept them happily, just as you do.

Giving honest compliments helps you to form the habit of looking for the good in others rather than paying attention to their

● We all like to hear good things about ourselves if we can think the good words are true. Make it a habit to give your friends honest compliments. *(Coronet Films.)*

faults. You, yourself, therefore become a better person.

Almost all the important habits that add up to success in friendships could be listed under the first point: liking and understanding others instead of thinking only of ourselves.

Traits that handicap friendships

Do you show consideration for others' rights? Or are you *inconsiderate?* The person who thinks, "I'm hungry this noon. I'll slip in up nearer the head of the cafeteria line" is not thinking about how hungry anyone else may be. In exchange for a quicker lunch, he has given up some of the respect and liking that other people in the cafeteria line may otherwise have had for him.

What about the person who borrows easily but never remembers to repay, the one who takes his time, says "Wait a minute," and makes someone else late for class; the one who promises to do something and then changes his or her mind and leaves you in the lurch at the last minute? All such things are lack of consideration for the rights and feelings of other people.

If you find some of your friends drifting away, examine your habits. Inconsiderateness for others can wreck friendships and can drive away people who might have become your friends.

Sometimes the people who want friends the most defeat their own wishes by *being too possessive* of the friends that they have.

Sally and Joan lived next door to each other and became good friends. Joan was friendly in her ways and often wanted to include other girls in plans the two made. But Sally worked to try to break

WHAT KIND OF A FRIEND ARE YOU?

	Yes	No
1. Are you usually cheerful when with others?		
2. Do you borrow money from your friends?		
3. Do you compliment others upon the good things they do?		
4. Do you frequently ask your friends to wait for you?		
5. Do you restrain yourself from repeating gossip that you hear about others?		
6. Do you find yourself resenting it when one of your friends is friendly to someone else?		
7. Do you make cutting remarks about others?		
8. Are you friendly to those who do not "rate" in your school?		
9. Do you spend much time telling your troubles to your friends?		
10. Are you a good listener?		
11. Would you like to have for a friend a person who had the same personality traits you have?		
12. Do you frequently quarrel with friends?		
13. Have you had one or more of the same friends for several months or years?		
14. Do you have more than one friend?		
15. Are you ever jealous of your friends?		
16. Do you make friends easily with both boys and girls?		
17. Do you trust your friends?		

up any friendships that Joan made with others. She would be sarcastic and cutting to anyone else who walked home from school with the two of them. She would discover unattractive things to point out in anyone else whom Joan liked. She would make fun of the clothes, the manners, or the speech of anyone who threatened to be competition for her with Joan. In some cases, when Joan began going around with some other girl, Sally would talk to the other girl about Joan, quoting or misquoting Joan in such a way that she managed to make trouble.

At last Joan found herself isolated with Sally. She said, "I always have liked Sally. But she just fences me in and everyone else out. It seems that I can't be friends with her and have any other friends at all — and I'm not satisfied with having it that way." The result was that Sally's possessiveness caused the end of the friendship that she was trying so hard to hang on to.

Possessive attitudes toward friends may easily have that effect. It is better to use your energy to overcome faults and be a desirable friend than to defend your friendships against competition.

REVIEW QUESTIONS

1. How important are friends to happiness?
2. Explain the differences between wanting friends for selfish reasons and wanting friends for unselfish reasons. Can you think of a case that will illustrate the point?

Making Friends   55

3. What is meant by "Make it a habit to be friendly"? Have you found this important in making friendships?
4. What is meant by calling cheerfulness a "habit"?
5. Do cheerful people necessarily have fewer troubles than people who are not cheerful? Explain.
6. What is flattery?
7. Do you think it is always possible to give *honest* compliments?
8. If you cannot think of an honest compliment, which would be better: to use flattery or to avoid saying anything?
9. Give several traits which are handicaps in making friends.
10. Summarize the whole chapter in a sentence or two, bringing out what is most important in making friendships.

KEY WORDS AND PHRASES

flattery   **possessiveness**

PROBLEMS AND ACTIVITIES

1. Think of the best friends you have ever had. Now make a list of the personality traits they had that you liked most. In another column list the traits you did not like.
2. Study the above lists and think about yourself. In both columns (traits liked and traits disliked) put a check by each of the traits you think you yourself have.
3. As John joined his group of friends who had been waiting for him to go to the show, he said, "I was late because Mother didn't have dinner on time, and I couldn't find my coat. Anyway, Dad is stingy and he wouldn't . . . ." You complete a personality sketch of John. Would he be a good friend?

FILMS

The Fun of Being Thoughtful — 10 minutes, sound, Coronet
Developing Friendships — 10 minutes, sound, Coronet
See reading list at end of Part Two, pages 118–19.

MORE ABOUT YOUR FRIENDSHIPS

7

Everyone wants at least one good friend. Even people who have many friends usually have one who is the "best friend." That is the one you know you can tell things to and be perfectly sure your confidences will not be broadcast through the school within a few days. Your best friend is the one who will not stand silently by and let someone else say damaging things about you. He will defend you even though he knows you do have your faults. A good friend does know your faults, but he likes you anyway, just as you like him, despite his faults.

One friend is not enough

During the high school years, you are developing a knowledge of people that will be important to you through all the rest of your life. You need to know and like many different kinds of people. The wide differences in people make them interesting. Not only will you improve your own personality as you learn to understand other people better, but you will enjoy your school life far more if you can enjoy a wide range of people.

Looking at it selfishly, you might call making friends with many different people, good "social insurance." You will never be left high and dry if you have more than one good friend. From any view it is worth while to work at enlarging your circle of friends rather than being content to concentrate on a twosome.

What about cliques?

In every school there are cliques, groups of people who are close-knit and exclusive in their friendships. Perhaps you are a member of a clique. If so, you can think of some good and some bad points about belonging to such a group.

If you are not now and have never been a member of a clique, you may be inclined to think there is nothing good about them at all. You may have noticed that some people attach too much importance to their group and imagine that it gives them special privileges or standing.

Cliques usually form more or less by accident. A few people get to be such good friends that they find themselves more and more doing things and going places together. Other friends they may have soon come to be included less and less often, so that finally everyone takes it for granted that those certain few are a group who depend on each other and do not need or perhaps want anyone else. They have become a clique whether or not they intended it.

If you belong to a separate group you need especially to remember that no clique lasts forever. You are going to need the friendship of many other people before you are through with school. No matter how much you enjoy your friendship with the small group and the security it gives you to know you can depend on their friendship, there are a lot of other interesting people in school whose friendship you are missing. Clique membership should not be allowed to crowd out your interest in other people. If you forget how big the world is and get to thinking everything centers in one small group, then it is too bad you belong to it, for you are losing more than you are gaining.

As people become more mature socially, they usually care less for clique membership. In most schools, the people who rate highest with the largest numbers of their schoolmates are likely

● You need to know and like many different kinds of people. (Hayward High School.)

● A clique gives security, but it may center all your interests too much in one small group and cut you off from other friends. (Luoma Photos.)

to be people who have many friends of all types. They are so busy and active in so many ways that they do not need or would not have time for membership in a small, tight, and exclusive friendship group.

Some of these people formerly may have been members of cliques but outgrew them. Others may never have belonged to such a group. Perhaps as underclassmen they may have wished they could be in such a group, but as they grew older they found that they enjoyed life more with a wider range of friendships, and they became successful enough not to need to depend on a clique.

GOOD FRIENDSHIP POLICY

1. Keep on your toes where your friendships are concerned. Don't take friendship for granted.

2. Value the friends that like you in spite of your faults, but keep working to get rid of your faults.

3. Keep in good repair the friendships you already have, but never stop working at making new friends.

4. Remember your school is full of interesting people, and most of them are worth knowing.

5. Get your mind off yourself and upon others and their interests, and you will not have too much of a friendship problem.

More About Your Friendships 59

• Have you learned how to say a definite "no" in a polite and friendly way? Well-liked people are those who live up to their own standards and beliefs without acting superior or critical of others. *(Coronet Films.)*

Choosing friends

The above discussion assumes that either now or later you will have developed ways that will help you have a choice in the friends you make. You will want to think about some further points.

People with standards different from yours. By now, you have given some thought to your standards of behavior. You have decided not to do some of the things that some others may see nothing especially wrong with doing. If you choose friends whose standards are not too much different from your own, they will help you to live up to what you think is right. In general, you may be happier with friends whose attitudes toward their obligations at school and toward honoring laws in the community are like yours and whose standards about points of behavior such as smoking and drinking are not far different from yours.

People who try to control you. You may find some friends whose background is far different from yours and whose standards on some things do differ from yours. You can still be good friends with them if both of you have an attitude of understanding and tolerance for your differences. But some people cannot resist trying to dominate and control those with whom they associate.

You can afford to avoid friendship with those who are too demanding, too possessive, or too determined in trying to control your activities and to influence your actions.

People of doubtful reputation. One's reputation is not always an accurate picture of what he is. Sometimes a boy or girl will get off to a poor start and become typed in a school as not a desirable character. Others may not wish to associate with him because of his reputation and, by their attitude, may drive him toward becoming worse than he really is. How much importance to attach to a person's reputation may be something of a problem in choosing friends.

Reputation does matter. Your reputation is what people believe you to be from what they have seen of your actions. Do people have reason to know that you habitually do what you believe to be right and that you are cooperative and interested in the best that your school offers? Or are you inclined to go along with what others do, regardless of whether or not the actions agree with your ideas of what is right or wise?

● When you choose friends, it is important to study yourself as well as others.

If you, yourself, are strong enough, you can have for a friend the person who has gotten off to a poor start and perhaps you can help him to overcome his handicap. On the other hand, if you find it hard to stand independently for what you believe, then it is wiser to avoid friendships with those whose reputations are already doubtful.

The important point in deciding, when questions arise about choices of friends, is to know yourself and your own strengths and weaknesses. Your friendships add to your enjoyment of life, but since they also contribute to growth and change in your personality, your choice of friends is very important as you are growing up.

REVIEW QUESTIONS

1. Why is it better to have many friends rather than just one friend?
2. What are the advantages and the disadvantages of belonging to a clique?
3. As people get older, they often do not feel the need of a clique. Why?
4. Why is it important to make friends among those who have standards similar to your own?
5. Is it good for us to make friends largely among those we can control? Explain.

KEY WORDS AND PHRASES

clique   reputation   standards of behavior

PROBLEMS AND ACTIVITIES

1. Are there many cliques in your school? If there are, do you think they are good or bad for the school? For the people in them?
2. If you are in a group that suggests doing things of which you do not approve, what is the most tactful way to handle the following situations?

   You are offered a cigarette and you do not smoke.

   The others want to say out until 2 A.M., but you have told your parents you will be home by 11:30 P.M.

   If the others are drinking beer, how do you refuse?

FILM

Feeling Left Out — 14 minutes, sound, Coronet
See reading list at end of Part Two, page 118.

More About Your Friendships

GROWING UP SOCIALLY

8

In this chapter, we shall think about your task of growing up socially, or learning to get along well in a world that will require you to live, work, and play among people of all kinds.

There are several kinds of maturity. John may be 16 years old chronologically (in years), but only 14 years old in his physical development. At the same time, he may be 18 years old mentally and only 12 years old socially. It is not unusual to find this wide range of "ages" in one person. It is easy to be unaware of the different kinds of maturity and to be critical of the person whose growth in different lines varies from the average. Some of John's friends may look at his actions at a party and say, "What's wrong with him? He is 16 years old, but he doesn't act like it." The truth is that he is 16 years old in years, but years are only a small indication of his real maturity. In his social experience, he is at the 12-year-old level.

Developing social maturity

During the years when people are working at growing up socially, some common difficulties and problems arise. The feelings of uncertainty or of self-consciousness that sometimes bother you probably trouble almost all of your friends at times. The table that follows shows how other high school students have said that they feel in certain social situations. You can do certain things to overcome unpleasant feelings. You can learn specific ways to help your social growing up. Years, in themselves, will not by some magic bring poise and self-confidence. You must make good use of the opportunities for growth that come along.

63

BOYS	YES %	IN THE FOLLOWING SOCIAL SITUATIONS:	YES %	GIRLS
🏃🏃🏃🏃🏃	57%	DO YOU FEEL AT EASE IN INTRODUCING PEOPLE ?	69%	🏃🏃🏃🏃🏃🏃🏃
🏃🏃🏃	39%	IN GENERAL, IS IT DIFFICULT FOR YOU TO CARRY ON CONVERSATIONS WITH THE OPPOSITE SEX ?	37%	🏃🏃🏃
🏃🏃🏃🏃	51%	ARE YOU AFRAID LEST YOU MAKE A MISTAKE AT A SOCIAL AFFAIR ?	55%	🏃🏃🏃🏃🏃
🏃🏃🏃	43%	ARE THERE SOME MEMBERS OF YOUR CLASS WHOSE COMPETENCY AND FEARLESSNESS IN SOCIAL AFFAIRS MAKE YOU FEEL INFERIOR ?	51%	🏃🏃🏃🏃
🏃🏃🏃🏃	45%	BOYS: DO YOU FEEL AT EASE IN ASKING A GIRL TO ATTEND SOME SOCIAL AFFAIR WITH YOU ?		
🏃🏃🏃	34%	BOYS: DOES IT BOTHER YOU MUCH TO WALK ACROSS THE FLOOR TO ASK A GIRL FOR THE NEXT DANCE ?		

Adapted from Percival W. Hutson and Dan R. Kovar, "Some Problems of Senior-High-School Pupils in Their Social Recreation," *Educational Administration and Supervision*, 28:503-519, 1942.

● A study of 2,163 students in one high school revealed that feelings of self-consciousness and being ill at ease are common to many students.

Self-consciousness

Everyone knows what self-consciousness is, because everyone has felt it at times. Some people do not appear to be bothered at all with the feeling; but if you could see their inner feelings as well as their outward actions, you would know that they struggle with that feeling just as you do.

It comes over Bill all at once that everyone is looking at him, that they can all see what a time he is having making his feet go as they should in the dance step, or that people can see how scared he is when he is giving a talk in class. He feels that they can even hear his throat muscles crack when he tries to swallow.

And Jane, who has to walk across the front of the room to take her seat in class, feels that everyone in the room is concentrating attention on the way she is walking, how she is carrying her hands, and how her skirt hangs. She is sure that all can see how awkward she feels.

Everyone knows what those feelings are like, and nobody enjoys the feeling.

What can you do about it? First, think this way of the situation in which you are self-conscious: What are all the other people around you doing? Are they not concerned about how they look to you and what you are thinking about them? You are not worrying about how *they* look; you are thinking about yourself and your feelings. What makes you think they are any different from you? Why should they be concentrating on you any more than you are concentrating on them and their actions and appearance?

When Bill is worrying about how he looks on the dance floor, he would feel less self-conscious if he could realize that all the others are busy with their own concerns. They are either enjoying the music and the dancing or concentrating on worrying about whether others notice their footwork trouble. They have not time to notice how Bill is doing. He might as well relax.

And when Jane feels so self-conscious as she walks into a class, she would feel better if she could realize that all the others are probably as self-centered as she is. They are more aware of how they look and of what they are doing than they are of her. Her feelings are *within*, and it is her feeling of self-consciousness that is bothering her, not that anyone is really watching her critically.

But, of course, feelings are powerful things, and just to tell ourselves that others are not watching us or aware of our troubles may not cure the feeling of self-consciousness. You can take more positive action.

● All of us feel self-conscious at times.

Growing Up Socially

● To overcome self-consciousness, be prepared to do well what you are doing. *(Coronet Films.)*

Work at doing, not feeling. Prepare for the things you have to do and concentrate on the thing you are doing, not on your feelings.

If you have to give a talk before the class, be thoroughly prepared. Think of what you have to say, and work at saying it in a way that will interest your listeners. Watch the other class members to see if they seem to be getting the points you are making; concentrate on putting over your points. If your mind is on your subject and on your audience, you will not have time to think of yourself. Self-consciousness will gradually disappear.

Learn social skills. That same rule applies to all situations. You can learn to make the correct move in social situations, so that you gradually gain confidence. You can learn, by practice, to be a good dancer, so that you can pay attention to enjoying the music and the rhythm and forget about whether others are looking at you. You can learn to make introductions smoothly. You can cultivate the habit of paying attention to others and to the task at hand, rather than concentrating on your inner feelings.

Good manners

What are good manners? Are they a bag of tricks that we learn in order to build up our self-confidence? Is it possible for one who is very selfish and self-centered, concerned only with the impression he is making, to have good manners?

One can follow specific rules that will help in developing good manners, but the true basis of all good manners is consideration for other people. The girl or boy who is honestly interested in seeing that others have a good time, or that others are comfortable or at ease in a situation, will practice good manners even if he or she has not learned all the specific details of etiquette. If his thoughtfulness for others is dictating his actions, he will never be far off from doing the "right" thing according to rules for accepted behavior.

Ann invited several of her friends to her house for an evening. She baked a cake to serve to them. She had not baked many cakes, and this one was not very successful. When she offered it to her friends, Jim looked at it and then took a very small piece.

Alice, who was a good cook herself, merely said, "No, thank you, I don't care for any."

Alice's brother, Peter, enthusiastically took a good-sized slice and, a little later, asked if he might have another piece.

On the way home, Alice criticized her brother's manners. She said, "It isn't good manners to ask for a second piece of cake. That cake wasn't fit to eat, anyway. I just politely refused when she offered it to me."

Peter said, "I noticed that you did, and your refusing was one reason why I asked for a second piece. Ann had baked that cake,

● Good manners mean thoughtfulness for others. *(Luoma Photos.)*

● A part of social growing up is to learn to think of the feelings of other people. The childish person thinks only of himself and his own feelings. *(Coronet Films.)*

and how do you suppose she was going to feel if everyone 'politely' turned up their noses at it as you did? It really was not such a bad cake and I asked for a second piece so she'd feel that someone appreciated her baking."

Whose manners were basically good, regardless of any social "rules"?

On another occasion Alice criticized Sally's manners because Sally looked up, smiled, and said "Thank you" when a waitress set a plate of fresh rolls on their table in a restaurant. Alice said, "The waitress was merely attending to her work. You aren't supposed to thank her for what she does. That is taken care of when you pay the bill and leave a tip." Sally said, "But I didn't stop to think. It just seems natural to show you appreciate it when someone bothers to do something for you."

Whose manners were basically better, Sally's or Alice's?

Two important rules in forming good social habits are: (1) Put yourself in the other person's place. What would you want him to say or do if you were in his place? (2) *Say* the good or thoughtful or kind word that comes to your mind. Don't hold back for fear it is the other person's place to speak first, or for fear you might be doing the wrong thing. It is *never* incorrect to show appreciation, as long as it is sincere.

HOW DO YOU RATE AS A CONVERSATIONALIST?

	Never	Some-times	Usually	Always
	0	4	7	10

As a conversationalist, I:

1. am prepared to discuss many different topics.

2. draw out the other person on his interests.

3. let the conversation stay on one topic long enough to let all express themselves.

4. shift to a new topic of conversation only when others in the group are ready to change to a new topic.

5. keep the conversation on a high level.

6. show that I hear what the others are saying.

7. am alert and take in all that is being said.

8. keep the "I's" in my conversations at a minimum.

9. notice whether what I am saying is of interest to the group or to myself only.

10. am alert to do my part to make a group conversation a success.

Total each column

Total points

Conversation

Learn to do your share or more in conversation. Think of what the other person is interested in and start from there. Don't wait for him to draw you out. Everyone loves to talk about his own interests to a good listener. Many of the people who are known as wonderful conversationalists are just good listeners. They get the other person started talking of his interests, and then they listen and encourage. They control their urge to grab the conversation and take it to their own interests. Of course, sometimes you may find a person who is really so shy that he or she will not talk much, and it is up to you. All right, go ahead. But even then, give the person a chance. If he seems to have anything at all to say, be ready to listen.

● Do you have trouble with introductions?

Introductions

Introductions often bother people. You know that there are right and wrong ways of introducing people, and you may feel that you always stumble around while you are trying to get the right kind of introduction out.

Remember that the purpose of introductions is a very practical one. Two people are standing looking at each other, and each wants to know who the other is. So you tell them. Just one thing you need to remember: You introduce one person *to* the other; the boy *to* the girl: "Mary, this is John." Your friend *to* your mother: "Mother, this is Peter." Always you introduce the man to the woman, or the younger, or less honored person to the older or more respected person. That is all that is really necessary.

Later, after you have formed your habit of making introductions simply and correctly, you may want to add a few pleasant flourishes. It always helps when you introduce two people if you know something to say that will help them get off to a quick start in talking to each other: "Dad, this is Bill. Bill is building a boat in his garage something like the one you built last year." Dad and Bill will not have to search for a subject to talk about.

It may be true that most people have a few moments of uncertainty in some situations even when they have lived for many years. But those moments become fewer and less troublesome for people who have built habits based on thoughtfulness for others and who have paid a reasonable amount of attention to common social practices.

You may be interested in reading some of the books that deal with a great many specific details of what to do and not to do in social situations. Some of these books are probably to be found in your school library.

You can help to overcome self-consciousness by taking time to learn what actions are generally accepted as socially correct. Nevertheless, some people who know enough never to use the wrong fork at a dinner table still are small children socially.

It is your habitual attitude around other people — your kindness and your ability to think of the feelings of others — that is the measure of how well you are growing up socially.

REVIEW QUESTIONS

1. How may one person have several different ages?
2. Why are we sometimes critical of the person who does not act his chronological age?

3. What is self-consciousness?
4. Give some common symptoms of self-consciousness.
5. List some specific things to do to overcome self-consciousness.
6. What is the basis of good manners?
7. Give some important steps in becoming a good conversationalist.
8. Give some of the rules for making introductions.
9. What is even more important than knowing what rules Emily Post gives on specific points of social behaviour?

KEY WORDS AND PHRASES

social relationships   chronological age
social maturity   self-consciousness
introductions

PROBLEMS AND ACTIVITIES

1. A person who is physically mature at 14 years might have problems that a physically immature person of 14 would not have. What are some of these problems?
2. Study the pictograph on page 64 which gives some situations in which a large group of senior high school students said they felt ill at ease. Now add to this list situations in which you sometimes feel ill at ease.
3. Review the techniques discussed in this chapter for overcoming self-consciousness. Add to this list any good techniques you have learned either by experience or through observing others.
4. Tell of some situations in which you thought people showed good manners although they may not have followed specific rules of etiquette.
5. It is often hard to remember afterwards the names of those to whom you were introduced. What system have you for remem-

bering names? If you do not have a system, have you heard of others who have worked out effective ways to remember names? How do some men in public life manage to remember the names of thousands of people?

6. *Role playing.* Be prepared to introduce two people at the next class session. You may introduce two people as themselves, or you may have them play the roles of entirely different people. You may introduce one as your mother and the other as your boy friend. Tell each something about the other when introducing them, so they will have a cue for conversation.

7. *Role playing.* Imagine that you are at a dance. Illustrate the right way and the wrong way for a boy to ask a girl for a dance. One couple may show both the right and the wrong, or two couples may take part, one couple doing it right and the other wrong. Show also what you do at the end of a dance number.

FILMS

Shy Guy — 14 minutes, sound, Coronet
Social Courtesy — 10 minutes, sound, Coronet
Mind Your Manners — 10 minutes, sound, Coronet
Good Table Manners — 10 minutes, sound, Coronet
Self-Conscious Guy — 10 minutes, sound, Coronet
See reading list at end of Part Two, page 118.

YOUR EMOTIONAL GROWTH

9

Growing up emotionally means becoming able to have thoughtful control of your actions rather than letting actions and attitudes be controlled mostly by feelings.

Emotional growth cannot be measured exactly, as chronological growth can be measured. Many different levels of emotional maturity can be seen in people of the same chronological age.

A description of the stages of growth that one's feelings of love or affection go through may help you to understand your emotional development.

Growth of affection

From the day of birth until old age, the need for love and affection is as necessary as food is to all of us. The ability to give as well as receive affection is a growing process that begins very early and progresses in a widening circle. The baby loves himself; he does not know anything of the needs of others, but he responds to their love for him. The love that he receives is important to his growth in infancy. Gradually, he branches out and can include his mother in his affections instead of only himself. Later, he includes the other members of the family, and his love for others contributes also to his emotional growth.

As children get to the pre-adolescent age (9-12) they have expanded their circle still farther and now are affectionate toward friends of their own sex outside their family. Boys at that age like boys and usually do not care much for girls, and girls at 9-12 are partial to girls. However, as boys and girls enter the teens, a new turn is taken in their development, and their affection begins to be directed toward people of their ages of the other sex.

74

If you are a girl you know that perhaps only a year or two ago it seemed that most boys were mere pests, but they seem to have changed. Now many of them are quite wonderful, and almost all of them are at least endurable. If you are a boy, something similar has happened. More of the girls are now fun to be with and fewer of them are just nuisances. This means that you have grown into a new stage emotionally.

In general, girls become interested in boys earlier than boys begin to be interested in girls. Ages at which such interests develop vary greatly, just as people differ greatly in their physical growth.

Most of you are now at the age when you are, or soon will be, shifting your interests to boys or girls outside of your family. This will continue until sooner or later you will find *one* person of the other sex who becomes permanently the center of your affection, and you will marry. Marriage makes it possible for strong affectional needs to be satisfied permanently. Later, children are born and the whole cycle begins over again. As parents, you will show affection for the self-centered baby; the baby, in turn, will learn to love others than himself, and the cycle we have described will be repeated. If this process goes well, each person gradually develops habits and traits that help him to mature emotionally.

● "Sure I love you, Fletcher, but I can't go around getting engaged to everyone I love!" (Emmy Lou *by Marty Links*.)

Your Emotional Growth   75

● "Do you think it's possible to fall in love with the whole senior class at once?" (Emmy Lou, *by Marty Links.*)

Self-centeredness

Sometimes progress is not as good as it should be in affectional development; some people do not grow beyond the baby stage of love. Like the baby, they crave love for themselves but cannot love anyone else. As the baby is completely self-centered in his interests and demands, so some people who are no longer babies in years are completely self-centered. They often feel that they are not appreciated enough by others, and they may become jealous and critical of others. It is hard for them to show consideration for anyone except themselves.

If you have brothers and sisters, your parents have been forced to work toward helping you to become other-centered, more than if you had no brothers and sisters. When there is only one child in a family, it is easy for parents to continue making the one the center of attention long after he should be learning to think of others. If you are an "only" child, you may have to work especially hard to overcome self-centeredness in yourself, no matter what your parents may do or have done.

Crushes

After you are in the stage in which your feelings of affection are beginning to center outside your family, you may at some time find that your affection for some one person becomes quite overwhelming. Perhaps it is your best friend, a person of your own sex, or it may be your boy-friend or girl-friend, not of your own sex. It may be your favorite teacher or some other older person who attracts you greatly. At this time, your affection for this person may be so strong that you feel it will surely last a lifetime.

If you have already had such an experience (some people call it a "crush"), you have found that gradually you changed in your feelings about the person. As time passed and you continued to grow up emotionally, you outgrew that emotional attachment. While it lasted, it was wonderful; or if your love was not returned, it was, perhaps, quite unbearable. But it served its purpose and came to an end. The experience was a stage in your growth.

Actually, such crushes probably help you to understand yourself better. You learn that you can feel a terrific emotion over someone and still get over it. Later, when you reach the age for marrying, you may be less likely to marry hastily the first person you fall violently in love with. Since you will have already learned that feelings can change, you will stop to think of other important things before you marry. You will think of whether or not you could really live with this person day in and day out for a lifetime or whether the two of you have ways, beliefs, likes, and dislikes so different that you might become terribly bored with each other if your emotions should change.

Love for parents

We have seen that the second stage in emotional growth is the love for parents, which develops when the baby begins to outgrow his self-love. Your love for your parents changes as the years pass and as you grow up. The person who is grown up in years and who is also emotionally grown up loves or respects his parents for all that they are as individuals. He appreciates what they have tried to do for him. He may or he may not enjoy their companionship, but he becomes able to see them as individuals somewhat as if

● How old is he emotionally?
(Luoma Photos.)

they were not his parents. As an adult, if your development has continued satisfactorily, the real center of your affection will be your husband or your wife and your children, not your parents.

Sometimes parents themselves are immature in that they find it hard to encourage their children to become independent of them emotionally. Parents may cling to their children and make it hard for sons or daughters to love someone they might marry.

On the other hand, you may sometimes feel that your parents are clinging to you or trying to hold you back more than they really are doing. At this stage of your growing up, problems arise for your parents and for you. Your parents are anxious to help you avoid mistakes that you might later regret. At the same time, they have to work to accept the fact that you are growing up and must gradually free yourself from your emotional dependence upon them. You, as well as they, need patience and a good understanding of what it means to grow up emotionally.

Coping with feelings

Another part of growing up emotionally is learning to cope with feelings that might control our behavior in undesirable ways.

Anger. When you see others who have not learned self-control, you can easily recognize their behavior as a sign of "retarded development." Though past that age, they are acting like babies.

If you still have difficulty outgrowing the habit of giving way to anger, the following steps may help you:

(1) If you do get into a situation that is provoking you to anger, look back at some other time when you were very angry about something. Remember how quickly it passed? Perhaps you were glad afterwards that you did not get the thing you thought you wanted so much at that time. Did you regret your anger later — feel that you made a fool of yourself? Looking back may help control present anger.

(2) Study others who become angry. Have you a friend who loses his or her temper? How do you feel toward him when he behaves so? Do you feel like giving in to him, or do you gradually get more and more hardened so that you feel like avoiding him when he is angry? How do his temper spells affect his popularity?

(3) When you get angry, your body prepares for physical combat. Anger produces a feeling of energy, so that you may feel like a fight. Then use that sudden energy some other way. Plunge into some type of physical activitiy to work off this energy. Do something with your hands. Take a walk, or run. Get into a game that requires vigorous activity. Even wash the dishes or the car! The extra energy which your body has suddenly given you need not be used in useless expression of anger. Your anger will disappear quicker if you use the energy in a way that gives you satisfaction rather than a later feeling of having made a fool of yourself.

Fear. Another emotion that concerns us as we grow up is fear. We all have fears that are the result of past experiences. By the time you reach your teens, you have some useful fears and some that are a handicap to emotional maturing. Fear is a good thing when it helps to prevent dangerous or foolish actions. You avoid exposing yourself to poison oak, for example, because you fear its effect on you. You obey traffic regulations, not only in order to be a good citizen but also because you fear the results of disobedience — traffic fines and highway accidents.

Fear is useful in another way. When you are suddenly frightened, you may act quickly and automatically to escape a real danger. Emotionally mature persons learn to look at their fears

● Most of us have developed unnecessary fears.

and to know which ones are useful, intelligent ones to which attention should be paid, and which fears are unreasonable, emotional reactions that they should try to outgrow.

Can you think of some of each type of fear? Can you figure out how you came by any unreasonable fears that you may have?

Bodily reactions to emotions

Do you ever lose your appetite just before some important event? Or possibly your stomach feels sick just before you take part in a play or an important game. Remember the time you were coming home from a friend's house after dark and you heard a strange sound or thought you saw something unfamiliar? Your heart started pounding so hard that you could almost hear it beat. Suddenly, you had extra energy for fight or flight. Possibly you started to run and you actually ran faster than you could have run if you had not been frightened. There are a number of ways in which our bodies react when we are faced with any sort of experience that makes special requirements upon us. There are the stomach symptoms mentioned above, the rapid beating of the heart. Many people find that they perspire excessively, they "break out in a sweat." Some lose control of their voices when they especially need good voice control. The saliva glands seem to stop working, and the mouth gets dry when one needs to speak freely.

BODY CHANGES WHICH TAKE PLACE TO PREPARE THE BODY FOR ACTION, RUNNING, OR FIGHTING

When one is angry or fearful

1. The liver releases extra sugar to provide energy to voluntary muscles for action, fight or flight.

2. Heartbeat and breathing become more rapid to get extra food, sugar, and oxygen to the entire body.

3. Blood supply is decreased to involuntary muscles and increased to the voluntary muscles where it is now needed for fight or flight.

4. Digestion is slowed down because energy is being directed to voluntary muscles.

5. The body becomes tense because it is ready for action.

6. The adrenal glands release extra adrenaline to keep the body ready for fight or flight.

All those bodily reactions are common experiences. As people grow up, they learn specific ways of coping with such bodily reactions. The first step is to become able to recognize such symptoms for what they are and do something constructive about them, rather than to let them control actions. The reason why public speakers are usually given a glass of water while speaking is that even the most experienced speakers sometimes find that their mouths get dry or their voices change pitch, and they need a drink of water to relax their throats. Athletic coaches habitually have players "warm up" before going into the game. The warming up gives the player a chance to work off some of the bodily symptoms that might bother him.

Sometimes athletes will say after a game, "I was so 'tied up' during the game that I could not play well." What they mean is that several body symptoms were so strong that they could not overcome them. Possibly you have had this experience on other occasions, such as, for example, when you wanted to ask someone for a date. Perhaps, like the basketball player, you "tied up," and

HOW OLD ARE YOU EMOTIONALLY?

	Never	Some-times	Usually	Always
	0	4	7	10
1. I control my temper.				
2. I act in a reasonable way when I do not get what I want.				
3. I respect others even if they disagree with me.				
4. I have friends among both sexes.				
5. I try to see myself as others see me.				
6. I can see the other person's point of view.				
7. I accept responsibility for my mistakes.				
8. I respect my parents' judgment but am developing independence from my parents.				
9. I am fairly free from jealousy.				
10. I can profit from criticism.				

Total each column

Total points

found that it was very hard for you to go ahead with the game.

As you are maturing emotionally during the teens, it is good to look at your emotions and to understand the bodily reactions that go along with your emotions. It is important to learn to know the difference between a real illness and a stomach which is simply reflecting a fear or excitement or tension in connection with an event or challenge. The person who is growing up emotionally does not let the bodily symptoms control. He does not take to his bed when he feels such symptoms. You learn by experience that you can work off the symptoms by warming up before a game, by preparing well for whatever you have to do, by meeting challenges with a positive action rather than by running away from them. The symptoms are natural. They are just a part of the way human bodies function. Fortunately, as time passes and you learn to cope with such bodily reactions to emotion, the symptoms become less and less of a bother. Many of them may stop occurring at all. Understanding them and knowing how universal they are among people can help you.

As you have read this chapter, have you been able to recognize some stages in your own emotional growth?

REVIEW QUESTIONS

1. Trace the growth of love or affection from babyhood to adulthood.

2. What is self-centered love? At what period in life is it a natural stage of development?

3. How does having brothers and sisters make it easier to develop "other-centered" love?

4. What part may a "crush" play in a person's growing up?

5. How does love for parents change as people become mature?

6. Give several specific steps one may take to help overcome habits of giving way to anger.

7. Give several physical symptoms that may occur when people are fearful, excited, or under pressure.

8. What things can one do to "work off" the physical symptoms that accompany emotions?

KEY WORDS AND PHRASES

emotional maturity   affectional need   emotional immaturity
affection   self-centered love   anger
pre-adolescent   other-centered   fear
   physical symptoms

PROBLEMS AND ACTIVITIES

1. If there is a baby in your family, observe it closely for a few days and make a list of the ways in which the baby shows self-centered love. Also make a list of any ways in which the baby shows the beginnings of learning to show love for others.

2. Most of us know people who become angry. What are some of the very foolish things you have noticed people do when they were angry?

3. Do you remember the last time you really became angry at home? What did your parents do to help you break your habit of anger? If you have not had a personal experience, do you know how some other family handled such a problem? Were their methods good or bad?

4. Mary complained in the middle of the afternoon that she felt sick, her stomach seemed to be tied in a knot and her lunch had not digested. She said she had quarreled with Nancy at the lunch counter at noon. Before noon, she had been feeling fine. What might be the emotional and physical basis for Mary's feeling ill? What could she do about it? How could she prevent such illness in the future?

FILMS

Control Your Emotions — 14 minutes, sound, Coronet
Act Your Age — 14 minutes, sound, Coronet
Overcoming Fear — 13 minutes, sound, Coronet
See reading list at end of Part Two, page 118.

   Your Emotional Growth

DEVELOPING SKILLS IN SOCIAL RELATIONSHIPS— DATING

10

Most other countries do not have dating customs like ours in the United States. In many countries, a young girl is never alone with any boy until she has reached the age for marriage. In some countries, an older person is always present even up to the very day of marriage. Sometimes travelers from other countries are very puzzled when they see young American boys and girls going about together in couples. The travelers may believe that the American way of early pairing off or "dating" is dangerous or harmful and that boys and girls should not be allowed to associate together so freely as our customs allow.

Whatever anyone may think about the custom, no one can doubt that "dating" is here to stay. It is just as accepted in American life as are hot dogs and hamburgers, highways crowded with cars, or the Sunday funnies. Nevertheless, as you reach the dating age, you face many questions that are not definitely answered for you by our social customs.

Your responsibility for deciding what you will do about many points that arise in the dating years is much greater than the responsibility of boys and girls in countries where their every move is controlled and supervised. This chapter will discuss some questions that arise in dating. You will think of others that should be brought up in your class discussions.

Why date at all?

To some of you, "Why date?" may seem an odd question. You would answer at once, "It's fun," or "Everyone does it." But there are other reasons why your dating in high school is worthwhile, if you want to make it so.

Through dating, you can get to know many different kinds of people. You can take part in more social activities than you would if you never dated. You can learn much about getting along smoothly with others. Through your dating experiences you can develop social skills and become more adept in social situations. As time passes, and as you date different people, you will gradually begin to understand yourself better and to form ideas that will help you eventually in choosing the kind of person with whom you could build a successful marriage.

● Dating provides an opportunity to learn about personality and the types of people with whom you get along best. Dating also gives an opportunity to develop social skills. *(Luoma Photos.)*

When should you begin to date?

The age to begin dating differs with different people in the same school. Just as people differ in their rate of physical growth — of two men six feet tall, one may have reached six feet at fifteen years of age, the other may have been eighteen or even twenty years old before he attained his height — so people differ in the age at which their social interests develop.

Age to begin dating differs also in different parts of the country and in different schools and towns. The figure on page 92 shows the percentages of freshman and senior boys and girls who were not dating at all in a large study of dating in twelve high schools in nine states. The figure on page 87 gives the ages that a national sample of high school young people thought were about right for the first date.

AT WHAT AGE SHOULD WE START DATING ?

AGE	%	
UNDER TWELVE	3%	
THIRTEEN TO FOURTEEN	44%	
FIFTEEN TO SIXTEEN	43%	
SEVENTEEN TO EIGHTEEN	5%	
OVER EIGHTEEN	1%	

* 4% did not report. Adapted from *The Purdue Opinion Panel*, Lafayette, Ind.: Purdue University, 10:2, December 1950, p. 34.

● At what age do young people start dating in your community? One national study of high school youth showed that almost half thought it was all right to start at thirteen or fourteen. Do you agree?

Some communities have dance groups or dance classes for almost all youngsters, even at the sixth grade level. In such communities, boys and girls will be likely to grow into the dating stage at younger ages than if they lived in communities where the planned recreation did not include activities that encourage pairing off.

In sections of the country where many of the parents are of foreign background, the boys and girls may not date as early, since their parents may not approve of early dating.

In some communities, even when many girls and boys date at fourteen or fifteen, some parents will not accept the custom. They may set the age at sixteen or older and refuse to permit their children to have single dates before that age. Attitudes of parents have to be reckoned with.

Some people cannot even remember accurately at just what age they really had their first date, because they associated with a group, and the change from having fun with several or a group, to being a foursome or twosome, was so gradual that they did not think of any one occasion as being a "first date." That is the most

Developing Skills in Social Relationships — Dating   87

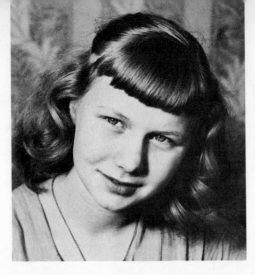

● When am I old enough to begin dating? *(Luoma Photos.)*

natural way to begin dating. You are probably at the age to begin dating when you have been having fun with groups of boys and girls, and it comes about naturally that you begin to spend more time with certain boys or girls whom you like. Then just two of you may begin to agree in advance on your plans; and before you know it, you are dating.

Getting dates

It often happens that girls begin to think about having dates before the boys of their age have become interested in dating. Girls can plan parties and invite groups of boys and girls. Both boys and girls enjoy this group stage of having fun, and (if you are a girl) it is better not to be in a hurry to move on to the next stage in dating.

Some girls "push" too fast and take too much initiative toward dating. Although these girls may get dates sooner than some other girls do, their aggressiveness may handicap them in their later dating. Boys like to feel that they are taking the initiative in dating. Even if a boy may find it hard to ask for dates (most boys do find it hard, especially at first), he still is likely to shy away from girls who pursue him too openly. A girl can show her liking for boys, or a boy, by being friendly and by being good company. There are many ways of making a boy feel liked and appreciated, but according to present American custom, girls have to learn how to show liking and appreciation without making a boy feel chased or cornered.

If you are a boy, you have a different problem. One fifteen-year-old girl said, "I'm glad I'm a girl. It's easy to be nice to boys, but I'd dislike doing the asking for dates. A boy has to walk right up to you or call you on the 'phone and say 'Would you like to go to this or that with me?' and take a chance that you'll be glad to say 'yes' instead of 'no.'"

That is true. Boys do have to take a chance and *ask*. But there are certain good rules that a boy can follow that will save embarrassment for himself and the girl he may ask for a date. After a few times, most boys get used to "taking a chance" and asking. In fact, a boy learns to read the signs well enough so that often he can be pretty sure, before he asks, whether or not a girl will be glad to say yes.

Boys: When asking for a date, be specific about what you are inviting a girl to do before you ask her if she is busy. Don't say "What are you doing Friday night?" Lay your cards on the table right off by saying, "I have tickets for the play Friday night. Would you like to go with me?" or "Tom, Harry, and I are planning to go to Playland Saturday afternoon. Tom and Harry are taking Jane and Sue. Would you like to go with me?"

You will feel better yourself if you are direct. It is easier to say something specific than to beat about the bush. When you are direct, you can expect a direct answer from a girl; and if she knows

9TH GRADE	%	DATING PROBLEMS	%	12TH GRADE
	50%	1. I SELDOM HAVE DATES.	32%	
	21%	2. I DON'T KNOW HOW TO ASK FOR A DATE.	9%	
	25%	3. I DON'T KNOW WHAT TO DO ON A DATE.	12%	
	28%	4. HOW DO I REFUSE A DATE POLITELY?	27%	
	18%	5. HOW DO I BREAK OFF GOING STEADY?	18%	
	20%	6. SHOULD I GO STEADY?	22%	

Adapted from *The Purdue Opinion Panel*, 8:3, April 1949, p. 10.

● It seems that as one goes from the 9th to the 12th grade, he has fewer dating worries. However, seniors worry about certain dating problems as much as freshmen. They, too, are worried about going steady, how to break off, and how to refuse a date politely.

Developing Skills in Social Relationships — Dating   89

SHOULD GIRLS ASK BOYS FOR DATES?

BOYS	%*		%*	GIRLS
	48%	YES	27%	
	33%	NO	54%	
	12%	UNDECIDED	14%	

* 7% of boys and 5% of girls did not report. Adapted from *The Purdue Opinion Panel*, 10:2, December 1950, p. 32.

● Far more boys than girls think girls should be free to ask boys for dates. What do you think? What problems might arise if girls were freer to ask for dates? What is the practice in your school?

all the plans, it is easier for her to make up her mind promptly how she wants to answer you.

Girls: A straight request for a date requires a prompt and direct answer. You cannot expect to get by with keeping Dick dangling, waiting for an answer, while you work on getting John, your first choice, to ask you to the big party. News of such tactics travels, and soon even your second, third, and fourth choices will be asking other girls instead of you for dates.

When you are asked, you must make up your mind whether to say "no" in the hope that your first choice will later ask you, or to say "yes" and then stick to your agreement even if a more attractive chance turns up later. This is a chance one must take. If it becomes known that Sally will let a boy down or break a date with him if a better date turns up, Sally will find fewer and fewer of the better dates turning up. So when he asks for a date, say "Yes, I'd love to go," or say "no" in a friendly way that makes him feel that you appreciate his having asked you. If you later regret the answer you gave, you can do differently the next time.

● Boys still feel that they should take the initiative in dating.

Girls: If you wish to refuse a date, remember that every request for a date is a compliment to you. Whether or not you like the boy, he has paid you a compliment by asking you, and you owe him courteous appreciation. Never refuse a date in such a way that a boy feels you have thrown his invitation back in his face. That is just as rude as it would be if your mother insulted someone who telephoned to invite your parents to a party.

If you do not want to accept, you can always be friendly and pleasant in the way that you say you are "busy" that night, or that you have to study, or have other plans. Whatever the reason you give for refusing, be sure you give it graciously, in the way you would want to be answered if you had to do the asking for dates.

How often should you date?

When several thousand high school young people were asked the question, "How often do you date?" their answers ranged from not at all to over ten times per month. This study made in twelve high schools in nine states is summarized in the figure on page 92.

Many boys and girls have dates only for special occasions such as class or school parties. That means that they date only about once in several weeks. Others feel that Friday or Saturday night is meant for dating; so if there is no special occasion set, they plan a date for the show or a record party or some other sort of activity-party. This once-a-week pattern becomes fairly common in many schools by the time people are juniors or seniors, but customs differ.

Developing Skills in Social Relationships — Dating   91

Whatever the pattern in your school or among your friends, you have found or will find that the demands made on your time by your other interests and activities are likely to set limits on how often you can date and still keep your activities balanced and organized.

If you have homework on several nights a week, and if you belong to any organization that takes some of your evening time, one date a week or less may be all you have time for.

Your dating will be a lot more fun if you arrange your plans so that you are keeping up with your other obligations and feel free to enjoy the dates that you do have without having to worry about work left undone. Most people find that dates on school nights do not work out very well, except on very special occasions.

In addition to considering the requirements of your school work, you must also take into account your need for sleep during the school week as well as your other activities and interests. How often you should date will depend also on your parents' attitudes about it. Do they object to school-night dates? How often do they think it is a good idea for you to have dates? Talk it over with them. You will enjoy your dating much more if your parents are satisfied with the way you plan your time. Even if they may be too conservative in their ideas about your dating, talking it over will probably help you and your parents to come closer to each other's views on the subject.

HOW FREQUENTLY SHOULD YOU DATE ?

FRESHMEN	%	FREQUENCY OF DATING:	%	SENIORS
👤👤👤👤👤	53%	DON'T DATE.	18%	👤👤
👤👤	21%	ONE TO FOUR DATES A MONTH.	25%	👤👤👤
👤👤	17%	FIVE TO TEN DATES A MONTH.	31%	👤👤👤
👤	9%	OVER TEN DATES A MONTH.	26%	👤👤👤

Adapted from Harold H. Punke, "Dating Practices of High School Youths," *NEA Bulletin of Secondary School Principals*, 28:48, 1944.

● The percentage of young people who date increases rapidly from the freshman to the senior year of high school. Over half the freshmen in a study of 5,628 students in high schools in 9 states did not date at all, but less than one-fifth of the seniors were not dating.

● Your dating will be a lot more fun if you arrange your plans in keeping with your other obligations.

REVIEW QUESTIONS

1. How are dating customs in the United States different from those in some other countries?

2. How does our system of dating demand that American young people take more responsibility for their actions than young people of some other countries?

3. What are some things that you should learn through dating?

4. What things influence the age to begin dating?

5. How does "group" dating lead to single dating?

6. Who gets interested in dating first, boys or girls? Why? (Think of the discussion in Chapter 5.)

7. Is it all right for the girl to ask for dates?

8. How can a boy know whether a girl will accept a date with him before he asks for the date?

9. What are some rules to remember in asking for a date?

10. What are some rules to follow in responding when you are asked for a date?

11. Is it fair to expect a girl not to break a date with one boy if a "better" date turns up later?

12. Name several things which should determine how often you date when in high school.

KEY WORDS AND PHRASES

dating customs   social customs

PROBLEMS AND ACTIVITIES

1. Interview someone in your community who has come from a foreign country. Ask about the dating customs in the person's homeland and report to the class. Possibly you can get some-one from a foreign country to come and talk to the class about dating, courtship, and marriage customs in the country of his birth.

2. *Class survey.* Study the figure on page 87, which gives the age at which other high school students think teen-agers should have their first date. Make a similar study in your class and compare the percentages with those in the national study (4 per cent gave no response in the national study.)

3. *Class survey.* Find out what the members of your class be-lieve about whether girls should be as free as boys in asking for dates. Compare your class beliefs with the national study given in the figure on page 90.

4. Make a list of reasons for and against girls' being as free as boys to ask for dates.

ROLE PLAYING

Several couples demonstrate the right and the wrong ways to ask for dates and to accept or refuse dates, in person and by tele-phone.

FILMS

Dating: Do's and Don'ts — 14 minutes, sound, Coronet
See reading list at end of Part Two, page 118.

DATING: GOING STEADY
AND HOURS TO GET IN

11

After you have been dating for a while, you may find yourself going out with one person more often than with others. The two of you get along well. You like each other and have fun together on dates, and for both of you it becomes easier to continue to go out together than to arrange for dates with different people. You may talk it over and agree to go steady. That means that both of you know that you can depend on each other for dates for all important occasions and for quite regular dates in between special occasions, and neither of you will date other people while you are going steady. It is an arrangement with both advantages and disadvantages.

Some advantages of going steady

If you are a boy, going steady means you can probably get by with being a little more careless about asking for dates very far in advance. You can take it for granted that Sue will be willing when you want a date. If you are the girl, you now have more freedom to suggest things you would like to do or places you would like to go. If you say, "Some Saturday soon, let's have a picnic and then go roller skating," he will not think you are taking too much for granted, as he might if you made such a suggestion when you were not going steady. You also know you can count on John for the Saturday night party, even if he has neglected to ask you for the date as far ahead of time as he would have done before you were going steady.

Another advantage for both of you is that by going steady you may get a better understanding of yourself and of others. When you go steady with a person you learn to know him or her better

95

● When you first start dating, you may want the security of going steady. After you are used to dating, you will see advantages in dating many different people in order to learn about different types of personalities. *(Luoma Photos.)*

than in more casual dating. You act more natural with each other and you become aware of your true feelings and attitudes about many things. After you have gone steady with more than one person you may be able to choose more wisely later when the time comes for a permanently serious love affair and marriage.

Disadvantages of going steady

There are also disadvantages for both of you in going steady. Sue may feel that since they have been going steady John has become altogether too relaxed and casual about asking her for dates ahead of time. He takes it too much for granted that she will always be ready and willing when he wants a date. Since he does not ask for dates fairly well ahead of time, she is often inconvenienced in making plans for her other non-dating activities.

For both of you, there is the danger that one of you will become too possessive, will become jealous or sulky if you show your usual friendliness to other boys and girls. No one likes the feeling of being fenced in, and it is easy for one or the other of you to begin to feel that going steady has fenced you in.

Boys are often quick to resent any possessiveness on the part of the girl. The very thing you like about going steady — the com-

● Going steady has disadvantages as well as advantages. Sometimes people begin to resent possessiveness on the part of a steady girl or boy friend. *(Hayward High School.)*

fortableness of knowing you can depend on each other — may be the thing that begins to take the zest out of your friendship and make the ties of your friendship feel more like chains.

How does going steady end?

Another disadvantage of going steady is that when you go with one person for very long you fail to get acquainted with other types of personalities as you should be doing during dating years. There is always the problem of ending your going steady agreement without hurt feelings or hurt pride for one or both of you. When you started going steady, of course you knew it was not to last forever. But almost always one becomes ready to end the agreement before the other is ready.

John goes away for a summer vacation and meets a new girl who suddenly seems to be a lot more fun than Sue is. Sue is at home with not much to do except to think of John and write him letters.

Or perhaps a new boy comes into school and Sue begins to think how much more interesting it would be to have a date with him for the class party coming up than to wait for John to decide whether or not he can go to it. On some Saturday nights, John has to work anyhow, and Sue dislikes staying home when John works.

No matter how good your reason for deciding not to go steady any longer, it is hard to tell someone, "I don't want to go steady with you any longer," without making him or her feel letdown and discarded. But that is the way almost all going steady agreements made in the early teens will end eventually. Some boys and girls face this at the beginning and try to avoid grief by agreeing to go steady only for a set length of time; for example, "until school is out" if they begin dating in the spring; "until the end of the basket-ball season" or "until Christmas vacation ends" if they begin dating in the fall. Even in those cases, one of them is likely to be anxious to continue going steady longer; but at least if a time limit is set on the going steady agreement, there may be less hurt pride and perhaps fewer hurt feelings.

Parents — and going steady

One reason your parents may object to your going steady is that the meaning of the term "going steady" has changed since your parents were young. When they were teen-agers, going steady was a

● Parents may not approve of going steady.

Dating: Going Steady and Hours to Get In

step toward marriage. When couples decided to go steady, they were usually several years older than "going steady" couples are today. When they began going steady they knew it meant that they might soon think of marrying each other if they continued to go steady. Today, the term does not mean that to most high school young people. You know that when you begin going steady with a person, it probably is a temporary arrangement, no matter how much you like each other. Many parents cannot understand that viewpoint. It is hard for them to recognize that you may want to go steady because it is a pleasant social custom in your school and that you know as well as they do that marriage is still a number of

---

REASONS SOMETIMES GIVEN FOR AND AGAINST GOING STEADY

Which of the advantages and disadvantages do you believe are important?

Advantages	Disadvantages
Dating security.	It is hard to break up.
Evidence of dating success.	It is hard to get back into circulation.
Can know each other well.	Do not get acquainted with many young people.
Can know another family well.	Family arguments and misunderstandings.
Costs less money.	Don't like being taken in by another family.
Family feels more confident since they know boy or girl.	Families worry about our being too serious.
Don't have to be on best behavior.	It costs more.
Don't have to dress so well.	One may be too serious, and the other has difficulty breaking up.
Don't have to plan ahead for dates.	Take each other for granted too much.

Dating: Going Steady and Hours to Get In 99

● "Walter has begun to bore me . . . especially since he's started going steady with Enid." (Emmy Lou by Marty Links.)

years in the future and not a consideration in your going steady. Purdue University polled high school young people in all sections of the country and found a great difference in thinking among parents and children on steady dating.

Hours to get in

Many boys and girls have difficulty with their families over the hours at which they get in from dates. It is often hard for parents and sons and daughters to agree on this point. Parents cannot help but think of the rules that applied when they were dating, and they may feel that those rules should apply for their children.

Such factors as where you live and what means of transportation you have to depend on for getting home have to be considered in setting the time for getting home at night. If you talk over the whole matter, you and your parents can probably understand each other better and agree fairly well about hours to get in.

The best thing you can do is to be perfectly frank with your parents. One reason parents seem to be stubborn or unreasonable on such matters is that if they do not know the places you are going to be and the people you are going to be with, they will worry about you and feel that they must set arbitrary limits on when you must be in. If you tell them exactly what your plans are and they know that they can trust you to use good judgment, they will be less worried and can be more reasonable.

If you live in a small town and are going to a moving picture, most parents will agree that from a half hour to an hour is all right for getting cokes or food and getting home after the show, unless the show runs unusually late. You know ahead of time when the show will end, and you can set a definite time for getting home.

If you live in a city, it is true that it is not safe or acceptable for high school-aged people to be on the streets at late hours, either in cars or in public means of transportation. In urban areas, even liberal parents are likely to feel that only a very exceptional occasion justifies your being out later than midnight. Many cities have "curfew" laws requiring people under 16 or 18 to be off the streets after certain hours, unless they are with adults. In small towns and in the country, it may be somewhat different. Take a poll of the parents of your class to learn what they think about hours to get in. Are their ideas reasonable? Consider the results of your poll and decide what you, as a class, can agree upon as reasonable hours. Keep it anonymous, so that none of you feels conspicuous if your parents are stricter than the rest. But ask them to say at what hour they think you should, as a rule, be in (1) from a moving picture show, (2) from a private party at a home, (3) from parties or dances at school or public places. How well do they agree?

It is usually the girl's responsibility to say at what hour she must be in. The boy is obligated to do his best to see that she gets home at the time she has agreed upon with her parents.

IS IT ALL RIGHT TO GO STEADY ?

STUDENTS	%*		%*	PARENTS
	44%	USUALLY	15%	
	42%	SOMETIMES	53%	
	11%	NEVER	29%	

* 3% of students and 3% of parents did not report. Adapted from *The Purdue Opinion Panel*, 9:1, November 1949, p. 41.

● In a national study of high school students, the students were asked to give their opinion and their parents' opinion about going steady. You will notice that students think differently from their parents on steady dating.

Dating: Going Steady and Hours to Get In   101

WHAT TIME SHOULD YOU BE HOME FROM DATES ?

NINTH GRADE	%		%	TWELFTH GRADE
	15	10:00	2	
	33	11:00	15	
	24	12:00	41	
	3	1:00 OR LATER	13	
	25	NO SET TIME	29	

Adapted from *The Purdue Opinion Panel*, 7:3, April 1948, p. 14.

● Parents and children have many conflicts over the hours the children should get in from dates. The pictograph summarizes the results of a national study of freshmen and seniors on what they think about the right time to get in from dates. Have you got together with your parents on when you are to be in?

Are your parents too strict?

Do you feel that your parents are too strict? They will probably outgrow it as you get older and as they become convinced that you are responsible. The truth is that your friends will think nothing of your parents' strictness if *you* have a good attitude about it. If you say to your date, "I have to be in by eleven o'clock. I hope that is all right with you" and then make sure you are good company for the time that you are with him, your social standing will not be hurt at all.

The boy or girl whose popularity suffers is the one who complains bitterly about his parents to his friends and insists on staying out so late that the friends get into difficulty with their parents, also.

You will probably be able to get your parents to relax their requirements more quickly by cooperating with them, while demonstrating that you are dependable and can be trusted to have more leeway in what you do. To resist and refuse to cooperate with their ideas may only make more conflict and postpone the time when they will relax their requirements.

● It's up to the boy to help the girl get in on time.

REVIEW QUESTIONS

1. What does the term "going steady" mean to you and to others in your school?
2. What are some of the advantages of going steady?
3. What are some of the disadvantages of going steady?
4. Why is it sometimes a problem to stop going steady with a person?
5. How has the meaning of the term "going steady" changed since Mother and Father were teen-agers? Ask your parents and your grandparents what it meant when they were in high school.
6. Why do parents oppose steady dating more than young people oppose it?
7. How can parents and children get together on hours to get in?
8. Why do parents worry when their children keep late hours?

KEY WORDS AND PHRASES

steady dating   curfew laws

PROBLEMS AND ACTIVITIES

1. Study the lists of advantages and disadvantages of steady dating as given on page 99. Add to these lists several other advantages and disadvantages that you have thought of.
2. Discuss the term "steady dating" with your parents. If they have opposed your steady dating, is a misunderstanding over the meaning of the term part of the cause of their opposition?
3. *Class survey.* What does your class think about going steady and about hours to get in? Make an anonymous study of your class and compare the results with the national studies of high school young people as given on pages 101 and 102. When the national study asked the question this way, "Should or should not boys and girls 'go steady' while in high school?" 42 per cent said they should, 35 per cent said they should not, and 23 per cent were undecided.
4. *Parent survey.* It would be interesting to give the above class survey to your parents and then to summarize it and compare parent opinions with class opinions on hours and steady dating.

ROLE PLAYING — SOCIO-DRAMA

Have a panel discussion of the problems centering around steady dating, hours to get in, use of the family car, and other dating problems. Have several students play the role of the parents and several others the role of young people.

FILMS

Going Steady — 10 minutes, sound, Coronet
See reading list at end of Part Two, page 118.

DATING MANNERS

12

Some of your friends may seem to be always perfectly poised and smooth in their social behavior. You admire them, for it seems that they just naturally know what to do on all occasions. But you cannot see the uncertainties that they may have underneath their smooth actions. The social poise that you see in them does not just come naturally for them any more than for you. They are, no doubt, working hard at learning to do the right thing at the right time on dates and on other occasions.

An earlier chapter suggested that self-confidence comes to one who learns what is expected of him in social situations and practices doing the right thing. You have a date for Friday night. What are some of the rules that you should know, that will help you feel at ease throughout the evening?

The first and most important rule for good manners on all occasions, whether you are a boy or a girl, will bear repeating here: Think of the other person, not yourself. Take pains to do and say the thing that will make the other person most comfortable and at ease, and you will not go far wrong on details of etiquette.

Nevertheless, there are certain rules that are followed as a part of custom in most parts of our country. Knowing them will help you in your dating.

For boys: calling for your date

Never ask your date to meet you somewhere unless some extremely unusual circumstance should make that necessary. Call at her house for her.

When you call for her, go up to the door and ring the bell or knock at the door. Sounding a car horn or standing on the side-

● Bill calls for his date at the door and takes her to the door at the end of the evening. *(Coronet Films.)*

walk whistling for the girl has been tried! But your date and her family will not appreciate it.

Should you take flowers?

Only on very special occasions, when you know that it is the custom in your school, should you take flowers. In many schools now, there is general agreement that no flowers are given for any school parties. In other schools, there may be one or two school or class parties each year when it is the custom for the boy to get flowers for his date to wear. Find out what the custom is in your school and follow it. If the occasion requires flowers, ask your date ahead of time what color her dress is to be, so that you can get flowers that will not clash. Then bring the flowers when you call for her, unless in your school it is the custom to send the flowers a few hours ahead of time. In most schools, however, on the rare occasions when flowers are given, the boy takes them with him when he calls for the girl.

Transportation

It is up to you to arrange for transportation. In states that have high age limits for issuing drivers' licenses, many boys are dating before they are old enough to drive a car. If that is true in your case, you may use public transportation, or perhaps your parents or an older brother will drive you and your date to the party.

It is a good idea to tell your date ahead of time how you and she are going to get to the party, whether by bus or whether someone is going to take you. Her parents will want to know, and the means of transportation may also make some difference in what she might wear. You pay any transportation expenses involved.

If you go in a car, you open the door for her and let her get in first, then get in yourself and close the door. (Yes, jumping in first and letting her shift for herself is sometimes done! It does not help a boy's popularity.)

● How do you call for your date?

Going to a movie

If your date is for a movie, a play, or another such public performance, you buy the tickets while she stands aside and waits for you. Then, as you enter to find seats, if there is an usher, your date follows him and you follow her. If there is no usher, you go ahead to lead the way to seats, then stand back and let her be seated ahead of you.

Eating after the show

Afterward, if you go somewhere to eat, you may suggest one or two places and let her choose, or you may just suggest the place you think would be a good place to go. The advantage of your taking responsibility for the choice is that you know how much you can spend, and you should limit the choice to the type of place you can afford to buy food in. In some schools, couples sometimes "go Dutch," each paying his or her share of the expenses. On such occasions, of course, the girl will take more initiative in making decisions.

It is correct in an eating place for you to give both your own order and your date's order to the waitress, after first asking the girl what she would like to have. However, it may be that in your community, the high school people habitually go to only one or two special places for their hamburgers and cokes, and in these places it is not the custom for the boy to order for both. If the situation is so informal that it would seem stiff if you insisted on ordering for her, she will speak for herself. In more formal eating places, however, the boy usually does the ordering.

When you take her home

If the time has come for her to be in, according to her agreement with her parents, don't linger on the porch talking until it becomes awkward for her to end the conversation and go in. Just tell her you have "had fun" or "enjoyed the evening" or whatever is easiest for you to say, then say good night and leave.

For girls: when he calls for you be ready

Whoever started the fiction that it was smart to be late, lest your date think you too anxious, was far off the track. Boys don't like to be kept waiting any better than you do. How would you like to be kept sitting talking to a pair of strange parents while *he* took his time getting ready?

Either answer the door yourself or have someone else go to the door, but be ready to appear and greet him promptly after he arrives.

If your parents are present, introduce him to them. You can do it simply by saying, "Mother, Dad, this is Jim. Jim, my parents." There are more flowery ways, but that much is correct.

If he brings you flowers

Show appreciation for them at once. He went to a lot of bother to try to please you with the flowers. Be sure you tell him at once how much you like them, and wear them proudly as a further way of showing your appreciation. Unless there is some good reason for delaying, you should pin them on at once. There is no exclusively "correct" place or manner for wearing flowers. That is up to your wishes. Depending upon the flowers, the occasion, and your dress, you may wear them in your hair, on your wrist, your shoulder, or at your waist.

A movie date

If you go to a movie, you will stand aside while he buys the tickets, then follow the usher to your seats. If there is no usher, don't rush ahead hunting seats; stand back and let the boy go ahead to find seats; follow him as you would the usher.

BOYS	DESIRABLE TRAITS FOR DATES	GIRLS
76%	IS PHYSICALLY AND MENTALLY FIT.	83%
65%	IS CLEAN -- IN SPEECH AND IN ACTIONS.	82%
71%	TAKES PRIDE IN PERSONAL APPEARANCE AND MANNERS.	80%
64%	IS CONSIDERATE OF ME AND OF OTHERS.	83%
72%	IS DEPENDABLE AND CAN BE TRUSTED.	83%
65%	ACTS OWN AGE AND IS NOT CHILDISH.	76%
69%	HAS A SENSE OF HUMOR AND GOOD DISPOSITION.	78%

Adapted from *The Purdue Opinion Panel,* 10:2, December 1950, p. 12.

● Do you have the traits that others like in dates? The above chart summarizes a national study of young people to find out the traits they like in others. Boys and girls seem to place high premium on the same traits.

SHALL WE GO DUTCH ?					
BOYS	%		%	GIRLS	
	37%	YES	36%		
	53%	NO	53%		
	10%	UNDECIDED	11%		

Adapted from *The Purdue Opinion Panel*, 8:1, November 1948, p. 37.

● Boys and girls do not differ in their thinking about going "Dutch." More than one in three are in favor. Are there certain types of dates on which you would favor going Dutch? Do you think that the boy or the girl should suggest going Dutch?

Eating afterwards

If you go to eat afterwards, let him decide where you should go. If he should ask you to choose a place, be sure you choose one in keeping with what he can spend. It is good manners to appear to ignore all financial considerations, yet to be very careful that you do not make choices that force a boy to overspend on a date with you. Even if you are going "Dutch" — each of you paying your own way — confine your spending to what will not put financial pressure on your date.

When it comes to giving an order, let him suggest something for you if he likes. Then wait to see whether or not he intends to go ahead and order for both of you. If he wants to observe the formalities and do the talking to the waitress, he will not appreciate your speaking up and taking the initiative any more than he would like it if you rushed ahead and opened the car door for yourself when he had intended to open the door for you.

Tell him at what time you have to be home

Cooperate by taking your full share of responsibility in seeing that you get home on time. Even if he may protest at the early hour, most boys appreciate a girl who lives up to her agreement with her parents.

Conversation

Take as much responsibility as you can for the conversation. (This applies to both boys and girls, but especially to girls.) Learning to draw another person out and to encourage him or her to talk of subjects that interest him most is a skill important to all social success and especially necessary in making dates a success.

Ask him about the game he has just played or some school subject in which he is interested. Perhaps the movie you have just seen suggests interesting subjects to talk about. Never be so anxious about the conversation, though, that you jump from one subject to another without giving any subject half a chance.

When he takes you home

Tell him how much you have enjoyed the evening. Put yourself in his place. If you had tried, as he has, to give another person an enjoyable evening, wouldn't you like to be told in an enthusiastic way that the evening had been fun? Some girls who learned when they were little, always, upon leaving a party, to tell the host or hostess what a pleasant time they had, fail to follow the same rule of courtesy when they leave a date. But the rule applies.

Saying good night

Say good night and go inside. He cannot very well leave until you make a move to go inside. One boy who came home very late from a date was reproached by his mother for keeping a girl out so late. He answered, "I didn't keep her out. She stood talking and talking on her front porch and didn't go in. I would have had to walk off leaving her talking if I'd come home any sooner." Perhaps he should have known how to make a gentlemanly getaway.

● Say good night and let him go home.

Nevertheless, he was right in assuming that the girl should have said good night and ended the evening when the time came for that.

During early dating, sometimes people wonder whether they should offer or expect a good night kiss. Boys and girls of college age have told us that as they look back, they feel that they made mistakes during their early teen years because they attached too much importance to whether they gave or were given a good night kiss. Many older young people feel now that because they were too anxious about growing up in dating situations, they overdid their emphasis on love and the expression of it in early dating.

Don't be afraid to be independent in your attitudes. Remember that the other person may be even more uncertain than you are, but may be trying to live up to what he or she thinks *you* expect.

A kiss is something special for a special person, even though among some groups that may not appear to be true. Almost all of your friends put a higher value on expressions of affection that don't come too easily and that are not given to too many people.

In the long run, if you are somewhat conservative about giving kisses, you will be more successful and comfortable in your dating. Think of it this way: which person do *you* think better of — the one who eagerly offers and expects kisses on all dates (with your friends as well as with you) or the one who, at least part of the time, has other interests in mind, and whose expressions of affection are rare enough to be a special compliment?

Remember the purpose of your dating. You want to get the most enjoyment possible out of associating with other boys and girls of your age. You want to better your understanding of yourself and other people. You want to learn to get along well with many kinds of personalities and also to discover which kinds of personalities are really not your type. You want to learn to express affection when you honestly feel affection toward someone — at the same time, using good judgment so that your dating will be a constructive, happy experience and leave you few regrets.

- "Alvin just can't be trusted. When I was out with Bernhard last night, he took Adele to the movies!" (Emmy Lou by Marty Links.)

YOUR DATING MANNERS (Girls)

	Never	Some- times	Usually	Always
	0	4	7	10
1. I give a definite acceptance or refusal when asked for a date.				
2. I treat it as a compliment when any boy asks me for a date.				
3. When a boy comes to my house, I ask him in and introduce him to my parents.				
4. I do not keep a date waiting after he comes to call for me.				
5. I think of the interests of my date and try to make him feel at ease.				
6. I am prepared to discuss many topics.				
7. I am careful to order inexpensively when my date takes me to a restaurant.				
8. I do not embarrass my date by talking too much or too loudly.				
9. I have learned to say good night without lingering too long.				
10. I dress appropriately for the occasion.				

Total each column

Total points

YOUR DATING MANNERS (Boys)

	Never	Some-times	Usually	Always
	0	4	7	10
1. I am specific in suggesting what we will do when I ask a girl for a date.	✓			✓
2. I concentrate on showing my date a good time.	✓			✓
3. I call for my date at her door.	✓			✓
4. I tell my date what type of a party it is so she will know what to wear.				✓
5. I go in the house and meet the girl's parents when she asks me to.				✓
6. I try to find out the hour when the parents expect their daughter home.				
7. I dress appropriately so I will not embarrass my date.				
8. I open doors, pull out chairs, and permit my date to go first.				
9. I see that my date gets in on time.				
10. I am prepared to discuss many topics, in conversation.				

Total each column

Total points

115

REVIEW QUESTIONS

1. How do you learn social poise on dates?
2. What is the basic rule for good manners on all occasions?
3. What should a boy do when he calls for his date?
4. Who arranges for transportation?
5. What are some rules for entering the car? A theatre?
6. Who orders in a restaurant? Is this a hard and fast rule?
7. Do you think punctuality matters in dating?
8. Should the girl always introduce her date to her family? What are different ways in which the introduction may be handled?
9. Who is to be responsible for hours to get home from the date?
10. Is it ever all right for the girl to pay expenses on a date? Discuss.

KEY WORDS AND PHRASES

observing formalities   social poise   affection
using good judgment   taking the initiative   courtesy

PROBLEMS AND ACTIVITIES

1. Study the list of dating problems on page 89, as revealed by the national study of high school students. Notice the differences in the problems of freshman and seniors. How would you explain these differences? What problems would you add to the list?
2. Make a list of any dating customs in your community that are different from the dating manners suggested in this chapter.
3. Study the two lists of traits boys and girls like most and least in the other sex as given in the tables on page 109. Do you think the students in your class would agree with this national

study of high school students? What traits would you add to each list as more important than those given?

4. *Class survey.* Take an anonymous poll of your class to see how they feel about "Dutch dates." Compare your class with the national study as given in the figure on page 110.

5. In many schools and communities there are few activities for couples on dates. Does your school and community provide enough things to do for young people? Can you suggest activities that you would like to see organized for dating couples in your school? Would you be willing to take an active part in the organization? Would you continue to support and feel responsible for the activity after it was organized?

ROLE PLAYING

Demonstrate the following situations: A boy calling for a girl and the girl introducing the boy to her parents; a couple going to a theatre with and without an usher present; a couple ordering at a restaurant; a boy taking flowers when he calls for a date and the girl receiving him and accepting the flowers.

FILMS

What to Do on a Date — 10 minutes, sound, Coronet
Date Etiquette — 10 minutes, sound, Coronet
How to Say No — 10 minutes, sound, Coronet

MORE ABOUT LEARNING TO UNDERSTAND OTHERS

ALLEN, BETTY AND MITCHELL P. BRIGGS, *Behave Yourself*. Philadelphia: J. B. Lippincott Company, 1950.

————, *If You Please!* Philadelphia: J. B. Lippincott Company, 1950.

BAILARD, VIRGINIA AND RUTH STRANG, *Ways to Improve Your Personality*. New York: McGraw-Hill Book Company, Inc., 1951, chs. 4–12.

BEERY, MARY, *Manners Made Easy*. New York: McGraw-Hill Book Company, Inc., 1949.

————, *Guide to Good Manners*. Chicago: Science Research Associates, Inc., 1952.

BETZ, BETTY, *Your Manners Are Showing*. New York: Grosset & Dunlap, Inc., 1949.

BILLETT, ROY C. AND J. WENDELL YEO, *Growing Up*. Boston: D. C. Heath and Company, 1951, chs. 7–8.

BLISS, WALTON B., *Personality and School*. Boston: Allyn & Bacon, 1951, Part III.

BOYKIN, ELEANOR, *This Way, Please*. New York: The Macmillan Company, 1948.

BRO, MARGUERITE HARMON, *Let's Talk about You*. New York: Doubleday & Company, Inc., 1949.

CARSON, BYRTA, *How You Look and Dress*. New York: McGraw-Hill Book Company, Inc., 1949.

COSGROVE, MARJORIE C. AND MARY I. JOSEY, *About You*. Chicago: Science Research Associates, Inc., 1952, chs. 4–9.

CRAWFORD, JOHN E. AND LUTHER E. WOODWARD, *Better Ways of Growing Up*. Philadelphia: The Muhlenberg Press, 1948, chs. 4–10.

CRAWFORD, CLAUDE C., E. G. COOLEY, C. C. TRILLINGHAM, AND EMERY STOOPS, *Living Your Life*. Boston: D. C. Heath and Company, Second Edition, 1953, chs. 5–7.

DALY, MAUREEN, *Smarter and Smoother*. New York: Dodd, Mead & Company, Inc., 1944.

DETJEN, MARY FORD AND ERVIN DETJEN, *Your High School Days*. New York: McGraw-Hill Book Company, Inc., 1947, chs. 9–13.

FEDDER, RUTH, *A Girl Grows Up*. New York: McGraw-Hill Book Company, Inc., 1948, chs. 1–5; 7.

HERTZ, BARBARA VALENTINE, *Where Are Your Manners?* Chicago: Science Research Associates, Inc., 1950.

KIRKENDALL, LESTER A. AND RUTH FARNHAM OSBORNE, *Dating Days*. Chicago: Science Research Associates, Inc., 1949.

McKown, Harry C., *A Boy Grows Up*. New York: McGraw-Hill Book Company, Inc., 1949, chs. 1–4; 7–8.

Menninger, William C., *Making and Keeping Friends*. Chicago: Science Research Associates, Inc., 1952.

Neugarten, Bernice L., *How to Get Along with Others*. Chicago: Science Research Associates, Inc., 1953.

————, Fred R. Bellmar, W. Russell Shull, Morris R. Lewenstein, William E. Henry, *Discovering Myself*. Chicago: National Forum Inc., 1948.

Pierce, Wellington G., *This Is the Life*. Boston: D. C. Heath and Company, 1951, Unit I.

Randolph, Helen R., Erma Pixley, Dorothy D. Duggan, and Fred McKinney, *You and Your Life*. Boston: Houghton Mifflin Company, 1951, chs. 18–20.

Reid, Lillian N., *Personality and Etiquette*. Boston: D. C. Heath and Company, 1950.

Shacter, Helen, *Getting along with Others*. Chicago: Science Research Associates, Inc., 1949.

Strain, Frances Bruce, *Teen Days*. New York: Appleton-Century-Crofts, Inc., 1946.

Weitzman, Ellis, *Growing up Socially*. Chicago: Science Research Associates, Inc., 1949.

Welshimer, Helen, *The Questions Girls Ask*. New York: E. P. Dutton and Company, Inc., 1949.

Part Three

OBLIGATIONS

NEW PRIVILEGES AND
NEW OBLIGATIONS

13

One of the pleasant things about reaching the teens is that one begins to be freer than ever before to make choices and decisions, to come and go more freely, and to make one's own plans fairly independently of parents and family.

Growing up means new privileges and new obligations

Many new privileges become yours. You will soon reach the legal age for driving a car. You can stay out later at night than formerly. You can earn and spend your own money. But some people are slow to recognize that *with new privileges and freedoms come also new responsibilities and obligations*. That is true not only in your teens; it will be true all through life. Let us look at some of these obligations and privileges that balance each other.

Driving a car

The day that you get your driver's license and can begin driving freely will be a special day. Almost everyone enjoys being able to drive a car. But there is more to driving a car than getting behind the wheel and burning up the road.

Most people begin their driving with the family car. They are allowed to use it occasionally for dates. Dad has to drive to work in it, and Mother uses it for family shopping trips.

When you begin to use the family car, how much responsibility should you take for keeping it clean? Who has the most time and energy for washing and polishing the car, your father or mother or you? What about keeping it filled with gas and oil, and taking it to be greased when a greasing is needed, or better still, learning to

121

● If you take responsibility for caring for the car, your parents will feel freer to let you use it.

do the greasing job yourself? Any high school boy or girl can learn to do almost all of the minor upkeep jobs on a car.

If, from the time that you get your license, you take a serious interest in the care of the car, you will probably find your parents much more willing to let you use it when you need it. Most parents feel resentful if they have to take all the responsibility for looking after the car when the children are using it as much as the parents are.

Another responsibility that will come with the privilege of driving is to learn traffic regulations and observe them. The person who does not bother to find out what the laws are, or who knows them but thinks it "chicken" to be a careful driver, is too *young* to be driving a car, no matter how many years he has lived.

Another obligation is to show consideration for others when it comes to use of the family car. Who is to have the car if several members of the family happen to want it at the same time? It is easy to think that this date you have is far more important than Dad's lodge meeting or any plans Mother might have. Some families have a lot of conflict here. Certainly some family members are going to have to be willing to give up their plans or change their plans for the sake of others. It will help you to do your share

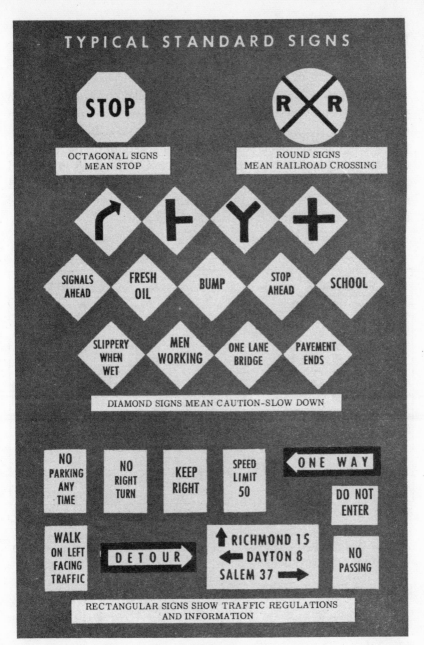

From Milton D. Kramer, *Deft Driving* (Dearborn: Ford Motor Co., 1952), p. 37.

● When you are old enough to have the privilege of driving the family car, you are obligated to learn the rules of driving.

New Privileges and New Obligations   123

of the giving up and compromising if you can consider honestly how much you contribute to the work and expense of keeping up the car and just how often other members do compromise by riding a bus or walking or staying at home so that you may have the car.

Planning ahead helps. Perhaps you can make an agreement with your parents and pass up some possible chances to use the car in exchange for the assurance that you can have it for certain important dates. The special dates can be marked up on the calendar far enough ahead of time to let other family members know and plan accordingly. The obligation to help work out, peacefully and reasonably, such complications balances some of the privileges that come with being old enough to drive a car.

WHEN YOU ARE OLD ENOUGH TO GET A LICENSE, SHOULD YOU BE ALLOWED TO DRIVE THE FAMILY CAR ON DATES ?

STUDENTS	%		%	PARENTS
👥👥👥👥👥	61%	USUALLY	23%	👥👥
👥👥👥👥	35%	SOMETIMES	63%	👥👥👥👥👥👥
👤	3%	NEVER	12%	👤

Adapted from *The Purdue Opinion Panel*, 9:1, November 1949, p. 12.

● Most families have some conflict over the use of the family car. The above national study shows what young people think about using the car and their view of what their parents think.

Earning your money

After you are in high school, you need and want a great many things that cost money. Your parents may not understand or sympathize with all your wants, even if they can afford the expense. The simplest solution is to begin to earn your own money, for

ARE YOU ACCEPTING NEW OBLIGATIONS
WITH YOUR NEW PRIVILEGES?

	Never	Some-times	Usually	Always
	0	4	7	10

1. When I have friends in, I help clean the house before and after.

2. If I use the car, I help keep it clean.

3. I accept my obligation to learn traffic laws and drive correctly if I am old enough to drive.

4. When someone offers to pay me for work, I do my best to earn the money.

5. I can work without being supervised.

6. I earn my spending money.

7. I am interested in getting good value for money I spend.

8. When I buy my clothes, I consider both quality and appearance.

9. I keep my room (or the room I share at home) neat.

10. When I accept a job or errand I can be depended upon to do it.

Total each column

Total points

125

most parents recognize your right to have a large choice in spending money that you earn yourself.

Perhaps your first job is baby-sitting. Boys as well as girls find baby-sitting a good job that does not interfere too much with their other activities. But it is easy to overlook the rights of the people who are hiring the baby sitter and to think only of the easy money.

Joan made an agreement with Mrs. Johnson, who lived next door, to baby-sit regularly every Thursday evening while the Johnsons were out. But if something interesting came up that Joan wanted to do on Thursday evening, she did not hesitate to tell Mrs. Johnson at the last minute that she could not come. On the evenings that Joan did go to the Johnsons' to stay with the baby, she usually invited a friend to spend the time with her, or she spent the evening talking on the phone to other friends. Sometimes, she used the occasion to wash and pin up her hair without bothering to leave the Johnsons' bathroom as neat as she had found it.

Was Joan giving Mrs. Johnson her money's worth? Joan's feelings were hurt when Mrs. Johnson ended their agreement and gave the job to a college boy who looked upon baby-sitting as a job as serious as caring for furnaces or cleaning science laboratories.

If you have a job delivering papers, do you accept the obligation to see that *every* customer gets his paper *every* day regardless of the weather, after-school games, or anything else?

Every job, no matter how big or small, is important to the person who is paying to have the job done; and when you take a job, you accept the obligation to give your employer his money's worth. That is a responsibility that comes with the privilege of earning your own money and having it to spend.

Spending your money

Once you begin earning money, you find yourself faced with many decisions in spending it. Some of the decisions will depend upon the situation of your family.

Probably the first expense that you will take over from your parents is your recreation. Most boys and girls begin to pay for

● When you have earned the money yourself, you like to consider values carefully before buying. (Hayward High School.)

their own amusements and recreational expenses when they begin to earn money. They have to learn to choose what they can afford and to do without what they cannot afford.

Others begin early to buy as many as they can of their own clothes. You can learn much about good values in style, appearance, and durability when you begin buying your own clothes. There is more incentive to consider carefully before you buy if you have earned the money yourself.

In some families, it is necessary for sons and daughters to begin early to help with the actual family expenses of food and shelter. But whether your family's income requires you to help all you can with family expenses, or whether it is such that they can pay all your expenses and let you save the money that you earn, when you begin to earn money you will want to get your money's worth in real value when you spend and you will have an obligation to give their money's worth to those who pay you for working. Straight thinking in matters relating to money — obligations involved in earning and spending it — will be important in your growing up.

New Privileges and New Obligations   127

● Once you begin earning money, you find yourself faced with many decisions in spending it.

Other obligations

As a small child at home you were told what you could and could not do. Your mother probably did all the work of keeping the house clean, even to picking up your things after you dropped them carelessly about. If you climbed on the furniture with your feet, she picked you off, and so on. You had few responsibilities. But now, in many ways, you live more like another adult in the family.

Whether you have a room of your own or with a brother or sister, you like to have a place for your own things, and you do not like anyone to bother them. Who, then, is responsible for keeping your room or your part of a room in order?

Perhaps you dislike being told what to wear. You may feel that your clothes are your own business. Who, then, is responsible for taking care of your clothes, keeping them hung up properly, and pressed and cleaned?

Girls, especially, tend to resent their mothers' having much to

HOW DO YOU RATE IN DOING YOUR PART AT HOME?

	Never	Some-times	Usually	Always
	0	4	7	10
1. I am neat and clean unless I am doing work that gets me dirty.				
2. I keep my belongings each in a definite place.				
3. I put my things away when I am through with them.				
4. I keep my clothes off the chairs, floor, and bed, and on hangers.				
5. My desk and locker are neat.				
6. My closet and dresser drawers are neatly kept.				
7. My soiled clothes are in the laundry bag, not lying around my room.				
8. I clean the washbowl and tub and hang up the towels after using them.				
9. When I read a magazine or the newspaper, I leave it in good condition for others to read.				
10. I do my part to keep things picked up at home.				

Total each column

Total points

Courtesy National Dairy Council.

say about their clothes. It is true that some mothers are not quick to realize it when their children are old enough to be independent on such matters. If your mother is that way, you will have to be patient until she learns. But there is an obligation other than just to be patient. No mother can be blamed for offering suggestions and advice about what a daughter wears if the mother still has to do the washing, ironing, and mending for a high-school-age daughter. The easiest way to have independence in the matter of clothes is to accept the responsibility for taking care of your own clothes.

In other words, any kind of freedom and independence brings with it certain responsibilities or obligations. You demonstrate that you are becoming an adult when you willingly accept obligations because the new privileges you get in return are worth it.

● "Mom — Dad and I insist you're working too hard lately — come on in and rest before you wash the dishes." (Emmy Lou by Marty Links.)

REVIEW QUESTIONS

1. What is meant by saying that with each new privilege or freedom come new responsibilities or obligations?

2. What new obligations come with the privilege of learning to drive a car? Can you think of others not given in the text discussion?

3. How can children demonstrate to their parents that they are responsible when it comes to driving the car?

4. If there is one car in the family, in what ways can parents and children get together so there will be little conflict over use of the famliy car?

5. What responsibilities come with the privilege of earning your own money? How did Joan show that she did not recognize responsibility on her baby-sitting job with Mrs. Johnson?

6. How can you show that you are becoming a "wise" spender?

7. What are some things you must do at home if you are to be recognized as able to accept the responsibilities of an adult family member? Can you think of some others not discussed in this chapter?

KEY WORDS AND PHRASES

privileges   obligations

PROBLEMS AND ACTIVITIES

1. Think of the driving practices of young people you know. Now make a list of ways in which they are demonstrating that they realize the obligations which come with the privilege of driving. In another column, list all the ways in which you have seen them show that they are not accepting the obligations which come with the privilege of driving.

2. Think of any part time jobs you have had in the past. In parallel columns, list the ways in which you lived up to the obligations of having a job and the ways in which you did not. Have you noticed growth in the way you live up to the obligations of working since you had your first job?

3. Are you becoming a wise spender? Contrast how you spent money as a child with the way you spend it now. How and why have you learned to spend more wisely?

4. List the ways in which you show that you have become more adult in assuming obligations at home. List also the ways in which you can still improve.

SOCIO-DRAMA

Two family scenes. In the first, bring out the conflict between two teen-age people and their parents over the use and upkeep of the family car. In the second scene, the same problem, but this time show parents and children talking over their problem and arriving at an understanding.

Scene in which a group of young people discuss their part-time jobs. Show mature and immature attitudes about privileges and obligations.

FILMS

Sharing Work at Home — 10 minutes, sound, Coronet
Wise Buying — 10 minutes, sound, Coronet
See reading list at end of Part Four, page 190.

OBLIGATIONS TO YOURSELF
AT SCHOOL

14

Although you spend only from six to seven hours out of the twenty-four at school, most of your interests center in your school. In some ways, your school life is almost your whole life at the present time. Are you getting the most possible in enjoyment and in good development out of it from day to day?

Your scholarship

Since school life offers many kinds of attractions, it is sometimes easy to forget that the key to the most inviting doors is good scholarship. Social life, athletic participation, and, in most schools, your participation in many school or class activities all depend upon satisfactory work in your studies. That does not mean that every one must be a straight "A" student or qualify as a "brain." But it is important to your happiness and success now and in the future that you have your class work under control. You can organize your studies rather than let them disorganize you.

More important than the brain you were born with are the habits that you form. Some people, who happen to have great natural ability, may not do well in their studies because they do not have systematic habits for handling their work. Others with average ability may excel in their studies and have time also to enjoy many outside activities because they have an efficient plan for using their time and energy.

Classroom habits

One high school senior boy said, "What you do *in class* is the whole thing. I can get by with very little studying outside of class

133

if I really make the most of every class period." It is true that good classroom habits can cut down greatly the study time required outside of class.

The following rules will help you to form the right kind of classroom habits:

1. *Leave your social life outside when you enter a classroom.* You will get along better in class if you do not sit near any of your best friends. Agree with your friends to separate and scatter out so that you will not be tempted to pay attention to each other instead of to the business of the classroom.

2. *Have the materials with you that you need in each class.* The student who finds himself in class without the needed text-book, notebook, or writing materials is only half present. He cannot do efficient work any more than a carpenter or plumber could work if he left his tools at home.

3. *Work at building a habit of listening.* It is easy to concentrate on what is passing outside the window or to let one's thoughts wander to the party last night, or to the game coming after school today. You will have to make a specific effort to form the habit of paying attention to the business at hand in class. Good attention habits don't just come naturally without any effort; they result if

9TH GRADE	STUDENT STUDY PROBLEMS	12TH GRADE
51%	I WISH I KNEW HOW TO STUDY BETTER.	40%
51%	I HAVE DIFFICULTY IN KEEPING MY MIND ON MY STUDIES.	54%
22%	I DON'T KNOW HOW TO PREPARE FOR TESTS.	20%
19%	I HAVE TOO MUCH HOMEWORK.	16%
39%	I HAVE DIFFICULTY EXPRESSING MYSELF IN WRITING.	40%
43%	I HAVE DIFFICULTY EXPRESSING MYSELF IN WORDS.	38%
44%	I WOULD LIKE TO KNOW MORE DEFINITELY HOW I AM DOING IN SCHOOLWORK.	20%

Adapted from *The Purdue Opinion Panel*, 8:3, April 1949, pp. 13-30.

● A national study of students in New England, the deep South, the middle West, and the far West shows that they all have about the same problems when it comes to getting their lessons. Freshmen and seniors also seem to have about the same study problems.

● One of the first steps in becoming a good student is to listen in class and to take part in classroom discussions. *(Coronet Films.)*

we work at building them.

4. *Participate in class discussions.* One girl said, "I don't like to be one of the eager ones, always raising my hand. I often know the answers, but I don't say anything unless the teacher calls on me."

She was taking a negative attitude toward her class work and depriving herself of the learning that comes from participation. She was not thinking about her responsibility to contribute whatever she could that might make the class more interesting for others as well as for herself. If you participate all you can, others will be more likely to do the same, and you know that the most interesting classes are those in which many of the class members take part in a good discussion.

5. *Take notes.* Have either a small notebook for each class or set aside a section in a large notebook and write down the things that are said that are important for you to remember from each class recitation. Some things may seem so interesting or important at the time that it seems unnecessary to write them down; you may think you will surely remember them. But once out of class, many

things leave your mind, and it is a help to be able later to look through class notes and be reminded of the important points that were made.

In taking notes, it is not necessary to take down everything said. Write down only keys to the important thoughts. Those who try to write down everything may be so busy writing that they miss other main points.

6. *Always write in your notebook the assignments that are made in class.* The inefficient student is the one who has to scramble to find out the assignment before he can begin studying or who offers as an excuse in class, "I didn't know what the assignment was."

If you build the habit of doing in class the six things listed above, you will have made a good start toward success in scholarship. School will be more fun, too. Nothing is so boring as to have to sit dully in a classroom for fifty or sixty minutes if you are not paying attention or participating and are only waiting for the time to pass. It is far more fun to put your best into each class period. Being a part of the activity is much more interesting than making yourself an outsider.

● Do you have good study habits?

Obligations to Yourself at School

SELF-RATING CHART ON DAILY
STUDY HABITS

	Never	Some- times	Usually	Always
	0	4	7	10
1. I write down assignments carefully as they are given.				
2. I plan the use of my study periods before beginning my study assignments.				
3. When I study at home, I am careful to choose good conditions for study.				
4. I keep a well-organized notebook.				
5. I keep the work in each of my classes up-to-date.				
6. In reading, I take notes and outline any difficult sections.				
7. Before writing, I outline what I plan to write.				
8. After studying an assignment I recite it to myself and review it before going to class.				
9. I make it a point to go to each class prepared to take part in discussion.				
10. I look up all unfamiliar words in the dictionary.				

Total each column

Total points

● Have a certain place in your home where you study. Make it a practice to start studying when you go to this place. Do your letter writing, day-dreaming, and listening to the radio in some other part of the house. You will find that when you go to your study place, you are ready to concentrate. *(Coronet Films.)*

Study habits outside of class

You know among your classmates some who are always behind in their work. They are worried and bothered and may spend more energy stewing about their studies than it takes you to do yours. You know others who seem to get along without half so much struggle. The difference is in the work habits of people.

If you have not yet given any thought to how you go about getting your lessons, try checking up on your system or your lack of system.

Sally, a high school freshman, had been complaining about her teachers' giving too much homework. She insisted that there were not enough hours in a day for her to do all the work that was required. Her older brother, Bill, decided one evening to keep a minute-by-minute record of how Sally did her homework. Without telling Sally what he was doing, Bill jotted down the record in a notebook. It was like this:

7:30 to 8:10: getting ready to start studying (mostly talking about how much homework she has to do and how hard it is).

8:10: flops down on bed and picks up English book; leafs through book.

8:15: goes to telephone and calls friend Jane to ask what English assignment is; talks to Jane for twenty minutes about what they are going to wear to school tomorrow.

8:35: goes back upstairs; lies down on bed; opens English book and begins reading.

8:45: runs downstairs to turn the radio up louder so she can hear the Hit Parade while studying.

8:45-8:55: argues with Mother, who thinks the radio ought to be turned off while Sally studies; Sally insists she can study better to music.

8:55: back upstairs, opens notebook and does some writing.

9:15: notices what time it is and moans that she has got to quit studying English and get at that awful Latin assignment or she'll never get it done.

9:25: runs downstairs to answer the phone, talks for twenty minutes to Judy, who called to find out the math assignment; they compare notes on what they plan to wear tomorrow.

9:45: back upstairs and to the Latin book again.

9:55: lays book aside, gets bobby pins from her dresser, props Latin book up beside the mirror, and begins to pin up her hair while keeping one eye on the book.

10:10: Mother comes up and says it is bedtime. Sally moans and says she is dead tired but has "hours and hours" of studying to do yet. Mother says, "You have to get your sleep or you can't do good work in school." Sally says that it looks like she'll fail her math anyway, since the assignments are so impossibly long, and she hasn't had time even to look at her math lesson yet, with so much other studying to do.

10:20: Sally lays down her Latin book, picks up her math book, leafs through it for a minute, groans, turns off the light and gets into bed.

Do you know anyone whose homework habits are about like Sally's? Sally will continue to be frustrated and unsuccessful in her studies until she organizes her time into a better schedule and develops a different set of work habits.

Systematic study habits

It is a good idea to make and follow a schedule, one that provides for a systematic way of getting your studying done. Here are some hints:

1. Study the *same subject* at the *same time* each day.
2. Study subjects which require library or other reference work *during your study time at school.*
3. When possible, study a subject just after or just before the recitation period.
4. Review lessons you studied the day before; preferably review just before the recitation.
5. Study the same subject in the *same place* each day. Have a certain chair and table in your home where you study. You will soon find you are ready for study when you sit in this place.
6. Schedule time in your day for other things, helping with the house work, your part-time job, and your recreation, so that you will not be tempted to take your study time for these things.
7. In planning, allow for your play, outside work, school activities, and the free time you need. Try to think of all the things that seem necessary to you in your week and balance them up in planning your time.

If you find that the days are not long enough to crowd everything into, then examine your daily activities carefully. Perhaps you are trying to do too many things. Something may need to be eliminated. Some people cannot hold part-time jobs and keep up their school work. Others must limit the school activities they participate in. Try to be realistic in making your schedule.

Stick to your plan

Once you have drawn up a realistic plan of study, make it a habit to follow it. You will not then have to waste time deciding over again each day what you will study at school and what at home. The habit will help you remember what books or materials to take home with you, since you will always be studying at home for the same class.

When the time comes to study, *study.* Don't let other things interfere. It may take a lot of determination to keep from talking on the telephone during study time. But your problem there is the same as that of all your friends. Many high school students do their telephoning early in the evening and let their friends

● Throughout high school, you will find many times when you need extra information. Learn to use your school library now. This boy is using the card catalogue. Do you know how to use one? Do you know how to find the books after you have found the information in the card catalogue? *(Coronet Films.)*

know that after a certain time they have to study. It can be worked out so that a group of friends will, by common consent, not call each other during certain hours and the agreement will mean that all of them will be able to organize their work better.

What about the radio?

Some people believe that they can study just as well (or better) with a radio or television turned on near by. But many students who have decided to try turning off the radio and concentrating on their work in a quiet room have found that they can get their work done quicker and better when the room is quiet. Actually, when they had the habit of studying with the radio on, they were either wasting part of their energy "blocking off" or ignoring the radio or they were letting the radio distract their attention, so that their studying was inefficient.

Noise, even radio music, uses up nervous energy that is needed for concentration. Experiments among workers under various conditions have proved that efficiency increases when noises are eliminated, even though the workers may have thought they were so used to the noises that they "didn't notice" them at all. The facts show that it is not true that one can study better with the radio on.

Obligations to Yourself at School   141

Reward yourself

In building up good study habits, make use of rewards. Everyone knows that it is easier to work if some reward is ahead to look forward to. The permanent reward of a more successful life is ahead if you build good habits now, but you can give yourself more immediate rewards.

If there is a certain television or radio program you like on Wednesday evening, tell yourself that you can enjoy listening to the program if you get your history lesson first. Or remind yourself that you can have the week-end free if you are efficient and get all your lessons during the week. But do not fool yourself. If you really do not have the history lesson, then be strong minded and deny yourself the pleasure of the radio or television program. The "reward" system breaks down if one gives in and says, "I have the lesson well enough" or "I will get it tomorrow" or "I will stay up late tonight and get it," and then goes ahead to enjoy a reward he has not really earned.

You will find a real satisfaction in making yourself accomplish what you have set for yourself and enjoying the rewards you

● Remind yourself that you can have the week-end free if you are efficient and get all your lessons during the week.

have promised yourself. That will be true throughout life. Perhaps you might be interested to know that when the authors were writing this book, they set themselves the task of getting a certain amount of the writing done each day. They promised themselves the reward of going fishing or swimming after the day's work was done, or getting to work with tools at building a room onto the cottage where they were writing. Since they could enjoy the rewards only after each day's writing was done, the pages of the book kept piling up until it was finished.

Studying a specific assignment

This chapter has talked of classroom habits and of out-of-class study habits. Here are some hints on how to attack a lesson assignment.

1. Look over any suggestions the teacher gave when making the assignment.
2. Look over the assigned pages hurriedly; read the introduction, the summary, the topic headings and possibly the review questions at the end of the assignment.
3. Have a general picture in your mind of what you are to look for in the material and what the material is all about.
4. Now read each topic in the lesson, looking for the main points under each heading. If you own the book, you may wish to underline the most important sentences or ideas. After reading the material on each topic, close the book and review, to yourself, in your own words, the most important thoughts in the material just read.
5. Read, study, and review all materials in the lesson, then try to *recite* the entire lesson to yourself.
6. Read for ideas, not words. Read as fast as you can, as long as you are getting the main ideas.
7. Re-read the study aids at the end of the assignment. Can you answer the review questions? Solve the problems? Do you know the vocabulary? If you feel confident after reading the teaching aids, then you probably have your lesson.
8. Review and review. Remember that we soon forget much of what we read. The secret of remembering, is to review often. Reading a lesson over and over without purpose is of little

value. The important thing is *studying* the lesson according to a plan.

You will see that the hours you spend are not the test of good study habits. Your success in your studies will depend upon all the habits you form both in and out of class.

REVIEW QUESTIONS

1. What opportunities are not open to those who do not have good grades in your school?
2. Do those who get the best grades always have the highest mental ability? Explain.
3. What are the six basic habits you need to cultivate in order to do good work in the classroom?
4. What minimum materials should be kept in your notebook?
5. List seven good study habits to follow.
6. Why is it good practice to study a subject just before or just after a recitation period?
7. Why is it important to study a subject at the same time and same place each day?
8. How might one handle the problem of phone calls during the evening?
9. What effect does any kind of noise have upon the amount of nervous energy used when studying or working?
10. How can one use "rewards" to help him improve his study habits?
11. Give the nine hints for preparing a lesson.
12. What is meant by the statement that the hours spent in studying are not the test of good study habits.

KEY WORDS AND PHRASES

| participation | realistic | study rewards |
| concentrate | study habits | study hints |

PROBLEMS AND ACTIVITIES

1. Keep a log of your classroom habits for one week. In your notebook, list the six suggestions given in the lesson; and after each class, for one week, give an honest evaluation of yourself on each suggestion.
2. Make an outline of your study habits as they are at present. How well do they conform to those suggested in your test? On what points could you improve? In what ways are your study habits like Sally's?
3. If you have good study habits, in what ways are they like and in what ways do they differ with those given in the chapter?
4. How do you study a lesson? Do you read your lesson more than once? Do you find review effective in remembering? What other study hints would you add to those given in this chapter?

FILMS

There are many excellent films available to help you develop good study habits. These treat such phases of studying as using the library and where to get outside information. It will be impossible for you to see all of these films. Below are listed four of the good films. Use the ones you think would be of most help. (They are from ten to fourteen minutes long, sound, and made by Coronet.)

High School: Your Challenge; How To Study; Know Your Library. Homework: Studying on Your Own.
See reading list at end of Part Three, page 190.

SCHOOL ACTIVITIES

15

In your school are many activities outside of studies. If you are to get the most out of school life, you will want to take part in some of these extra activities. Just as you organize your study time, you will need also to organize the rest of your time so that you can get a balance between your studies, extra school activities, and whatever requirements your home or family makes upon your time and energy.

Since it is possible to try to take part in too many activities, consider what the choices are in your school. What are your special interests? What activities, perhaps outside of your special interests, might help you to develop new skills or abilities?

Three good reasons for taking part in school activities are:

(1) for your own pleasure

(2) to learn new skills

(3) to add to the pleasure of other people and to the life of your school.

Can you think of other good reasons?

Activities for enjoyment

Naturally, the first reason for going into a certain activity is for recreation. If you have always enjoyed playing basketball, volley ball, tennis, or any other team sport, you will want to go out for the sport that you like. If you have been a camera fan, you will enjoy joining a group of your classmates who have the same interest. Special aptitudes or interests attract people to dancing groups and many other special interest clubs or organizations in school. One finds pleasure and social development in doing things with others who have some of the same interests.

Learning new skills

We grow as we get out of our own little groove and find new interests or learn new skills. For that reason it is a good idea, each term or year, to go into at least one activity that will give you new kinds of experience. Perhaps you feel that you have no interest in dramatics; you are not the dramatic type. That may be a good reason for joining a dramatic club, or trying out for your class play. Whether you get a small part or the lead, or whether you spend your time planning and helping with stage sets or doing any of the other work that goes with producing a play, you will learn all sorts of new and interesting things.

Perhaps, when it is all over, you may still be convinced that the stage is not among your main interests — or you may find out the opposite. In either case, if you gave all you could to the activity while you were at it, you will have had a profitable new experience.

So *try some new activity each year*. Don't just stick to doing the things that you know that you can do well.

There is another advantage in trying new things. Think of the people you know. Who are the really interesting ones that everyone likes to know? Are they people who cling to the security of

● It's fun to take part in school activities. Whether they are folkdancing, plays, debating, athletics, the school paper, or a class office, you will enjoy the activity, and the association with others will contribute to your social and emotional development. *(Luoma Photos.)*

the familiar, who do only what they can do well and associate only with people they know well? You become a more interesting person to others as you branch out and work at growing in every way that you can.

● Try some new activity each year.

Doing your part as a citizen in your school

The third reason mentioned for participating in activities is related to good citizenship. If your school is to be a good school, many different people have to take responsibility for keeping worthwhile activities organized and going.

People with athletic ability are likely to do what they can, not only for their school, but because of the individual rewards that come with athletic achievement. But many other less spectacular achievements are just as important to the life of your school.

The school paper needs reporters, from every class, who will be alert and energetic in their hunt for news that will picture your school as it is.

Moreover, there are never enough people in any school who

will serve faithfully on committees — clean-up committees as well as planning and decorating committees!

School elections are important, and this part of the democratic functioning of your school should not be left to a few who are old hands at putting up and electing candidates. If you think that "they" have elections and class or school offices all tied up, don't complain or lose interest. Get busy and organize; put up a "dark horse" candidate. Whether or not you elect your candidate, you will learn a lot about your school and classmates, and you will be helping democracy to function in your school.

What kind of a participator are you?

Whatever activity you take part in, you owe it to yourself and to the others to be *reliable*. If a practice is scheduled, *be there* and *on time*.

You know people who sign up for a club or an activity and are full of enthusiasm at the beginning of the term; but as soon as some other attraction comes along, they are off like a child chasing butterflies. No one can count on them for anything. Some people

SHOULD STUDENT GOVERNMENT:	YES	NO	DON'T KNOW
PLAN CONVOCATIONS AND ASSEMBLIES ?	81%	11%	8%
MAKE RULES ABOUT CONDUCT IN SCHOOL ?	72%	21%	7%
HOLD COURT TO TRY STUDENTS WHO BREAK RULES ?	59%	32%	9%
FINE OR OTHERWISE PUNISH STUDENTS WHO BREAK RULES ?	53%	36%	11%
PUBLISH A SCHOOL PAPER WITHOUT CONTROL BY TEACHERS ?	42%	49%	9%
COLLECT STUDENT RATINGS OF TEACHERS ?	44%	38%	18%
POLL STUDENTS ON WAYS TO IMPROVE THEIR SCHOOL ?	87%	7%	6%

Adapted from *The Purdue Opinion Panel*, 7:3, April 1948, p. 18.

● What part should students take in the government of their school? The students do much of the governing and rule-making in some schools. In others, the principal and the teachers carry the load. How does your school rate in student government? Are the students getting experience in a functioning democracy?

School Activities   149

● All students who hold offices in classes and student organizations in Hayward High School must register for a class in how to conduct and organize student organizations. Here the class is at work assembling their new booklet on how to conduct business meetings. *(Hayward High School.)*

will sign up for an activity because a boy friend or girl friend is interested in that activity and then drop out when a new friend becomes more important.

Friendships are important, but you need some interests that are independent of your friends and that continue regardless of changes in your friendship groups. The reliable person can be counted on to *finish what he starts* even if it may get to be a rather hard pull toward the end.

Your participation in activities with other people is an important part of your education. It stands very near your success in your studies, in what it can contribute to you and to others.

● You are developing attitudes of good citizenship now. *(Hayward High School.)*

HOW DO YOU RATE AS A CITIZEN
IN YOUR SCHOOL

	Never	Some-times	Usually	Always
	0	4	7	10

1. I take an active part in at least one school activity.

2. I try some new activity each year.

3. I vote in student elections.

4. I attend most home events in athletics.

5. I attend dances, plays, and parties sponsored by the school.

6. I campaign to see that the right people are elected to school and class offices.

7. I conduct myself so that I am a credit to my high school.

8. In general, I try to do the things that will make my school a better place for everyone.

9. My grades are up to my mental ability.

10. I try to understand and get along with my teachers.

Total each column

Total points

● The reliable person can be counted on to finish what he starts.

REVIEW QUESTIONS

1. What are three reasons for taking part in school activities?

2. How does one get social development out of school activities?

3. Why is it important to try new activities each year?

4. Why is it a part of good school citizenship to participate in some school activities?

5. What is an important trait in those who are successful in school activities?

6. Being a good citizen in school is preparation for active citizenship in the community after graduation. Why is this true?

7. How many activities should you have? Do you know of students who go in for more activities than they should?

KEY WORDS AND PHRASES

democratic functioning   participator   "dark horse" candidate

PROBLEMS AND ACTIVITIES

1. Make a list of the school activities you have taken part in during the past two years. Which of these did you like and which did you not like? What specific benefits did you get from the different activities?

2. Bill could win honors for his school in track, but he is not out for track this year because he wants to spend his after-school hours with Sally, with whom he is going steady. What do you think of his choice as viewed from Bill's own view point? From Sally's? From yours as a classmate?

3. After evaluating your activity program, what do you think you could do to make a more balanced program for another year?

4. As a class, make a list of all the activities open to students at your school and put these on the blackboard. Each student write down two activities which you think you would like and two which you think you would not like. Make investigations into the four activities you have listed and be prepared to report on the purpose of each group: what the members do, what the members learn, and any special advantages or disadvantages.

FILMS

Student Government at Work — 10 minutes, sound, Coronet
Parliamentary Procedure — 10 minutes, sound, Coronet
School Activities and You — 10 minutes, sound, Coronet
School Spirit and Sportsmanship — 11 minutes, sound, Coronet
See reading list at end of Part Three, page 190.

YOU AND YOUR
COMMUNITY

16

When you were a child, the kind of town or community you lived in was entirely beyond your control. You could do nothing but fit into the situation and be influenced by your surroundings.

You received from your surroundings ideas and attitudes, beliefs and prejudices which, as a child, you could not judge or measure. You could only grow up with them. Now it is different. Through your school and because of your contacts with a larger world, either by travel or by means of newspapers, radio, and television, you can look more as an outsider would look at your community and at the attitudes you have received from it.

At the beginning of this section of the book, we discussed the fact that with new freedom and with privileges come also new obligations and responsibilities. From now on, you have a responsibility as one member of the community to help in *setting standards*. You are no longer a helpless follower. The attitudes and standards of your town, school, or community are only the total of the individual standards of many people like you. You are beginning to accept your responsibility when you recognize that *what you think and what you do affects many other people as well as yourself.*

Being a responsible citizen

In our daily lives, many occasions arise in which we demonstrate how responsible we are as citizens.

Is your community a good one in which to grow up, to live, and to work? If you were looking for an ideal community in which to live, would you recommend yours? Not long ago, we received a letter from a couple who were strangers to us. They were, by

154

birth, American citizens, but were of a race and religion different from the majority of Americans. They had grown up in a South American country and had lived and worked there until now. But now that their three children were ready to go to school they wished to come to the United States to make their home. They wrote to us, saying:

We know that in the United States every good thing can be found if you search for it. We want to find a community in which our children may grow up well, a community where there is absolute tolerance for all religions; where our children will not learn to hate, but will learn to understand and respect people who may be different from themselves; where different races cooperate in the community with mutual respect, and where we ourselves can do our work and fit into the community without discrimination. Will you please recommend to us such a community?

Would it have been safe to recommend that the writers of the letter settle in your community?

There are many ways in which, as you become older, you have an obligation to take responsibility in your community. What does your community provide in housing? How is law enforcement in your town? Is there recreation for all groups?

BOYS WANT TO KNOW	BECOMING A GOOD CITIZEN	GIRLS WANT TO KNOW
25%	HOW CAN I HELP TO MAKE THE WORLD A BETTER PLACE IN WHICH TO LIVE ?	35%
13%	WHAT CAN I DO ABOUT THE INJUSTICE ALL AROUND US ?	18%
10%	I AM MIXED UP ABOUT WORLD AFFAIRS	18%
20%	WHAT CAN I DO ABOUT RACE PREJUDICE ?	30%
20%	IS THERE ANY WAY OF ELIMINATING SLUMS ?	27%
16%	WHAT CAN I DO TO HELP GET BETTER GOVERNMENT ?	14%
11%	WHAT CAN I CONTRIBUTE TO CIVILIZATION ?	12%

Adapted from *The Purdue Opinion Panel*, 8:3, April 1949, pp. 13-30.

● In a poll of students from all parts of the country, Louisiana, Kansas, California, and Maine, students expressed a desire to help make the world a better place in which to live. What would you like to do to improve conditions within your school, community, state, or nation?

Perhaps members of your class would like to form committees to investigate to find the answers to those questions and report your findings to the class.

In one town, the high school class in social problems made a survey of the recreation of the young people. The survey revealed that little was offered the young people other than the theatre and the pool halls. Student organization and action resulted in the building of a community recreation hall for all in that community. In many other cases, students have taken such action, showing that they are responsible citizens.

Respect for individual rights

The United States has been called a "melting pot" because our people have come from nations and races all over the world. No one can claim to be "pure American." Nevertheless, in some towns and communities, people of certain races and those having religious beliefs different from the majority of their neighbors are looked upon with doubt or suspicion. They may be discriminated against because they are a "minority group."

Discrimination against minority groups is contrary to the principles upon which our democracy was founded. Equal rights of all kinds were guaranteed by the Constitution to all Americans, regardless of race or religion. Nevertheless, because such rights have sometimes been withheld from minority groups, our federal

● Have I developed unfair attitudes and prejudices against certain Americans? *(Coronet Films.)*

● Would all people be welcome in your church? *(Luoma Photos.)*

government has now passed laws which make it specifically illegal to discriminate against people of any minority group by forcing them out of a living area, by depriving their children of equality in school privileges, or by depriving them of the right to do work for which they are qualified.

But laws can be effective only when individual people like you consider it a personal obligation to live up to the ideas that the laws are based upon. What can you do about it in your own neighborhood?

Keep in mind what is the real worth of any person. What abilities does he have that are worth something to himself and to others? What ideas and feelings does he have that can contribute to the thoughts and feelings of others? A healthy sense of humor, a good disposition, gentleness, and an understanding of others, a pleasant or witty way of speaking, any skill or ability, whether mental, physical, artistic, or mechanical — these are things that count in the worth of a person. None of them depends on one's race or color or upon the religious faith into which one is born.

Make sure that in your attitudes and in your treatment of every person there is no discrimination because of things that have nothing to do with his real worth. Even if your community is one that is full of prejudice, you can, by your thinking, as well as by your acting, begin to change attitudes.

In one high school class, when it came time for graduation and the class was lining up to march, two by two — a boy and a girl — some of the girls began maneuvering to make sure they would not have to march with John, a boy of a different nationality. Margaret, who was a popular girl in school, stepped up and said, "Would you mind walking with me, John?" Afterwards, someone said to Margaret, "It was good of you to march with John." Margaret said, "It's true that I did it to help John, I hated to see him embarrassed. But actually I think it was good of *John* to march with *me*. He has always been one of the best ones in the class to do his share and help keep things going, no matter what kind of work had to be done, while *I* often did only the things that I thought were fun or that I really wanted to do."

Margaret's attitude toward John was the same as toward any other classmate. She judged him by his actions and his worth as a person, not by some other standard.

Prejudice

At the beginning of this chapter, we said that as a small child growing up, you could only accept without much question the attitudes and standards of your family and community, but that now you are responsible for thinking through your standards and then helping to set standards, rather than merely following them.

It will help you in your thinking if you understand what some of the elements of prejudice are. Some discussion was given earlier of what it means to prejudge or to be prejudiced. Turn back to chapter 3 and read again the definition of prejudice. Americans believe that a man is innocent of a crime until proved guilty. However, in our dealing with minorities or with strangers in general, we may prejudge them. Before knowing any facts in the case or before knowing an individual at all, we may allow ourselves to act according to prejudices we have absorbed from others. Unfortunately, it is true that prejudices are usually most active against groups of people who are strong enough in numbers or in ability so that they are "competition" for the majority group. Some people then cling to their dominant position and try to keep the minority group down by enforcing unfair handicaps upon the minority group.

IS RACE PREJUDICE INBORN OR ACQUIRED?

NINTH GRADE		TWELFTH GRADE
26%	YES, IT IS	24%
42%	NO, IT IS NOT	60%
32%	I DON'T KNOW	16%

Adapted from *The Purdue Opinion Panel*, 8:1, November 1948, p. 18.

● One-fourth of high school students polled in all parts of the nation believe that race prejudice is inborn. Students in New England agreed with those in the South and the far West on this, and seniors did not differ with freshmen. What do you think? How can race prejudice be decreased?

The person who is prejudiced also jumps to a general conclusion about a whole group of people because of some notion he may have gained from or about one member of the group.

If you should hear a visitor from abroad say, "Americans are noisy and brash. They think the only thing that matters is money," you would resent it. You would say at once, "What does he mean? There are millions of Americans, and they are of all kinds. There's a quiet one for every loud one and a serious and wise American for every brash one. And how does this prejudiced foreigner know what 'Americans think?' Can he read minds?" Then you might go ahead and add, "All foreigners are ignorant anyway. They are just jealous of Americans!" You would be doing the thing you resent another's doing. One irritating visitor from abroad may make you feel like generalizing (drawing a general conclusion from one case) about the whole group, just as he has generalized about Americans from observing the actions of one or two.

Prejudice could not survive without that kind of generalizing. Many people, without thinking, accept such generalizations and then go on to attach labels to members of any group.

● It's easier to pre-judge people than to learn the facts.

At the present time, there is a tendency to lump all people with controversial political ideas together and to label them as communists. It is easier to do this than to get acquainted with what some people may really think and to distinguish between their thinking and that of communists. Do you ever express a prejudice by giving a label to an individual or group? Can you think of some commonly accepted generalizations that probably have no basis in fact? What are some labels commonly applied in your school or community that show prejudiced ideas? What implications, not necessarily true, are in such labels? One example might be: "She's a BRAIN." Think of others.

It is so common for people of one nationality to label individuals of other nationalities that governments, trying to do something to overcome it, are making it possible for students and teachers to go to other countries to live for a period of time and get acquainted with people of different nations. Under the Fulbright Act, hundreds of teachers and students go each year to all countries of the world to study and to teach. Students and teachers from other countries come to America. After a student has spent a year studying and living with young people in Italy or Turkey, he is not apt to come home saying, "All Italians are excitable" or "All Turks carry long swords." When he gets to know people as individuals in these countries, he can see that they differ as much as all of our people differ in their ways, their beliefs, goals in life, and tastes. Of course, a very narrow-minded person might not bother to get acquainted with individuals of another group but might just seek evidence to back up his prejudices.

During the war years, soldiers who were stationed in the East, West, South, or North, for the first time had a chance to get acquainted with boys and girls in other sections of our own coun-

HOW WOULD YOU RATE YOUR COMMUNITY ON THE FOLLOWING POINTS

	Never	Some-times	Usually	Always
	0	4	7	10
1. In my community, all nationalities and races have equal rights.				
2. Recreational activities are provided equally for all groups.				
3. Children of all nationalities and races are treated with equal fairness in the school system.				
4. The police enforce the law without considering wealth, nationality, or race.				
5. Good housing is available to all.				
6. I would recommend my community for the So. American family.				
7. In employing people, our industries treat all nationalities and races with equal fairness.				
8. Our newspaper is fair to all nationalities and races.				
Total each column				

Total points

try. Many now have a better understanding of all Americans.

Perhaps you are wondering what this discussion of prejudices and labels has to do with you and your community. Your community is only what you and your friends are. Your community is influenced by the way you think. Your responsibility is to be able to think clearly about the rights and obligations of individuals in our democracy and then to live up to your personal responsibility as one important unit in your community.

REVIEW QUESTIONS

1. In what ways have you, up to the present, accepted the attitudes, beliefs, and prejudices of your community? Discuss.

2. What is meant by saying that the standards of your community are only the total of the individual standards of many people like you?

3. What is a good indication of the fact that one has started to accept his responsibility as a citizen?

4. What is meant by calling the United States a "melting pot"?

5. What is a "minority group"?

6. How have minority groups been discriminated against?

7. How does the Constitution try to protect minorities?

8. Would there be discrimination against minority groups if we judged them according to the *real* worth of each person? Explain.

9. How did Margaret show that she was judging John according to his individual worth rather than as a member of a minority group?

10. Define the word "prejudice."

11. Why do we often prejudge minorities, foreigners, or strangers?

12. What do you understand by generalizing and labeling?

13. Illustrate how foreigners might generalize about Americans.

14. What is a common example today of generalizing about those who have doubtful or controversial ideas in America?

15. What is our government doing today to help rid people of their prejudices about other nationalities?

16. How does military service lead to breaking down prejudices about people in different sections of our country and people in other countries?

17. Why would you or wouldn't you recommend your community for the couple who wrote from South America?

KEY WORDS AND PHRASES

attitudes	melting pot	contribute	brash
prejudice	minority group	controversial	liberal
objectivity	discriminate	labeling	disrepute
precedent	depriving	generalizing	

PROBLEMS AND ACTIVITIES

1. We often read and hear about discrimination against minority groups in other countries. Do we have discrimination in our country? Make a list of types of discrimination you have heard about in different places in our country.

2. Can you think of times in your life when you have prejudged someone at first and then, after you got to know them, found that your prejudgment was entirely wrong?

3. Make a list of commonly accepted generalizations that probably have no basis in fact. Now try to figure out how these generalizations started and why they survive.

4. List commonly applied labels used in your school, community, or in our country, that are the result of prejudice.

5. Look up the word *liberal* in the dictionary. Then ask several adults whom you know how they would define a liberal thinker. Do their definitions agree with the dictionary? With each other?

6. What generalizations have you accepted in the past which you now know to be false generalizations?

7. *Special talk.* If there is a teacher or a student in your community who has had the opportunity to spend a year in another country on a Fulbright scholarship, possibly the person would be willing to discuss his experience before the class.

8. *Class project.* Study your community for possible improvements. After each class member has thought of what he considers serious community problems, have a class discussion and decide upon a few projects upon which you are going to try to get community action for improvement. Divide the class into committees to work on the different projects. Each committee will make a more thorough study of the problem and make a detailed report to the class on how to get action on the problem. (If one of the reports is especially good and the need for action is great, you may wish to take your project to the governing body in your community for action.)

9. What could or should be done for a German family with one elementary and one high school student who are emigrating to your community. (Note—they already speak English)

SOCIO-DRAMA

A group of students participate in a discussion of other nationalities, races, or religions. Part of the students will play the role of the prejudiced and will state many false generalizations and apply false labels. The other students will play the role of unprejudiced people and question many of the generalizations of the ones playing the prejudiced roles.

FILMS

Who Are the People of America? — 10 minutes, sound, Coronet
Are You a Good Citizen? — 10 minutes, sound, Coronet
See reading list at end of Part Three, page 190.

YOUR ATTITUDES TOWARD LAW AND RIGHT AND WRONG

17

You do not make the laws in your town now. Later, you will be responsible for helping to do that. Your responsibility now is to know and respect the laws that affect you.

What are some of the laws that affect you as an individual? Why do you owe it to yourself and your community to observe the requirements of the laws?

Laws on age for driving

The law that sets the age at which you can drive a car differs in different states. Whenever laws are changed on this point, the tendency seems toward setting a higher age. In several states, one can drive at fourteen; in some states, the age is eighteen.

Whatever the legal age for driving, there are always some boys and girls who believe that they are exceptions to the rule, that although they have not had the right birthday yet, they are well enough qualified to drive a car. The only problem they see is to avoid getting into trouble with "the Law" if caught driving a car without a license. Unfortunately even some parents do not think straight on this point. Occasionally, a parent will believe that his or her child is exceptional, and the parent will permit the child to drive the car while he is still under the legal driving age.

Perhaps we might agree, for the sake of the discussion, that certain people are unusual, that they might be better qualified than other under-aged people to drive. Nevertheless, before laws on age for driving are passed, careful studies are made of the average maturity and driving qualifications of people of various ages. Age limits are set according to the age at which *most* people are ready to drive safely.

165

Could it safely be left to all individuals to decide when they, themselves, are qualified to drive, and whether they are more advanced in their abilities than the average of others their age? Are even the parents of a person able to judge accurately just how exceptional their own child is? If it were left to individuals, perhaps those who would be the most dangerous on the highway because of their immature judgment might be the first to decide they were well qualified to drive. Therefore, each one of us can only protect his own safety on the highway by adhering strictly to this, as well as to all other, traffic laws. Laws are for our own protection.

By respecting the law ourselves, we support law and make easier the enforcement of all laws that are for our protection. Actually, all laws are our safeguards, although some of them may seem to limit personal freedom of action. How are laws against trespassing meant for the protection of those who might trespass as well as for the protection of property owners?

What about laws against playing ball in streets or riding bicycles at night without proper lights?

What about laws that require you to keep your dog licensed and under control if you live in a city?

● **We respect the laws to protect ourselves and others.**

From *Man and the Motor Car* (New York: Prentice-Hall, Inc., 1954.)

How are you personally protected by the laws against turning in false fire alarms?

Can you think of other laws that seem to restrict freedom but that serve to protect even those who are restricted?

Why respect laws?

Sometimes you may not see any sensible reasons for some law. You may be inclined to think that since this law does not seem to

Your Attitudes Toward Law and Right and Wrong   167

● How honest are you? Bill was given more change than was due him when he bought his new pen. Should he call attention to the mistake or pocket the extra money? What would you do? *(Coronet Films.)*

have any logical basis, you have no obligation to respect it. Everyone has a right to protest against laws of which he disapproves. There are democratic processes provided in our government for changing unsatisfactory laws. But as individuals, we are either law-abiding or we are not. If we allow ourselves to ignore or to break certain laws of which we do not approve, it means that we do not realize how important the whole system of law is to our safety and comfort. By deliberately breaking any law, we are destroying rather than supporting a value that is important in our community. So you, as one person, have a responsibility for helping to form the attitudes of respect or disrespect for law in your town.

Moral decisions

When it becomes necessary to make a moral decision, how do you make the decision? One winter night, five boys left the school gymnasium after basketball practice. As they started up the street, they made snowballs and threw them at each other, at trees, and at a mailbox. Just as they turned into a block that was lighted by a row of ornamental street lights, Peter said goodnight and left his friends, since he lived in a different direction. A minute later, Tom impulsively threw a snowball at one of the globes of a street light. He missed, but snatched up another snowball and said, "Ready, aim, fire!" The other three promptly joined in and began throwing. One of the boys, Henry, deliberately missed the lights every time he threw, because he really didn't want to do damage. Before anyone stopped to do much thinking, all the ornamental globes in the whole block were broken. Later, the city spent $400 to repair the damage.

The next morning, as soon as Peter reached school and before he had talked to his friends, he was called into the principal's office and questioned about the broken lights. He realized that his friends were the guilty ones and that only his having to leave had kept him from being in on the mischief. He told the principal only that he knew nothing about it, that he had left the other players shortly after leaving the gym, since he lived in an opposite direction. The other boys, knowing that Peter was being questioned, agreed that when their turns came they would all deny any knowledge of the broken lights and would stick together and tell stories that agreed.

● The moral decisions that you make now determine what standards you will live by, now and later.

Your Attitudes Toward Law and Right and Wrong   169

● These people are cheating on an examination. Is it easier to cheat or to do wrong when you are in a group than when you are alone? What is conscience, and how is it developed? Does conscience always tell us what is right and what is wrong? *(Coronet Films.)*

Their coach had reason to be quite sure which boys were involved, but he refused to have anything to do with the investigation, claiming that there was nothing he could do about it. He told his wife, "If they should find out those four boys are guilty, I'd lose my four best team members." The four boys boasted to others about how well they had made their stories hang together, so that nothing could be proved in the investigation.

Before long, most of the boys in their class knew all about what had happened, but everyone who was questioned was careful not to say anything that would get the boys into trouble. Soon some of the parents also knew what had happened. But they said, "It would be too bad for the boys to be put off the team. They were just having fun and were carried away with excitement."

Henry was bothered when he thought about it all. He talked it over with a close friend and said, "If I had actually broken any of the lights, I would feel that I should tell my father about it, and I know my father would think we ought to help pay for the damage. But I don't think I broke any of the lights. I aimed to miss every time. I only lied to Mr. Grey to cover for the other boys. I had to do that much, didn't I?"

Perhaps you have been in a similar situation. You had to make decisions about what was right or wrong to do. You had to think of what you owed to your community, to yourself, your friends, your school.

What moral decisions were involved for each person in this case: Peter? Henry? The other boys? The parents who learned the truth? The coach? Mr. Grey, the principal? What right or wrong decisions were made? Was it right that the damage was charged to the taxpayers in the community instead of being paid for by the boys and their families?

Perhaps you wonder what such an incident has to do with citizenship. The moral decisions that you make, now, determine what standards you will live by now and later. Perhaps it happens that there has been a serious accident on a downtown street, caused by a driver's carelessness or recklessness. Sometimes, in such cases, it is very hard to get witnesses who will admit that they saw the accident. Many people will refuse to take any responsibility for helping to see that justice is done, although it would cost them nothing to testify about what they saw.

Whenever any one of us holds back and protects himself or any other one person at the expense of the larger community as a whole, he is helping to destroy values in our democracy.

Democracy is "government by the people" and the only way it can work so that the interests of all are protected is for each person to act as a committee of one to do his part in seeing that the rights of all are protected. Any action which is against the interests of the group should be brought to the attention of the group. This applies to the damaging of public property just as to violation of individual rights guaranteed in the Constitution. When you think of it that way, it becomes easier to find the answers to some of the questions that arise about the moral decisions made by the different people in the light-breaking incident.

REVIEW QUESTIONS

1. Who makes the laws in your community?

2. At what age can you get a driver's license in your state?

HOW HONEST ARE YOU?

	Never	Some-times	Usually	Always
	0	4	7	10

1. If a store clerk accidentally gives me too much change, I call it to his attention.

2. If a mistake is made in my favor in grading an examination, I report the mistake to the teacher.

3. When I find a lost article, I make a serious effort to find the owner.

4. If I hear things about people that I know are untrue, I refrain from repeating them.

5. When I do wrong to another, I attempt to correct the wrong.

6. I refrain from cheating by giving help on tests or examinations.

7. I refrain from cheating by getting help from others on tests or examinations.

8. When reporting on an incident, I tell exactly what I believe to be the truth.

9. I pay back what I borrow.

10. I recognize that to tell the truth means to tell the whole truth.

Total each column

Total points _____

3. Do you think it would be better to let individuals decide when they are old enough to drive?

4. How can laws limit our freedom and yet be for our own protection and give us greater freedom?

5. Explain how, by deliberately breaking a law, an individual is destroying an important value in his community.

6. What have some student groups done to show that they are becoming responsible citizens?

7. What are "moral decisions"?

8. In the case of the basketball boys breaking the ornamental street lights, what do you think was the right moral decision for Peter? Henry? The coach? The parents? Other students who knew who broke the lights?

9. How can citizens help make a democracy work?

10. Would a democracy work if all people thought and acted the way all of those did who were involved in the street light incident?

KEY WORDS AND PHRASES

moral decisions   democratic processes   public property

PROBLEMS AND ACTIVITIES

1. How well do the young people in your community respect the driving laws? List all the ways in which you think they show respect for the driving laws and ways in which you think they could improve.

2. Can you think of laws in your community which citizens ignore much of the time? If you can, do you think these laws should be obeyed? Changed to fit the practice? Done away with entirely? Obeyed by some but ignored by others? What other solution would you suggest?

Your Attitudes Toward Law and Right and Wrong   173

3. What is the right procedure for getting an undesirable law changed or for getting a desirable law passed? Find out how a referendum works and report to the class.

4. Find out what are the qualifications for voting in your local elections and in state and national elections.

5. Consider each of the following traits in the chief participants in the basketball team—snowball incident: loyalty; honesty; citizenship; conscience; trustworthiness.

6. *Special report.* Ask a police officer to talk to the class on good citizenship.

7. What percent of eligible voters voted in your last municipal election?

8. *Special talks.* Have people who work at "politics" on the precinct level speak to your class. Ask them to explain to the class what each person's responsibility is as a voter.

FILMS

Why We Respect the Law — 14 minutes, sound, Coronet
Respect for Property — 10 minutes, sound, Coronet
Right or Wrong? (Making Moral Decisions) — 10 minutes, sound, Coronet
See reading list at end of this section, page 190.

WHAT DO YOU BELIEVE?

18

Your beliefs will determine what life means to you now and later, for your beliefs are an important part of your personality. As time passes and you have new experiences, you will change in some of your beliefs; but, gradually, you will find that you are living by a certain "philosophy of life" that has grown out of all the things that you believe.

What do you believe about yourself as a person? Do you think that what you do or think matters to the larger world outside of yourself and your immediate circle? What do you feel that you owe to the world and that the world owes to you?

What do you believe about the rights of people in our society? Does the word "democracy" mean more to you than just that it is the name given to our form of government?

What do you believe about religion? Have you thought about what your religion means in your life?

As a little child, you probably accepted from your parents many parts of their philosophy of life. Just as philosophers throughout history have developed ways of thinking to explain the universe, the purpose of life, and the future, so each one of us develops his way of looking at life. Your philosophy of life grows out of what you have been taught and what, from your own experience and observation, you believe to be true. Eventually, you may not believe just as your parents do, but you will have been influenced by their attitudes and beliefs.

Your beliefs about yourself and others

If you believe that what you think or do matters in the world about you, then you are growing toward being a responsible citizen in your society. You probably will also accept the responsibility

175

for learning all you can about facts in your world; you will try to get at truth so that you will not be "off the beam" in what you think and do. There is the kind of person who says, "What does it matter what I think? I'm only one person and nobody is much interested in what one person does. My life is my own, anyway, to live as I please." That person is not going to have a very useful influence in his neighborhood. Nor is he likely to be very happy himself.

What Do You Believe?

True, you are just one person. But you can accomplish some things that no other person can. In a small town, two young housewives heard that the new manager of the neighborhood gasoline service station had fired a boy from his job because of his race and religion.

Mrs. A. said, "I don't think that's right. If he's a good, honest worker, his race or religion should have nothing to do with his keeping his job. It's too bad such things have to happen." Then she forgot about the incident.

The other woman, Mrs. B., went to the service station manager and asked him the facts about the case. She wanted to know for sure whether what she had heard was true or was only hearsay. The man explained that he felt his customers objected to the boy's living and working in their neighborhood, and he said he had acted only to keep his customers satisfied. Mrs. B. said, "I can't believe that you are right about the feelings of the people in this neighborhood. Will you keep the boy on for a while and check to see whether your business increases or decreases?" The man agreed, and Mrs. B. spent an hour or two each morning for several days calling on people she knew and explaining to them exactly what had happened. She told each one that she was sure that if people knew about it, they would be glad to give that station their business in order to prove that they valued good, honest work and held no prejudice against any person because of his race or religion.

Mrs. A. and Mrs. B. were different in their beliefs about their responsibility as individuals. Mrs. A. thought that, as only one person, her ideas about some person's job in the neighborhood would not make any difference. But Mrs. B. believed that she ought at least to find out the truth about what she had heard. After checking with the station manager and getting the truth, she had enough confidence in her neighbors to think that when they knew the facts, they would do what they felt to be right. When she asked the service station manager later how his business was going, he answered, "Why, it is better than ever. I guess I was wrong about how people in this neighborhood feel on some things. The boy is a good worker, and, from now on, that's the basis I'll hire and fire on."

Do you believe that every person is responsible for thinking

What Do You Believe?   177

straight and then acting according to his beliefs? There may never be a time when you can or need to do anything spectacular, but by simply knowing what you believe and taking whatever small or large responsibility is yours as one person, you will have a far larger influence in the world than might seem to be possible.

Your philosophy of life

What you believe about yourself, your obligations to others, and their obligations to you are important parts of your philosophy of life, or of the code that you live by. Your philosophy of life will affect all of your relationships with other people.

Bill says, "I have learned by experience that you have to get the best of the other fellow before he gets the best of you. I intend to look out for myself because no one else is going to do it."

His friend, Jim, answers, "I don't feel that way. It seems to me that you have to think of the other fellow's interests as well as your own. I've found that most people will be fair with you if you are trying to see their viewpoint as well as your own." Bill

● Your marks, not the other fellow's, will put you ahead in this work-a-day world.

What Do You Believe?

● Are you developing a philosophy to live by? (*Luoma Photos.*)

and Jim have opposite philosophies of life. Which do you think will have more difficulty in his dealings with other people?

Of two businessmen, one says, "Honesty is the best policy. It pays to give people good value for their money." The other says, "Business is business. I'm here to make money, not to worry about whether or not some people spend their money foolishly." How much are the two men showing about their philosophies of life?

Think of some of the people you know. From their attitudes toward others, can you tell what philosophy they live by? How do their beliefs seem to work out in their lives? Are they loved by others? Successful in their work? Happy? Useful in their town or school?

Your beliefs about the rights of others and of yourself in a democracy

The first ten amendments to our nation's Constitution are called the Bill of Rights. These amendments to the Constitution guarantee specific rights to the American people. (Before reading this section check the following test "What Do You Believe?")

WHAT DO YOU BELIEVE?

	Agree	Disagree	Uncertain
1. Newspapers and magazines should be allowed to print anything they want except military secrets.			
2. Religious belief and worship should not be restricted by laws.			
3. The government should prohibit some people from making public speeches.			
4. In some cases, the police should be allowed to search a person or his home, even though they do not have a warrant.			
5. Some criminals are so bad that they shouldn't be allowed to have a lawyer.			
6. Some religious groups should not be allowed the same freedom as others.			
7. If a person is accused of a crime, he should always have the right to know who is accusing him.			
8. Certain groups should not be allowed to hold public meetings even though they gather peaceably and only make speeches.			
9. Foreigners in this country should always be allowed the same basic freedom that citizens have.			
10. Local police may sometimes be right in holding persons in jail without telling them of any formal charges against them.			

11. In some criminal cases, a trial by
    jury is an unnecessary expense and
    shouldn't be given.

12. In some cases, the government
    should have the right to take over
    a person's land or property with-
    out bothering to go to court.

13. The police or F.B.I. may sometimes
    be right in giving a man the "third
    degree" to make him talk.

14. Persons who refuse to testify against
    themselves (that is, give evidence
    that would show that they are
    guilty of criminal acts) should either
    be made to talk or be severely pun-
    ished.

15. Some of the petitions which have
    been circulated should not be al-
    lowed by the government.

After checking the test, get the answers at the end of the chapter and
compare your answers with those of other high school students from
all parts of the country who took this test. (Adapted from *The Purdue
Opinion Panel*, 11:1, November 1951, pp. 2a-12a.)

Some of the rights guaranteed in the Constitution have been
accepted and practiced for so many years that safeguards against
their violation no longer seem necessary. Such a right is the third
article, which says that soldiers cannot be quartered in private
homes in peacetime without the consent of the home owner.

Others of the amendments are very important to us today.
Articles I, IV, V, and VI guarantee rights that are basic to our
freedom now and that have been lost by people in some other

parts of the world. If we should lose the rights that these amendments seek to guarantee, we would have lost that which Americans have always valued most highly.

Most Americans would say, "Of course I believe in the Bill of Rights," but many of them could not tell you what it contains. Every American should know the Bill of Rights. If you have not yet studied it, now is a good time to study it. Then you should think about whether you, personally, accept as right the guarantees that these amendments to the Constitution make and are willing, as far as you can, to help make certain that every person is given his guaranteed rights.

In a mid-western city, not long ago, just as an experiment, a man had a copy of the Bill of Rights typed on a large sheet of paper. Then he stood on a street corner and asked passers-by, "I am trying to get signatures of people who are willing to give moral support to this document. Will you sign it?" Many people refused, giving various excuses.

Some said, "It sounds all right to me, but I wouldn't want to go on record for it. I'll have to think about it." Others said, "Oh, I believe in what it says there; but I don't want to get mixed up in any controversy."

Where do *you* stand on your beliefs about the rights guaranteed to Americans by the constitution? Read the Bill of Rights, which follows:

AMENDMENTS TO THE CONSTITUTION

(First ten amendments, the Bill of Rights)

Article I

Congress shall make no law respecting an establishment of religion, or prohibiting the free exercise thereof; or abridging the freedom of speech, or of the press; or the right of the people peaceably to assemble, and to petition the Government for a redress of grievances.

Article II

A well regulated Militia, being necessary to the security of a free State, the right of the people to keep and bear Arms, shall not be infringed.

Article III

No soldier shall, in time of peace, be quartered in any house, without the consent of the Owner, nor in time of war, but in a manner to be prescribed by law.

Article IV

The right of the people to be secure in their persons, houses, papers, and effects, against unreasonable searches and seizures, shall not be violated, and no Warrants shall issue, but upon probable cause, supported by Oath or affirmation, and particularly describing the place to be searched, and the persons or things to be seized.

Article V

No person shall be held to answer for a capital, or otherwise infamous crime, unless on a presentment or indictment of a Grand Jury, except in cases arising in the land or naval forces, or in the Militia, when in actual service in time of War or public danger; nor shall any person be subject for the same offense to be twice put in jeopardy of life or limb; nor shall he be compelled in any criminal case to be a witness against himself, nor be deprived of life, liberty, or property, without due process of law; nor shall private property be taken for public use, without just compensation.

Article VI

In all criminal prosecutions, the accused shall enjoy the right to a speedy and public trial, by an impartial jury of the State and district wherein the crime shall have been committed, which district shall have been previously ascertained by law, and to be informed of the nature and cause of the accusation; to be confronted with the witnesses against him; to have compulsory process for obtaining witnesses in his favor, and to have the Assistance of Counsel for his defense.

Article VII

In suits at common law, where the value in controversy shall exceed twenty dollars, the right of trial by jury shall be preserved, and no fact tried by a jury, shall be otherwise re-examined in any court of the United States, than according to the rules of the common law.

Article VIII

Excessive bail shall not be required, nor excessive fines imposed, nor cruel and unusual punishments inflicted.

Article IX

The enumeration in the Constitution, of certain rights, shall not be construed to deny or disparage others retained by the people.

Article X

The powers not delegated to the United States by the Constitution, nor prohibited by it to the States, are reserved to the States respectively, or to the people.

Study especially Articles I, IV, V, and VI. What specific rights are guaranteed that are important to every one of us? In the light of these amendments to the Constitution, should any American ever be afraid to express his religious or political views? Should he be afraid to attend a "protest meeting," regardless of whether he disagrees or agrees with what is being "protested"? Should he be afraid to sign a petition for fear of being involved in a controversy? Do you believe that every American should have the rights guaranteed in the Constitution, regardless of whether or not you personally agree with his ideas? Should we abolish the Bill of Rights in cases of people who hold views that are wrong?

Bill of Rights Week Is Set

SACRAMENTO, Dec. 8.—(P)—Governor Knight urges Californians to familiarize themselves with the Bill of Rights and "support to the fullest possible extent the basic freedoms it guarantees to all Americans."

He did so in proclaiming December 9-15 as Bill of Rights Week in California, December 15 will be the 162nd anniversary of the adoption of the first 10 amendments to the U.S. Constitution. The amendments are generally referred to as the Bill of Rights.

"This most important addition to our national constitution throughout its history, and the principles it establi

What Do You Believe?

If America is to continue to be a "land of the free and the home of the brave," you must know what our freedoms are and have the courage to defend them in your everyday life. A man who loved liberty once said, "I disagree with every word that you say, but I will defend to the death your right to say it."

Freedom of speech, freedom of the press, the right to assemble in protest against things some people object to, the right to petition for changes that some people think should be made — all these rights have been under attack in recent years in many parts of the world. Countries dominated by believers in communism or fascism feel that it is not safe to allow their citizens the right to think for themselves and to express their thoughts freely. But our democracy is based upon respect for the individual's intelligence, his ability to think for and help govern himself, and upon the belief that free men will cherish their freedom and will have a far greater loyalty to their country than people whose liberties are not protected.

Americans do not always agree on what are the best ways to defend democracy. But surely one of the best ways to protect human rights in a democracy is to see that no person's rights are taken from him, regardless of what we may think of him or his ideas. When one person is deprived of his rights, then a part of freedom has been damaged, and every one of us has suffered a loss.

Your religious beliefs

People all over the world and from ancient times to the present have had religious beliefs that are important to them. People disagree on many points of religious belief, but the beliefs held by the majority of the people in any country have a very great influence upon what life is like in that country.

While there are many differences in the beliefs of different religious faiths, there are also some important points on which the three chief religions of our country (Protestant, Catholic, Jewish) agree. If you are Protestant and have Catholic and Jewish friends, or whether you are Catholic or Jewish, you have found that in some ways your friends are not so different in their beliefs. For all of you, religion centers in the belief in God as a supreme Being who is concerned with the world and its people and with you as an individual.

What Do You Believe?   185

What your religion means to you

At this point in your life, you will want to do some thinking about what your religion means to you and whether or not you are willing to live according to its teachings. Most people reach the point where their religion becomes their own, rather than simply the religion that their parents have taught them when they were small children.

Does your religious belief have any effect upon the way you get along with other people? A belief in God leads to an acceptance of the importance of all people and should, therefore, make it somewhat easier for you to think of the other person as well as of yourself. At different times in this book, we have mentioned the value of getting a "perspective" view of life or of any of its problems. (See chapter 19, page 194, to get a better understanding of what perspective is.) One of the chief things that your religious beliefs may do for you is to help you get a perspective of life. You may begin to see the world as larger than yourself; to see yourself not as the center of the whole universe but as a responsible person among many other people who have rights and needs.

Another thing that your religious belief may do for you is to give you some feeling of security or sureness about the meaning of life. From the beginning of history, people have always been puzzled about many things in the world. It is natural to wonder what life is all about, why we are here, and what the future holds. Your religion offers explanations for the unknown and hope for the future. This may give you a confidence which makes life more worth living all the way through.

As you study history, you will learn that people have done many terrible things in the name of religion. And you have probably already seen for yourself that people in our own country often are intolerant and cruel toward others because of differences in religion. When people are bitter and intolerant over religion, they lose for themselves and others almost all that is worthwhile in their beliefs. They have perhaps accepted the outward forms of religion without understanding the true meaning of a religious faith.

For you, as you are growing up, the most important thing is that you know what you believe in all the areas discussed in this chapter and what your beliefs can contribute to your life and to the lives of others around you. Beliefs that would make you cruel or intolerant in your attitudes toward others need to be changed as you build the philosophy of life by which you will live. Beliefs that have meaning and worth, that help you to understand yourself and others better and to be a more useful person in the world, or that give you a secure confidence about life now and in the future — those beliefs you need to keep and live by.

● From ancient times, people all over the world have had religious beliefs that are important to them.

REVIEW QUESTIONS

1. What is a philosophy of life?
2. Where do we get our philosophy of life?
3. Why is it important for you to believe that what you think and do matters in the world?
4. Contrast the ways in which Mrs. A. and Mrs. B. reacted when they saw a wrong against democracy in their neighborhood.
5. What contrasting philosophies may be expressed by people who have been successful in business?

What Do You Believe?   187

6. What are the basic beliefs in our democracy as stated in the Bill of Rights?
7. Why is it that some people do not accept the ideas in the Bill of Rights?
8. How common is a religious faith among people all over the world?
9. Do Catholics, Jews, and Protestants agree on certain basic religious beliefs? Discuss.
10. Give some of the important things that one should get from his religious beliefs.
11. Should one get along better with others if he follows the teachings of his religion? Explain.

KEY WORDS AND PHRASES

beliefs	constructive	faiths
philosophy of life	Bill of Rights	perspective
democracy	infringed	intolerant

PROBLEMS AND ACTIVITIES

1. Mimeograph the test over the Bill of Rights from pages 180–181; ask another teacher in school to have her classes check their beliefs. Do not state that it is the Bill of Rights they are checking. Compare the results with the natioual poll of high school students.

2. *Assembly program.* Your class might use the results of the above study for an all-school assembly program on Democracy. Different students in class could take up the different civil rights guaranteed in the Bill of Rights, show how students in your school and in schools all over the country feel about these rights, and then stress the importance of all knowing and accepting the guarantees in the Bill of Rights if our democracy is to mean anything.

What Do You Believe?

3. Try writing out your philosophy by giving what you believe on the following: religion; honesty; government; what is worth striving for in life.

4. *Special talk.* Have representatives from the Catholic, Jewish, and Protestant faiths come to class and present the basic beliefs of their faiths.

5. Write or give to the class a short sketch of a person you know whose philosophy of life seems to have a strong effect (good or bad) on the way he gets along with others.

6. Re-write the ten amendments using only words a grammar school student can easily understand.

7. Collect newspaper articles involving incidents pertaining to the first ten amendments.

KEY FOR TEST
What Do You Believe?

Percentages of beliefs as expressed by national sample of high school young people. The italicized answer corresponds to an interpretation of the Bill of Rights.

	Agree	Disagree	Uncertain		Agree	Disagree	Uncertain
(1)	*45*	41	14	(9)	*54*	32	14
(2)	79	13	8	(10)	17	*76*	7
(3)	34	*53*	13	(11)	12	*76*	12
(4)	26	*69*	5	(12)	8	*88*	4
(5)	15	*79*	6	(13)	58	*27*	15
(6)	7	*87*	6	(14)	33	*47*	20
(7)	*81*	13	6	(15)	34	*34*	32
(8)	25	*60*	15				

FILMS

Our Living Constitution — 10 minutes, sound, Coronet
How Honest Are You? — 10 minutes, sound, Coronet
Developing Your Character — 10 minutes, sound, Coronet

MORE ABOUT OBLIGATIONS

BARUCH, DOROTHY WALTER, *Glass House of Prejudice*. New York: William Morrow & Co., 1946.

BENNETT, MARGARET E., *High School Handbook*. Chicago: Science Research Associates, Inc., 1951.

BILLETT, ROY O. AND J. WENDELL YEO, *Growing Up*. Boston: D. C. Heath and Company, 1951, chs. 6, 9, 11–12.

BLISS, WALTON B., *Personality and School*. Boston: Allyn and Bacon, 1951, Part II.

CLARK, THADDEUS B., *What Is Honesty?* Chicago: Science Research Associates, Inc., 1952.

CRAWFORD, CLAUDE C., E. G. COOLEY, C. C. TRILLINGHAM AND EMERY STOOPS, *Living Your Life*. Boston: D. C. Heath and Company, 2nd ed., 1953, chs. 1–3, 9, 11.

DETJEN, MARY FORD AND ERVIN WINFRED DETJEN, *Your High School Days*. New York: McGraw-Hill Book Company, Inc., 1947.

GERKEN, C. D'A., *Study Your Way through School*. Chicago: Science Research Associates, Inc., 1952.

HARK, MILDRED AND NOEL McQUEEN, *Make Your Pennies Count*. Chicago: Science Research Associates, Inc., 1953.

HUNT, ROLFE LANIER, *High School Ahead*. Chicago: Science Research Associates, Inc., 1952.

LASSER, J. K. AND SYLVIA F. PORTER, *Money and You*. Chicago: Science Research Associates, Inc., 1952.

LETTON, MILDRED C. AND ADELE M. RIES, *Clubs Are Fun*. Chicago: Science Research Associates, Inc., 1952.

LINDQUIST, E. F., LAUREN A. VAN DYKE, AND JOHN R. YALE, *What Good Is High School?* Chicago: Science Research Associates, Inc., 1953.

McDowell, Nancy E., *Your Club Handbook*. Chicago: Science Research Associates, Inc., 1951.

McKown, Harry C., *A Boy Grows Up*. New York: McGraw-Hill Book Company, Inc., 1949, chs. 9–11.

Merriam, Robert E., *Politics for Boys and Girls*. Chicago: Science Research Associates, Inc., 1952.

Neugarten, Bernice L. and Paul J. Misner, *Getting along in School*. Chicago: Science Research Associates, Inc., 1951.

—————, W. Russell Shull, Fred R. Bellmar, Morris R. Lewenstein, William E. Henry, *Toward Adult Living*. Chicago: National Forum Inc., 1951.

—————, *High School Life*. Chicago: National Forum Inc., 1949, chs. 1–19.

Pierce, Wellington G., *This Is the Life*. Boston: D. C. Heath and Company, 1951, units 3–4.

Randolph, Helen R., Erma Pixley, Dorothy D. Duggan and Fred McKinney, *You and Your Life*. Boston: Houghton Mifflin Company, 1951, chs. 1–6.

Taylor, Florence, *Why Stay in School?* Chicago: Science Research Associates, Inc., 1952.

Wrenn, C. Gilbert, *Practical Study Aids*. Stanford: Stanford University Press, 1951.

YOU AND YOUR
FAMILY

Part Four

YOUR PARENTS

All through this book as we have been considering you and your life, the discussions have included your parents and your family. For, as you know, your personality, your attitudes and habits, and all your beliefs and experiences are so closely tied up with your family that it is not possible to study about the process of building your life without studying about your family.

Now we will think more specifically about some of the things in your family living that may make problems for you at this stage in life.

Are your parents inclined to be old-fashioned? Do they ever embarrass you by things they say or do in front of your friends? Are they often unreasonable?

If so, perhaps you have tried to keep your feelings about it to yourself. But if you have talked to your friends about your difficulties with your parents, you have found that your friends have most of the same complaints that you have.

Perhaps Mary Jane's mother seems to you to be quite attractive for a woman of her age. She always looks neat and speaks pleasantly, and you have never seen her act unreasonable or peculiar. But Mary Jane has a lot of trouble with her mother and with her father, too. She says, "They never want to let me do anything that I want to do. They always ask questions about all my plans. They make unreasonable and old-fashioned rules, and they will never listen to my side of it. They say I'm being impudent if I try to tell them what I think about their ideas."

If you and your classmates would all write on slips of paper the three things that bother you most about your parents and then have a committee summarize the results, there would probably be a large measure of agreement on troublesome traits in parents.

Why do parents behave as they do?

Is there any way that you can help them to change?

Getting a perspective on the problem

In your art classes, you have learned to view a scene in *perspective;* that is, you see distance as well as foreground, depth as well as height and breadth. It is also possible to view a problem in perspective, that is, to see it in its true proportions and in its relationship to other facts. Sometimes, problems viewed in perspective turn out to be not so much problems as just natural and logical stages of growth.

Let us see how this can be. When you were under two, you had the task of learning to walk. As you learned, you took some tumbles. You often had bruises from bumping into chairs or table legs. Your parents were very proud of your progress. They probably bored some of their friends by boasting about what an active child you were and at what a young age you were learning to walk. When they felt like snatching you up to save you from tumbles, they held themselves back because they knew that you would make better progress if they did not hinder you with too much protection. They knew that your task at one-and-a-half was to learn to walk.

Now you are in your teens, and your task at this age is to grow into a mature person who can eventually stand on his own feet in life without support and control from his parents. Your parents also have a very special task at this time. Their job now is to let you grow into independent adulthood at your own pace and still to give help and control when you really need it. It was fairly easy for them to hold back and let you learn to walk alone when you were little; it is many times more difficult for them now to know how to act wisely. Situations are much more complicated now.

In each new situation that arises, your parents must make a new decision, asking themselves, "Is this a thing that is really Bill's (or Jane's) own business and not mine? Or is this something about which I must raise an issue and assert my authority in order to keep my child from making a serious mistake?" Naturally, par-

● It's important to see things in proper perspective.

ents do not always find the right answers to these questions.

By looking at the matter in this way, is it not possible to see that perhaps difficulties that arise now between you and your parents are not so much "problems" as they are just signs of natural development and growth on the part of both your parents and you? *You* are trying to get on with the business of growing into an independent adult, and *they* are trying to grow toward their future role of being the parents of a young adult instead of the parents of a child. Almost all growth involves some awkwardness and fumbling.

"Seeing the matter in perspective may be a good idea," you say, "but it is still just as aggravating to have to try to cope with parents who boss too much, who set old-fashioned and unreasonable standards, and who don't realize that a person has a right to some privacy in life! What can I *do* about it?"

Let us look at some of the specific points of conflict and see if there is anything that you can do.

Some problems

Many parents find it especially hard to know which choices you should make for yourself and which ones they should help you make or even make for you. You probably feel that you should

● Is this appropriate for the occasion?

get to decide for yourself on many things.

In many families, conflict arises over the question of clothes. Girls like to choose their own clothes and make all their decisions about what to wear, but many mothers feel that they have had more experience in judging values in clothes to be bought, and that they know more about what is becoming and what is not. They also are used to managing the money for family clothing, so they may insist on taking the responsibility for decisions about daughter's clothes. With boys, the problem is somewhat different, because many boys are not so much interested in clothes as girls are. With boys, the trouble may arise over what is to be worn on certain occasions.

The Bowmans might be a fairly typical family. John, at fifteen, liked to wear Levi's almost everywhere he went. His parents felt that Levi's were not suitable for school or for any social occasions. They bought him slacks, shirts, and ties to wear to school.

John's father said that he had driven past the school and observed that some of the boys entering and leaving the building looked very neat in slacks and shirts and seemed to him to be much more suitably dressed than the boys in Levi's.

John's mother said, "We've spent good money for decent school clothes for you, and you are letting them hang there unworn while you outgrow them. Soon they'll be too small, and the money will have been wasted."

But John said, "I didn't want those slacks in the first place. You didn't have to spend the money for them. All I wanted was some more Levi's and sweaters. And if a few boys want to wear slacks, that's their choice. *Most* boys in my school wear Levi's, and that's what I'm going to wear."

When they went to church on Sunday, John would appear wearing the slacks and an open-necked shirt with no tie. His parents would insist that he put on a jacket and a tie. John said, "I'm not wearing a tie. I'd rather be choked." The argument would go on until they were all late to church.

Neither John nor his parents would change their views. John continued to go tieless and coatless to church, although his parents were embarrassed by his appearance. He continued to wear a bat-

SHOULD PARENTS CHOOSE THE KIND OF CLOTHES YOU WEAR ?								
		%	STUDENTS	%	MOTHERS	%	FATHERS	
USUALLY	BOYS	11%		28%		13%		
	GIRLS	5%		24%		24%		
SOMETIMES	BOYS	42%		52%		44%		
	GIRLS	47%		59%		44%		
HARDLY EVER	BOYS	47%		16%		40%		
	GIRLS	47%		14%		41%		
DON'T KNOW	BOYS	0%		4%		3%		
	GIRLS	1%		3%		3%		

Adapted from *The Purdue Opinion Panel*, 9:1, November 1949, p. 16.

● Students in this study told what they thought about choosing their own clothes and then gave what they believed to be their mothers' and fathers' thoughts on whether the children should choose their own clothes. Both boys and girls feel they should have greater freedom than they are given by their parents, especially their mothers.

tered up pair of Levi's to school and to show a sulky face every morning at breakfast because he could feel his parents' disapproval.

John's sulky face was hardly noticed on many mornings, however, because his parents were too much involved with his sister, Ann. Every morning, Ann came to breakfast wearing a different combination of blouse and skirt, or sweater and skirt, and contrasting colored neck scarf. Mrs. Bowman disapproved of Ann's choices of color combinations. She would say, "Ann, *what* are you trying to do? Attract attention to yourself? That green scarf with that purple sweater is simply awful. And *why* that ribbon around your neck? Of all things!"

Then Mr. Bowman would say, "Wipe off some of that lipstick. No daughter of mine is going to appear on the street looking like that."

Ann would say, "*I* know what looks good on me. I'm the one that's wearing these clothes. What difference does it make to you? You aren't going to have to look at me today." On some days, she would yield to her parents' wishes. On others, she would snatch up her books, slam the door, and go to school.

The worst battles came when Ann needed new clothes. Most of the time, she felt that she needed new clothes, and her mother would point out that she had plenty of clothes hanging in her room if she would only wear what she had. After many arguments, Ann and her mother would go shopping. They could not agree at all on what to buy. Mrs. Bowman insisted on buying things that were "suitable" for a 14-year-old girl, while Ann felt that her mother's choices were "childish." Mrs. Bowman wanted to consider quality and ease of upkeep, while Ann wanted what all the other girls were wearing, even if it might not be as durable or washable as the things her mother would choose. Both would be exhausted with the conflict after a few hours of trying to shop for Ann's clothes.

How to solve the problem

What solutions can you think of for the troubles the Bowmans were having over decisions about clothes?

Do you think it might be possible for all four to agree that it

● Some families can discuss the problem of clothes and appropriate dress and reach peaceful agreements. If you can discuss rather than argue about the subject, it may help your parents to see the problem from your point of view and you to see it from their point of view. *(Luoma Photos.)*

was too bad to spoil so much of their home life with this kind of conflict and to reach some kind of compromise that would be satisfactory to all of them?

They would have to consider such questions as: What is really the custom in John's school today regarding school clothes? Have ideas about what is suitable changed since Mr. Bowman was in high school? What is most generally considered the right way to dress for church for boys of John's age? Was John making unnecessary embarrassment for his parents by insisting on wearing something different from what most people accepted as the right dress for church? Should the parents have bought school clothes for John without consulting him?

Just how much money could the family afford to spend for clothes and what share of it should be spent for Ann, John, and each parent? Can you suggest how Ann and her mother could compromise about their different ideas on what is suitable for a 14-year-old girl to wear? Is it possible that both were partly

Your Parents

wrong, Mrs. B. trying to keep Ann a little girl too long and Ann tending to handicap her own attractiveness by trying to dress in too "old" a way?

If they couldn't agree, who should make the decision? If Ann makes her own decisions in buying clothes, should she also have the privilege of discarding a garment and getting another new one if she later decides she doesn't like the choice she made?

Emotional conflict over problems

When we look, as outsiders, at such problems that others have, it is often fairly easy to see how they should be able to work them out. When we, ourselves, are in the midst of such problems, we are likely to get emotional and to feel like "fighting it out on these lines if it takes all winter," rather than trying to find a reasonable compromise.

The next chapter will discuss some points that may help you solve problems with your parents in thoughtful rather than emotional ways.

HOW DO YOU RATE AS A FAMILY MEMBER?

	Never	Some-times	Usually	Always
	0	4	7	10
1. I am cheerful at home.				
2. I save some time to do things with my family.				
3. I show an interest in what others in my family are doing.				
4. I make a sincere effort to understand my parents' viewpoint and discuss important matters with them.				
5. My parents can count on me to carry out unpleasant decisions without sulking.				
6. I try to have my friends and my parents know each other.				
7. I take time to tell my parents about my activities outside the home when they are interested.				
8. My parents can count on me to do my best to take advantage of the opportunities they make for me.				
9. My parents can depend on me to be responsible for taking care of my own health.				
10. I try to keep from asking for special favors that others in my family don't get.				
Total each column				
Total points				

Courtesy National Dairy Council.

REVIEW QUESTIONS

1. What is meant by seeing a problem in perspective?

2. How do you explain the fact that some problems viewed in perspective are no longer problems at all?

3. How would an outsider, who has perspective, view the problems that arise between young people and their parents?

4. Compare the behavior of parents when you were learning to walk with their behavior toward you now.

5. Compare the reaction of the baby in learning to walk with your behavior now, when your parents become concerned about what you are doing.

6. Are parents always sure about what is best for you? Are they always consistent in their disciplining? Why or why not?

7. Review the conflicts the Bowmans were having over clothes. Have you known of such conflicts in your family or in other families?

8. When should you make your own decisions on what you are to wear?

9. When should you have full responsibility in buying your clothes?

10. Who was right, John Bowman or his parents, in their difference over what he should wear to church and to school? Was either entirely right?

11. Can a girl think of quality in clothes if she is to keep up with current fads in dress?

12. Have ideas about wearing lipstick changed since Mrs. Bowman was in high school? Discuss.

13. Why is it easier to see other people's problems in perspective than our own?

14. When a friend has a problem that is similar to one you have faced, do you find that you are able to take a calmer, saner view of the situation, now? Are you even able to see the humor in some cases? Do you try to do this sort of "standing aside" to look at problems of your own?

KEY WORDS AND PHRASES

impudent   decisions
perspective   natural processes

PROBLEMS AND ACTIVITIES

1. *Class survey*. Each student make a list of the things which bother him most about his parents. Do not sign your name. Have a class committee summarize the results and put the ten highest parent problems on the blackboard. Leave these on the blackboard for the days you are studying parent problems.

2. Talk to your parents or other adults about what were acceptable styles in dress and make-up for high school people when they were in school. What changes have occurred? What fundamentals of good taste still remain?

3. Do you know a family who has problems similar to the Bowman's? If you do, can you see the problem in proper perspective? This means that you would probably see the problem from the point of view of both parents and children. Seeing both sides of a question is a sign of maturity.

4. *Problem for homework*. Mary is plump, and she insists on wearing plaid dresses because they are in style. Her mother has suggested that she should wear different clothes but cannot tell Mary why because Mary is sensitive about her figure. As a result, there is constant conflict over Mary's clothes. How could Mary and her mother get together?

5. *Special report*. When you come to class tomorrow, be prepared to tell the class about some incident or happening at home in which good manners (either your own or some other family member's) helped to avoid friction or helped to put a stop to friction or confusion that was already started. Kind words or a sense of humor may have accomplished the same purpose.

SOCIO-DRAMA

A discussion of the parent problems discussed in the chapter, or better yet, those brought out in your class survey (problem 1 above). Have four students play the roles of parents and four play the roles of young people. Through your role-playing, try to get the parents to see the point of view of the young people and the young people to see the point of view of the parents.

PANEL DISCUSSION

Instead of using students to represent the parents, have four parents come to class to participate in the discussion of parent problems, using the result of your survey as a basis of discussion.

FILM

You and Your Parents — 14 minutes, sound, Coronet
See reading list at end of this section, page 223.

YOUR FAMILY AND YOUR
20 DECISIONS

In daily living a number of points arise around the issues discussed in the preceding chapter. You feel that you know your own needs and your own situation better than your parents do, and that therefore you should have a right to decide many things for yourself.

It will help to avoid conflicts with your parents if you can find answers to certain questions about the situations that sometimes cause trouble.

Some of the following questions are important: Is there any reason why, if I decide and make a wrong decision on this point, it would harm the rest of the family by wasting my parents' money, by causing extra work, or by depriving some others in the family of something they ought to have?

If I make the wrong decision, am I willing to accept the consequences of my choice?

Is this a point on which I ought to make the decision because, whether right or wrong, I can learn things I need to know by thinking it through and deciding for myself?

If you can find the answers to those three questions, you may be willing on some matters to give up making your own decision. On other matters you may be able to talk it over with your parents (after you have thought it through) and get them to see your viewpoint and agree that you should make your own decision in this case.

It helps if you will remember that your parents do not like conflict any better than you do. They would like very much to feel that they could relax their authority and leave to you many things for which they are now taking the responsibility. But they may not have seen any evidence that you are able to make choices

● Problems are easier to solve if you can be thoughtful rather than emotional in your approach to them. *(Luoma Photos.)*

wisely and follow through with what you attempt. If you can talk questions over together, problems will work out easier for all.

What about choosing your own friends?

Perhaps your parents seem to you to try to influence your choice of friends too much. They may discourage certain friendships and encourage others, and you may feel that they are interfering in your personal affairs.

Try to figure out why they have the attitudes they do about your friends. Parents are people with faults just like the rest of us. It **is** possible that they are being swayed by prejudices in their attitudes about your friends, but it is more probable that they are thinking of things that seem to them to be important to your happiness and good development. Consider whether or not you may have chosen some friends whose values in life and whose standards are so different from yours that in their company you may do things that could bring trouble to yourself and to your parents.

Your parents may be more conscious than you are that you will be "typed" in your school by the friends you have, and they may be anxious and worried if they see that you have chosen some friends whose reputations are not good. They may also discourage a friendship if they see that you are allowing one certain person to monopolize you and cut you off from other friends.

Such reasons may cause parents to want to take a hand in your affairs. The best thing you can do about it is to try to use as much wisdom as possible yourself in managing your friendships. Gradually you can probably help your parents to see that you are growing up in your own way and that you, as well as they, are aware of important considerations in choosing friends.

What about your right to privacy?

Jack, who lives with several other family members in a very small apartment, and Sally, who lives in a large house with only her parents, both have some of the same complaints. They both say, "My parents want to know who called me on the phone, or whom my letter was from. I call it prying!" Jack says, "I have no place for my own things." And Sally says, "My mother walks into my room any time she wants to. She inspects my dresser drawers and criticizes the way I keep my things."

Right now, because you especially want your parents to realize that you are no longer a child, you are likely to look upon any natural interest in your activities as prying or invading your right to keep your affairs to yourself. But your parents have not changed as much as you have in the last two or three years. They have

● "It's the old story, boy meets girl, boy meets girl's parents, boy can't see girl anymore." (Emmy Lou by Marty Links.)

● Talk it over with your family before you make the decision to smoke. A lifetime decision should not be made hastily or when you are being pressured into it by friends. Get the facts, as you do when making other decisions. *(Coronet Films.)*

always been interested in what you do, and they still are. They may be baffled and puzzled because now, suddenly, you resent what seems to them to be their usual interest in your activities. As time passes, they will probably learn not to ask questions you resent, and you will also become more able to accept their interest in you. You will find it easier to share freely with them experiences that they would enjoy hearing about and to keep to yourself other matters that are important to you as personal and private.

Decisions about your behavior

Your parents may be very anxious for you to live according to standards that they believe in. Yet, all around you, you see others who have different standards.

Many of your choices and decisions are made more difficult by the fact that pressures are put upon you from various directions to behave in certain ways.

For example: Some of your friends may have begun to smoke cigarettes, and advertisements in magazines and on the radio and television constantly suggest to you that it is time you began smoking too. But whether or not your parents are smokers, they

208   *Your Family and Your Decisions*

may feel that you should not begin the habit. Should you make that decision for yourself now? What must be considered in making the decision? Is it one of the important decisions that your parents have reason to be concerned about, or is it one of the less important ones that is no one's affair except your own?

First, the decision to begin smoking now is a more important decision than it at first appears to be, for it means beginning a lifetime habit. Few people ever stop smoking later, if they begin smoking while in their teens. Any policy or habit that is to be followed for the rest of your life deserves some careful thought before you take it up. You owe it to yourself and your parents to talk it over with them and consider their views before you make a decision.

They may point out to you, for one thing, the cost in money. The average smoker spends approximately $100 a year for cigarettes. If several in a family smoke or if one smokes very heavily, the costs increase proportionately. Some families who feel that they could not afford the expense of keeping and feeding a dog could keep a dog and also finance the cost of some interesting hobbies at less cost than their cigarette money. Or rather than thinking of the cost of smoking in terms of feeding a dog, your father may see the expense in terms of life insurance. The cost of one or two persons' smoking in a year would easily pay the premiums on a $5,000 to $10,000 life insurance policy.

So in thinking about beginning to smoke, you can look ahead and think about whether you might prefer to spend the money that over the years would go for tobacco in some other way that might be worth more to you and your family.

Another thing that you will want to think about before you begin the habit is whether or not smoking will have an undesirable effect on your health. You know that statements are made by tobacco advertisements which try to show that smoking is not harmful in any way. Nevertheless, successful athletes know that they cannot be at their best if they smoke. Training rules for all competitive sports prohibit smoking. Such rules are not made from prejudice but are based on known facts about the effects of smoking.

Doctors have long argued over whether or not smoking actually causes or aggravates certain diseases. There are very good doctors

Four Reports Link Cancer, Cigarettes

Exclusive to The Chronicle
From the New York Times

NEW YORK, Dec. 8 — Four medical reports in which the link between cigarette smoking and disease, particularly lung cancer, was pointed out without the usual qualifications and hedging were presented here today.

The correlation between smoking and cancer was stated in unusually strong terms by medical specialists speaking at the 29th annual Greater New York Dental Meeting.

The meeting marked one of the first occasions in which medical researchers, reporting before a professional group, have joined in insisting firmly that it is smoking and not some other environmental factor, that has caused the great increase in lung cancer among males noted in disease statistics of the last two decades

IN ANOTHER 50 YEARS

Dr. Alton Ochsner, chairman of the surgery department at Tulane University School of Medicine in New Orleans, said medical men are "extremely concerned about the possibility that the male population of the United States will be decimated by cancer of the lung in another 50 years, if cigarette smoking increases as it has in the past, unless some steps are taken to remove the cancer-producing factor in tobacco."

What this factor may be is not know, Dr. Ochsner said. It appears to be some substance in tobacco tars.

A report of 13 independent studies of lung cancer and smoking was presented by Dr. Ernest L. Wynder of the Memorial Center for Cancer and Allied diseases.

A 20-FOLD RISK

More than 5000 patients with cancer of the lung have been studied in England, Germany, Switzerland, Denmark, Czechoslovakia, and the U. S., Dr. Wynder said. There were some variations in the independent studies, he reported, but the ultimate conclusion is that "the prolonged and heavy use of cigarettes increases up to 20 times the risk of developing cancer of the lung."

The connection between smoking and the onset of diseases of the heart and blood vessels was discussed by Dr. Grace H. Roth of the Mayo Foundation at the University of Minnesota. Extensive tests, she said, indicate it is nicotine, and not other factors in smoke, which cause increases of blood pressure and pulse, and decreases of skin temperatures in susceptible persons. She said any person with a tendency toward blood or vascular diseases should stop smoking.

All speakers agreed that th[e] causative factor in lung canc[er] is smoking, and not pollu[ted] city air or some other envi[ron]mental condition. Dr. Och[sner] added that cigarettes a[re the] cause, not pipes or ciga[rs be]cause cigarette smoke i[s usual]ly inhaled and pipe [and cigar] smoke is not. On [the other] hand, he continued, i[t has been] shown there is a [connection] between cancer [of the lip, tongue, and mo[uth and the] smoking of pipes [and cigars as] well as cigarette[s.]

Tobacco Firm Hits Cigaret, Cancer Links

NEW YORK, Dec. 9.—(P)—P. Lorillard Company, a leading manufacturer of cigarets, today assailed the scientific opinion which alleges a connection between cigaret smoking and cancer of the lung.

The company said it had "initiated a program of research which includes all facets thus far suggested that have a bearing on tobacco smoking and health." Its statement was signed by Harris B. Parmele, Ph.D., director of research.

Lorillard manufactures "Old Gold" and "Kent" cigarets. It followed the lead of Paul M. Hahn, president of the American Tobacco Company ("Lucky Strike") who last month characterized the alleged connection as "loose talk."

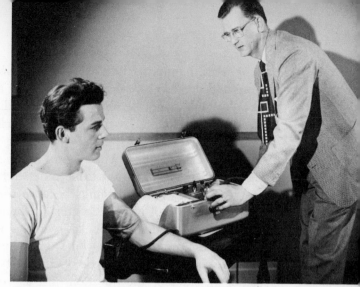

● Scientists have devised tests to learn the effects of tobacco upon the heart and nervous system. This young man is taking such a test. (Coronet Films.)

who will defend each side of the question. Meanwhile, research in medical institutions continues to bring out facts which show that there is a relationship between certain kinds of cancer and long-continued smoking.

Doctors who examined the records of lung cancer patients in British hospitals found only two nonsmokers among 649 men with lung cancer. Another recent study by doctors at Barnes Hospital in St. Louis compared the smoking habits of lung cancer patients with the habits of other patients. It was found that about three times as many of the lung cancer patients were excessive or chain smokers. Many doctors who have been studying this problem have concluded that it is heavy smoking of cigarettes, continued habitually over a period of years, that seems to lead to lung cancer. The Journal of the American Medical Association announced in December, 1953, that it would no longer accept advertising for cigarettes because tobacco advertisers have misquoted doctors on the real effects of cigarettes and because of the proven relationship between smoking and lung cancer. It is easier for you to look at facts thoughtfully before you have begun to smoke. For smoking, once begun, usually becomes habitual.

Another thing to think about is this: Just *why* do I want to begin smoking? Some people begin because they feel awkward in social groups. They don't know what to do with their hands, and they feel that smoking makes them less conspicuous. One 16-year-old boy who was a fingernail biter, said, "Tom is a chain smoker. I bite my nails. I suppose both habits are in the same class. We get nervous and don't know what else to do, so I bite my nails and he smokes!" Would it not be better to work at developing real social poise that would not depend on some such habit? Chapter 8 discussed many ways to work at developing social poise.

There are other people who begin smoking because others are doing it, and they are afraid to be independent in a group. The most successful people do things because they think the actions are wise or right, not because others do them.

Rather than starting to smoke secretly because the gang is smoking, and thus drifting into a habit which will be with you for life, it would be better to be open about it with your family. Consider all sides of the question, just as you would in making any other important decision in your life. One thing certain is that it will do no harm to postpone smoking and give yourself a chance to think it over. Work at developing your skills and at getting along with people without falling back on a prop like smoking. Your progress will be happier in the long run.

In this, as in other things, your parents will probably accept your ideas when they see that you are showing mature judgment in managing your own affairs wisely and are trying to think the matter out carefully rather than acting impulsively.

Show in every way that you can that you are a responsible person. Then, while your parents are growing to accept you on that basis, be patient. You will be happier later if you have not had too many bitter battles with your parents over the decisions that you make or want to make during these years.

REVIEW QUESTIONS

1. What are three important questions you should ask yourself when you are learning to make your own decisions?

2. Many parents have reasons for being concerned with their children's choice of friends. Discuss.

3. How can you get your parents to respect your choice of friends?

4. What is one of the best ways for you to show your parents that you are ready to make your own decisions?

5. Why is the decision about whether to smoke an important one?

6. How much does the average smoker spend on tobacco per year?

7. What are some of the effects of smoking upon the body?

8. What are some of the reasons why young people start smoking?

KEY WORDS AND PHRASES

emotional   cancer
prejudice   impulsively

PROBLEMS AND ACTIVITIES

1. How mature are you in making your own decisions? Think of the last several important decisions you have made. How many of these were good decisions? How many bad decisions did you make? If you made several bad decisions, why did you make them? Are you apt to repeat them or did you learn from your mistakes?

2. Have you known young people who were too dependent upon their parents; they always let their parents make all their decisions for them? Which do you think is worse, to make the wrong decisions once in a while or to let parents make all decisions?

3. Parents usually think making *good decisions* is more important than making *your own decisions*. Young people usually think it is more important to make their own decisions. Which is correct? How could a compromise be reached?

4. Why is it difficult to get the truth about the effects of smoking upon the body?

5. *Class project.* For your classroom bulletin board, collect all the material you can on smoking. In one place, put what science says about smoking; and in another place collect what tobacco advertisers say. Evaluate the cigarette advertising. Try to be objective. What claims may be true and what part of the advertising is open to question?

6. Talk to several people who smoke and ask them what they would advise for the young person who has not started smoking.

FILMS

Make Your Own Decisions — 10 minutes, sound, Coronet
Alcohol and Tobacco: What They Do to Our Bodies — 10 minutes, sound, Coronet (use with this chapter or with chapter 25).
See reading list at end of Part Four, page 223.

UNDERSTANDING BROTHERS AND SISTERS

21

If you had the power to change your family into an ideal family, what changes would you make? Would you eliminate all disagreements and conflicts? Would you have more brothers and sisters or fewer brothers and sisters than you have? Would you wish to be an only child, or the youngest, oldest, or middle child? Would you make changes in yourself as well as in the others in your family?

An ideal family might be one in which the mother and father love all children equally; brothers and sisters appreciate and love each other and are good companions to each other; and there is no conflict between parents and children or between brothers and sisters. But how many families fit this ideal? Almost all families at times have some conflict. It is often true that brothers and sisters are jealous of each other and sometimes quarrel bitterly. Most children feel at times that their parents do not appreciate them or do not love them enough.

Jealousies

If you are the oldest child in the family, you may feel jealous of your younger brother or sister. Perhaps you have not called your feeling "jealousy." It has only seemed to you that your younger brother or sister is a troublesome person. Your feeling probably began in happenings back farther than you can remember.

The oldest or the first child in the family is the center of attention in the home for two or more years, usually. Not only do the parents give him all their attention, but he may also have two sets of doting grandparents. The first child thrives on all the attention and affection he receives, and life is beautiful for him. Then one day, something happens to change things. A brother or sister is born and the parents and relatives seem to change suddenly.

If you were the oldest child, of course you noticed it when they began to give much of their attention and affection to the new baby. You fought for love and attention in some way, and you developed certain feelings about the new brother or sister who seemed for a while to be displacing you. If you have a dog, have you ever noticed how he acts when a neighbor's dog comes to your place, and you start petting the neighbor's dog? Your dog may growl at the other dog, he may push his nose into your hands to make you notice him, or he may bark and roll to call himself to your attention. The older child reacts in similar ways when he sees the baby getting attention that he is used to having himself. Whether or not you were the oldest child in the family, you may have gone through the same experiences when a younger brother or sister came into the family.

Perhaps you adjusted quickly to the new situation and kept no jealous feelings toward your younger brother or sister. But if you still are often resentful toward your younger sister or brother, some of your early experiences help to explain it. You may forget

● Try petting a strange dog in the presence of your dog.

experiences but keep traces of the feelings that began with them.

Another common reason for jealousies and misunderstandings between brothers and sisters is that children feel that their parents favor one above another. No matter how much parents love all their children, it is hard for them to act in exactly the same way toward each child. You and your brother are two very different people. You respond differently in different situations. You draw out different responses from your parents. It is easy for you to conclude that one or the other is a favorite because of the way the parents treat him or her.

John gets the idea that his little brother Jim is his mother's favorite. John has noticed that in any trouble between the two boys, Jim never seems to get the blame for anything. Or Sue thinks her parents favor her brother because he is allowed to stay out later at nights, and to do some things that she is not allowed to do.

If you could put yourself in your parents' places you would see that they probably struggle to decide what is right for each child. They must consider the special needs of your brothers and sisters as well as yours. Perhaps you can see things only from your own viewpoint, and what you feel and want crowds out your ability to think of the needs of others in the family. It is easy simply to conclude that your parents favor the other person when decisions fail to go your way.

June was critical of her parents because they expected her to help around the home, while her older sister, Helen, never did much of anything to help at home. June felt that Helen was favored by her parents. June complained to her mother, and her mother tried to explain the situation as she saw it. She said, "Your father and I feel that we were very unwise when Helen was younger. We did everything for her and let her grow to be very selfish. Now we are trying our best to help Helen change. But now that she is seventeen, she will have to do the changing herself. There is little we can do now about her selfish ways unless she really works to change herself. But, you, June, are five years younger, and we are trying not to make the same mistakes again. You will be a happier person if you are unselfish and cooperative. I'm thinking of *you* when I try to get you to do

● Rivalry in the family can bring out the good or the bad in us. *(Luoma Photos.)*

your share at home. Helen is handicapped by her selfishness. When I try to keep you from having the same handicap, it doesn't mean that I favor Helen."

June still sometimes feels resentful when her parents expect her to do things that they don't try to make Helen do, but she is able to see it from her mother's viewpoint. She understands at least that her mother does love her as much as she loves Helen and that her mother has a problem in dealing with two very different girls, one of whom is already somewhat "spoiled."

Rivalry

In some families, the brothers and sisters work to outdo or excel each other in almost all their undertakings. This, too, may be traced back to the time when they were very small children. If Bill, at four, saw that everyone was fascinated by the cute new baby, he may have climbed up on the dining room table and shouted, "Look at me! Look what I can do!" and then jumped off the table. Or if small Johnny felt that everyone admired the way big brother or sister was learning to read, Johnny may have worked hard to learn to pound nails into a board to show that he, too, had abilities.

Such competition between brothers and sisters, whether they are four or fourteen, is natural. In order to be happy all of us need to feel recognized for what we are and to feel appreciated for what we can do. Because of your need to compete with brothers or sisters, you work harder than you otherwise would do to develop the special abilities that you have.

Family rivalries can, however, work in several different ways. Sometimes jealousy may make the rivalry too intense. John may become so emotional over his sister's or brother's superiority in some line, that he does unreasonable things. If his brother greatly excels him in athletic ability, instead of doing his best and getting some enjoyment out of sports, John may drop all sports and spend his time in less profitable ways. Or if Jane's sister is more popular with the boys than Jane is, Jane may say she doesn't care for boys, anyway. And she may withdraw from activities that might help her to become more skilled socially and that might help her learn to get along better with others.

An important part of becoming emotionally mature is learning to accept ourselves and others without being upset about differences. You are doing good work at growing up when you can enjoy being proud of the achievements of your brother or sister, while going ahead to do your best in your own way whatever your abilities are.

Quarrels

Some of the quarrels that you have with your brothers and sisters may grow out of the jealousies and rivalries that began when you were very small. Other quarrels occur only because you are tired or hungry and your brother or sister is at hand to get the benefit of your irritated feelings. Some people feel that families — parents and brothers and sisters — are good "shock absorbers." That is, feelings of anger or frustration that we have to control when we are out among friends or strangers can be expressed at home where we are loved and understood.

Sometimes there are issues between brothers and sisters that cause frequent quarrels. Does your sister wear your clothes without asking you? Does your brother bother you or interrupt when you are using the telephone? Do you quarrel over whose turn it is to do the dishes or over which radio or television program is going to be on? Some quarrels serve a good purpose; they help people to become aware of unpleasant things that they do, and the quarrels may cause people to work to change their habits. Other quarrels accomplish nothing at all, except to make a home a less pleasant place.

Think of the last few quarrels that you have had with a brother or sister. Did they do any good? What good was accomplished? What harm was done? As you grow up, you will want to look for better ways than quarrelling to settle differences.

Values in brother-sister relationships

You have probably had nearly all kinds of feelings about your brothers and sisters. Perhaps you can sympathize with Marsha who appeared at a friend's house one day in a boiling mood and said, "I just had to leave my house to get away from my awful brother. Tom has mixed in every single thing I've tried to do today. He makes me so mad. *Why* wasn't I an *only child!*" Or perhaps you can understand Jim, who had just had a terrible time explaining to a girl friend something his sister Sally had quoted him as having said. He came home mumbling, "It's tough to have a sister around messing things up for you!"

But on another day, Marsha said joyfully to the same friend, "My brother Tom brought a new boy home with him today, and the three of us had the most fun while we were washing the car! And Tom asked me to go along when he took the new boy home at dinner time. I'm so glad I've got a brother! It's such a help!" And Jim, who on one day thinks it is tough having a sister around, on other days rushes into the house calling, "Sally, come on, let's have a game of Ping-pong." Or "Sally, *please* will you press my shirt. I've got to have it to wear in about two minutes." And he knows Sally will drop what she is doing and press his shirt for him or play the game of Ping-pong.

If you add up the times when you may have wished you were an only child and compare them with the times that you have been glad that you have brothers and sisters, you will probably conclude that most of the time you would not trade your brothers and sisters for anything in the world.

Moreover, in many ways that you may not have thought of, your brothers and sisters are a help to you. Even the quarrels and unpleasant times you have may help you to recognize your faults and to overcome some of them. People who grow up in a family of several children have an advantage all through life,

● Rivalries of early childhood tend to disappear, and brothers and sisters become good companions during the teen years.

for they have to learn early to get along with others and to adjust to the needs and wishes of others.

All through life, you will be a more successful and a happier person also if you have learned to take pride and pleasure in the achievements of others as well as in your own. You are proud of the accomplishments of your brothers and sisters. Their success in any line contributes to your own feeling of worth, and, in turn, whatever you do matters to them. These are special values that you get from having brothers and sisters.

REVIEW QUESTIONS

1. What is a picture of the ideal family? Do you know of any "ideal family"?

2. If the oldest child is jealous of the next younger child, what might be the origin of this jealousy?

3. How do parents sometimes try to make it easier for the oldest child when the new baby arrives?

4. Why does it sometimes seem that parents favor certain children?

5. When may rivalry between brothers and sisters be good? When might it be bad?

6. What is often the basis of quarrels between brothers and sisters?

7. What is meant by saying that the family may be a good "shock absorber" for you?

8. What are some of the things that brothers and sisters contribute to your development?

KEY WORDS AND PHRASES

jealousy	rivalry	shock absorber
favorites	fascinated	family unity

PROBLEMS AND ACTIVITIES

1. Describe behavior you have noticed in an older child when another baby was born into the family.

2. Do you have a dog? If you do, try an experiment. Show special attention to a strange dog by petting it in the presence of your dog. Make a list of the things your dog does to show that he feels neglected. How does your list compare with the behavior you have noticed in neglected people?

3. Think of several young people you know who think their parents show favoritism in the family. Do the parents show favoritism or is it that the children need different treatment in that family?

4. Tell about a case of rivalry between brothers and sisters which you thought was good. Give a case which seemed bad.

5. Think of the past quarrels you have had in your family. How many of these were caused by jealousy or rivalry? How many because you had had a bad day at school? How many because you were not feeling well? How many because you were hungry or tired?

6. Where do you come in your family: eldest, youngest, middle?

What special problems have you thought you had because
of your position in the family?

7. Sometimes brothers and sisters are ashamed of each others'
manners. Have you ever worked out a way of helping your
brother or sister to improve his or her manners? Explain.

FILM

Family Life — 10 minutes, sound, Coronet

MORE ABOUT YOU AND YOUR FAMILY

CRAWFORD, CLAUDE C., E. G. COOLEY, C. C. TRILLINGHAM AND EMERY
STOOPS, *Living Your Life*. Boston: D. C. Heath and Company, 2nd
ed., 1953, ch. 4.

DETJEN, MARY FORD AND ERVIN W. DETJEN, *Your High School Days*.
New York: McGraw-Hill Book Company, Inc., 1947, ch. 8.

FEDDER, RUTH, *A Girl Grows Up*. New York: McGraw-Hill Book Company, Inc., 1948, ch. 6.

JENKINS, GLADYS GARDNER AND JOY NEUMAN, *How to Live with Parents*.
Chicago: Science Research Associates, Inc., 1948.

McKOWN, HARRY C., *A Boy Grows Up*. New York: McGraw-Hill Book
Company, Inc., 1949, chs. 5–6.

PIERCE, WELLINGTON G., *This Is the Life*. Boston: D. C. Heath and
Company, 1951, unit 2.

RANDOLPH, HELEN R., ERMA PIXLEY, DOROTHY D. DUGGAN AND FRED
McKINNEY, *You and Your Life*. Boston: Houghton Mifflin Company, 1951, chs. 13–17.

ULLMAN, FRANCES, *Getting Along with Brothers and Sisters*. Chicago:
Science Research Associates, Inc., 1952.

———, *Life with Brothers and Sisters*. Chicago: Science Research
Associates, Inc., 1952.

WHITESIDE-TAYLOR, KATHARINE, *Getting along with Parents*. Chicago:
Science Research Associates, Inc., 1952.

Part Five

PHYSICAL AND
MENTAL HEALTH

GOOD HEALTH

22

On your way to school this morning, you probably passed at least one billboard that advertised some product by picturing a healthy, happy person. Whatever the billboards are trying to sell, they all base some of their appeal upon the fact that we associate good health with happiness and success.

It is true that good health is important to success in anything we try to do, even though many people do achieve outstanding success in life in spite of serious physical handicaps.

We can not buy good health by following the suggestions of the advertisers of products; nevertheless, each of us has a wide range of choice in determining his own state of health. Just as you can take the right care of a piece of machinery or equipment to get the maximum efficiency and enjoyment from it — so you can form habits of living that will make the most of the possibilities for good health with which you were born.

Your eating habits

When you were younger, you may have had little choice about what you ate. Families have eating patterns that the children naturally follow while they are small. Some families are more lacking in energy and vitality than others, with frequent illness, while other families seem to be full of energy and seldom ill. Eating habits are important in their effect upon family health. Now that you are no longer a child, you have more individual freedom of choice and consequently more responsibility for choosing wisely the foods that will serve you best. You choose your lunches while at school; your after-school snacks are your own affair, and at your

Get up early enough to eat a good BREAKFAST such as ☞	FRUIT OR TOMATO JUICE CEREAL OR TOAST, OR BOTH MILK ON CEREAL MILK TO DRINK AN EGG, IF YOU DO NOT HAVE ONE IN ANOTHER MEAL
VEGETABLE SOUP A GREEN VEGETABLE BREAD AND BUTTER SCRAMBLED EGGS POTATOES MILK PUDDING	Eat a good LUNCH at school or at home a hot lunch such as ☞
or a BOX LUNCH Don't hurry when eating. Play quiet games after- ward. ☞	SANDWICHES FILLED WITH EGG OR CHEESE OR MEAT AN APPLE, CARROT, OR OTHER RAW FRUIT OR VEGETABLE MILK AND COOKIES
MEAT, FISH, OR DRIED PEAS OR BEANS, POTATOES, A SALAD A YELLOW VEGETABLE BREAD AND BUTTER MILK PUDDING Some families eat their dinner or large meal at noon. Others eat their dinner in the evening. The important thing to remember is to have the *basic seven* foods in your meals every day.	Eat a good DINNER something like this ☞

Ruth Strang, *Ways to Keep Well and Happy* (National Tuberculosis Association, 1790 Broadway, New York 19, N. Y.)

● A well-balanced diet is essential to good health.

age your mother ought not to have to be responsible for seeing that you "eat your vegetable and drink your milk."

A good complexion, pep, endurance for daily activities, and a good disposition rather than irritability and touchiness all are at least partly the result of a good habitual diet. So much is said about the need for vitamins and minerals in the diet that many people forget that a diet properly balanced with proteins, carbohydrates, and fats does contain the vitamins and minerals one needs. Nutritionists point out that the place to buy vitamins is in the meat and vegetable markets, not in the drugstore. Many families spend for commercial vitamins and minerals money that they might better spend for good food. Commercial vitamins are valuable for people who for some reason need special supplements to their diet, but taking vitamin pills can never be a substitute for good dietary habits.

Good diet

You do not have to be an expert on nutrition, but you can have a good working knowledge of the fundamental facts about good diet.

Proteins are a class of foods that are extremely important in the diet of the growing person. The best protein-furnishing foods are meat, fish, eggs, milk, and cheese. Not all of those foods have to be eaten every day, but a good start for your day is an egg and a glass of milk for breakfast; or if you make your after-school snack a cheese sandwich instead of a coke or an ice cream soda, you are getting better health-and-growth value for your money.

Ice cream contains some milk, cream, and eggs, but it is a far better source of fats and sugars than it is of protein, and you need protein more than you need sweets and fats. Those, while they do produce energy, may also contribute to complexion problems, and they may dull your appetite for the foods that are more essential.

Carbohydrates are provided by foods such as potatoes, bread, cereals, sugar, and some vegetables. Carbohydrates are needed for energy, although they contribute less to growth and endurance than proteins do.

Fat is also an energy producer. Butter, cream, nuts, frying oils, and fat meats are high in fat content. Fat is important in the diets of people who live in cold countries and need great amounts of energy just to keep warm. In moderate climates, or in warm seasons of the year, we need less fat. If too much fat is eaten, the body stores it up, and we begin to worry about reducing.

A good diet will include some of all three of the food groups and will not be overbalanced by any one of the three. A good diet will include — in addition to milk — cereals or bread, and either eggs or meat, some fruit every day, and two or more vegetables.

An easy way to improve your diet is to make it a habit to eat an apple or an orange instead of a candy bar. And when you raid the refrigerator or cupboard, look for a stalk of celery or a raw carrot instead of cake or cookies. You will get double enjoyment out of such eating habits: the enjoyment of good foods and the pleasure of an improved complexion and a higher level of vitality.

Attitudes and eating habits

Much of your success in forming and maintaining good eating habits will depend upon your *attitudes* toward food and eating. Some people enjoy food almost entirely for the immediate pleasure

● "Vegetables, soup, ugh!" The right attitude toward food is a part of good eating habits.

Good Health

HOW ARE YOUR EATING HABITS?

	Never	Some-times	Usually	Always
	0	4	7	10
1. I enjoy my meals.				
2. My digestion is good.				
3. I eat at regular hours.				
4. I get up in time to eat a hearty breakfast.				
5. I take time to eat a substantial lunch.				
6. I drink at least four glasses of milk daily.				
7. I eat green or yellow vegetables daily.				
8. I eat three good meals a day.				
9. I am sociable but sensible about what I eat between meals.				
10. My table manners are acceptable to others.				

Total each column

Total points

Courtesy National Dairy Council.

in eating it. They will eat the foods they like, regardless of whether the food gives them any needed elements for health or even if they know certain foods to be harmful to them. Those are the people who will fill up on sweets, chocolates, and starchy foods between meals and have no room for meat and vegetables and fruits at meal times. They will, at the same time, worry over their lack of pep or their complexion troubles. Some other people are able to enjoy food not only for its good taste but also for the energy and sense of well-being that results from a properly balanced diet. They will think about what foods are good for them, as well as what foods they especially like, when they choose what to eat.

Sleep

"Nights, I sleep fine; mornings I sleep pretty well, but afternoons, I tends to git kind of restless." The character who said that, apparently worked at getting his sleep. You will not need to go so far as he did, but getting enough sleep is just as necessary as having enough to eat, if you are to have energy and endurance.

If you find yourself often tense and irritable during the day

● Most young people get their exercise.

Good Health

● Active sports are good for your mental and physical health. (Luoma Photos.)

or too tired when night comes, count up the number of hours of sleep you have been getting at night. You may find it is not enough.

People vary in their sleep requirements. During the teens, most people need nine or ten hours a night. Many people continue for many years to require about nine hours of sleep out of the twenty-four. You can determine for yourself what your sleep needs are. Enough sleep is the amount that enables you to wake up in the morning feeling ready to get up, with energy and enthusiasm for the day.

We have all heard of how Thomas Edison was able to get along with about four hours of sleep out of the twenty-four and accomplish his work efficiently. But Edison was one in a million. The rest of us will work and play more successfully and enjoy life far more if we get more than twice that much sleep.

Exercise

It seems hardly necessary to talk about the need for exercise because if you are eating a balanced diet and getting enough sleep, you probably would hardly be able to resist getting into activities that give you exercise. You may be interested in going out for the team sports of your school, or perhaps you like individual sports such as tennis, swimming, handball, or golf. It may be that you don't care for any sports, but you do enjoy romping with your dog or walking with your friends. Almost everyone of us can enjoy some sort of physical activity, regardless of whether or not we happen to be of the athletic type.

● Worry can make one ill. Have you known times when you became ill physically because of some worry or emotional upset? *(Coronet Films.)*

Your feelings and your health

The preceding discussion may have seemed to imply that if you follow a good plan of eating, sleeping, and exercising, you will be full of vim, vigor, and vitality, as surely as two and two equals four. But you know that in spite of sensible living and good health habits, illness does strike. Moreover, a person who eats a proper diet and goes to bed at a reasonable hour may still have difficulty sleeping or may be tense or feel tired in a way that takes the joy out of life. What is the explanation? What can one do about it?

Your feelings about health and illness, your general attitudes toward life and toward the daily problems and challenges that arise have as much to do with health as do food, rest, and exercise. Worry can cause loss of appetite or indigestion, no matter how digestible one's food is. An excessive fear of illness can actually make one ill. The close relationship between our attitudes, feelings, fears, worries, and physical well-being is one of the facts-of-life that we must understand and cope with.

Some people have an unhealthy fear of illness. They attach too much importance to every little ache or pain and, as a result, spoil their enjoyment of life just as much as if they actually had many serious illnesses. They may also look upon small aches and pains as excuses for avoiding hard or unpleasant tasks.

A sound approach to good health, then, consists not only in good habits of diet, sleep, and exercise, but in understanding yourself well enough to know when a lack of energy or an ache or pain is due to insufficient sleep or the wrong food and when it has its source in worries, fears, or in your approach to problems in life. No matter what the source, there are things that can be done

HOW WOULD YOU SCORE YOUR GENERAL HEALTH?

	Never	Some-times	Usually	Always
	0	4	7	10
1. I feel full of pep during the day, even when working hard.				
2. I am hungry at mealtime.				
3. I make sure my eyesight and hearing are O.K.				
4. I am free from frequent colds.				
5. I have regular habits of elimination without the use of medicine.				
6. I get at least nine hours of sound sleep at night.				
7. I keep from getting moody and easily discouraged.				
8. I am free from headaches.				
9. I have dental checkups regularly.				
10. I have a physical checkup regularly.				
Total each column				
Total points				

Courtesy National Dairy Council.

233

about it. Poor living habits can be corrected. If real illness occurs, there is medical help. And in dealing with problems, you can follow a policy that will promote good health.

The next two chapters will discuss further the relation between good health and your mental attitudes.

REVIEW QUESTIONS

1. Why do advertisements stress good health?
2. How do we develop our eating habits when young?
3. What is one cause of much illness in some families?
4. What is the best source of needed vitamins?
5. What basic foods are required in a balanced diet?
6. What are good sources of proteins? Carbohydrates? Why are they important in your diet?
7. What is meant by the statement that good eating habits depend upon your attitudes toward food and eating?
8. How many hours of sleep do you need? How can you tell whether you are getting enough sleep?
9. How can feelings and attitudes affect health? Illustrate.
10. Some families seem to have unhealthy attitudes toward health. Explain.

KEY WORDS AND PHRASES

| Synonomous | vitality | proteins, fats |
| potential | vitamins | carbohydrates |

PROBLEMS AND ACTIVITIES

1. Study the diet chart on page 226. Keep a record of what you eat each day for one week. Compare your diet with the balanced diet shown in the chart.

2. Notice your eating habits and those of your friends for one week. List all the good and poor eating habits you observe.

3. Keep a record of your hours of sleep for one week. Are you getting enough sleep for a person of your age?

4. Have you known some family that seems to be overly concerned about health? How do they show their unhealthy attitudes?

5. Can you think of a time when you became ill largely because of worry or fear?

SOCIO-DRAMA

1. Two family scenes: (a) The Jones family, the parents, and their four children, at dinner. The conversation will show how the parent Joneses pass on wrong attitudes toward food to their children, also how a family may develop a bad habit of letting table conversation dwell on food likes and dislikes. (b) The Smith family at dinner are the reverse of the Joneses. In this scene, try to bring out correct attitudes and feelings toward food and a better type of table conversation.

2. Two family scenes similar to above, but let these scenes bring out attitudes and feelings about illness. Ten-year-old Sally comes to the breakfast table complaining that her stomach hurts, and she doesn't feel like going to school. The two families react to Sally's stomach-ache in different ways in the two family scenes.

FILMS

First Aid: Fundamentals — 10 minutes, sound, Coronet
Rest and Health — 10 minutes, sound, Coronet
Exercise and Health — 10 minutes, sound, Coronet
Improve Your Posture — 10 minutes, sound, Coronet
See reading list at end of this section, page 282.

MENTAL HEALTH - SOLVING PROBLEMS

23

Since our attitudes, our feelings, our fears, problems, and worries are so closely related to our health, it is necessary to have specific and good ways of meeting problem situations in life, just as we follow a definite policy in diet, sleep, and exercise.

How to meet problems

Every one of us has his problems. Perhaps there is a teacher who seems to "have it in" for you. Perhaps you have wanted a certain person for a friend, and it is not working out. Or you have not enough spending money for the things you want badly. Or you are not happy about the clothes you have for school. Or your parents are making life rugged because they demand too much from you or put too many restrictions on what you can do and where you can go. It may be a brother or sister who is a problem in your life, or perhaps you are not progressing in a sport in which you wanted very much to succeed. Almost no one is without a problem of some kind. Although these problems are difficult, each one becomes less difficult when you have learned a system for meeting them.

Steps in meeting problems

The first step is to *face the problem.* Try to *look squarely at what the problem is.*

No matter how bad it may be, it will help if you can face the problem rather than trying to run away from it or refusing to think about it and letting it hang over you.

Try to figure out how the situation arose that is bothering you.

Is the trouble being caused by something you yourself are doing or not doing? Is your problem something that you are not responsible for, but that perhaps you could change if you gave enough thought to it?

The problems that we try to hide from ourselves by refusing to think about them are the ones that may cause us the most trouble. Sometimes the situation that may be causing one to feel listless and dull — perhaps with headaches or digestive upsets — may really not be so bad, once it is brought into the open in one's thinking.

The next step is to *do something about the problem.* If the difficulty is caused by something you yourself are doing, the solution may be fairly easy. For example, is it possible that the teacher has it in for you because you have been acting disinterested in her class, or have been paying more attention to your girl friend or boy friend, in the same class, than to the classwork? If that is the trouble, you will not have to worry about trying to change the teacher; you can go to work on changing your own attitudes in the class. The chances are good that even the slowest teacher will catch on pretty soon to the fact that you are doing your best — if you are. It really takes less energy to be cooperative in a class than to be uncooperative and have conflicts with teachers. Teachers also have problems of their own that they are trying to meet, and they may not have found the best ways for meeting problems any more than you have.

If the trouble is a conflict with your parents, try to figure out just *why* they have attitudes that are making things hard for you. Try to imagine how the situation looks to them.

They are probably honestly trying their best to understand you and your world and to make the decisions that seem to them to be for your best interests. It will take less energy and be less frustrating for you if you will work at trying to be frank with your parents and help them to help you, rather than bracing yourself and perhaps building up a situation that becomes a tug of war between you and your parents.

You will find some problem situations that really are beyond your power to change. Perhaps some other person is, in fact, prejudiced or a troublemaker for you because of things in his or her own life that warp his attitudes. Even in such a case you can

● It is important to learn to face problems and to think of what to do about them. *(Luoma Photos.)*

change the effect the behavior has on you by trying to understand that such an attitude is a worse problem to the person who holds it than it ever can be to you. You can center your interests elsewhere and time will help take care of the situation.

Whatever your problem, it is possible to decrease your feeling of frustration about it if you can *act* to change either yourself or the situation rather than just letting a thing get you down.

If you have faced the facts as honestly and carefully as you can and have found that there seems to be nothing much that you can do about something that is troubling you, the next step is to *look for a constructive way to relieve your feelings.* There are both healthy and unhealthy escapes from problem situations.

Healthy escapes from problems

Activities that require use of physical energy are good. They help you to release the tension that has been built up in your emotions. It is hard to feel very frustrated or upset when you are having a good swim, or playing a hard game of tennis. *Working* at something you are interested in is a healthy way to relieve your feelings. That is why people with many hobbies are less troubled by problems.

Organizing some collection you have, or making something with tools, or sewing, or baking a cake — even cleaning a room and rearranging the furniture — all can serve in a healthy way to shift your attention from your problems. The farther you can get

238   *Mental Health — Solving Problems*

away from a problem, the better you can see it as a whole, and often that helps to cut it down to a size that you can handle. Sometimes if we come back to a problem after we have found temporary escape through exercise or work, we can size up the problem more accurately and see how to solve it.

Outside help

There are times when most of us have problems which are too big for us to handle. You may need to talk with someone who can listen and perhaps help you to understand yourself or the problem. Does your school have a counselor trained to listen to problems of young people and to help with difficulties? Although each person thinks his problems different from those of other people, counselors find as they listen to students' problems that many people have the same difficulties. Troubles tend to fall into a "pattern." The experience the counselor has had in helping other young people face problems makes him able to be of more help to you.

If your school does not have a special counselor, a teacher in whom you have confidence may be able to help you. Sometimes parents or other adult friends can be very helpful with problems.

The wise person can learn to recognize when he does need help from others. You will want to face and solve your problems your-

● Sometimes a counselor can help with difficult problems. *(Hayward High School.)*

self if you can. But there are difficult times when an understanding person can be of great help to you. At such times it is worthwhile to hunt for such a person.

Feelings that cause trouble

We all have, at times, feelings of anger or antagonism toward others. Sometimes there is a good reason why we feel as we do toward someone. And sometimes there is no real justification for our feelings; the cause may be in ourselves. Whatever the reason, everyone has such feelings occasionally. The test of your success and happiness is whether you let such feelings make trouble for you or whether you can work them off in constructive ways.

Sixteen-year-old Jack once said, "It used to be that when something went wrong at school and I was 'burned up' about something I would take it out on my family when I got home. I would make it tough for my younger brother, and I would be rough around the house, and maybe accidentally mar up some of the furniture, until my mother finally lost her temper and told me what she thought of my actions. Then I would lose my temper too and blame her.

"But after I figured myself out, I quit doing that. Now, when I feel burned up about something I work it off before I go home. I'm out for track, and I go out and practice the broad jump until I feel tired enough that I've almost forgotten what I was mad about. Or I walk home instead of riding the bus, and that two-mile walk usually does the trick. If it doesn't, I get some good loud music on the radio when I get home. The louder the better and sometimes that helps."

Like Jack, you can figure yourself out and find the ways that you can best work off your feelings of anger or antagonism. There are dozens of ways that will work if you find them. It is usually better to work feelings out through action than to express them directly against the person who seems to be the object of your anger. To take out feelings on a person only makes an enemy or increases bad feelings and so creates future sources of ill-feeling. It seldom settles anything. You'll never have to apologize for the thing you have not said, and if you are not handing out black eyes you are not so likely to be showing one yourself. Certainly

● Have you found some activity in which to work off your feelings when you have had a bad day? If not, do others suffer because of your feelings? *(Luoma Photos.)*

anger creates an inner tension that calls for release, but the point is that there are good ways to release that tension without doing something that may cause more trouble in the future instead of dissolving the anger.

Good days and bad days

Even if you have the habit of meeting your problems constructively — facing them and trying to do what you can about them — and if you have found satisfactory ways of working off troublesome feelings, you may still find that on some days things just seem to go wrong. You may tend to have ups and downs in the way life looks to you. That is a common experience for most people. What to do about it?

Is there any good reason for this being a "bad day"?

Are you hungry? It is wonderful what a good meal can do.

Have you had enough sleep? If not, get through the day as well as you can, and tonight get to bed early and catch up on sleep.

Are you behind with your work or your studies so that some assignment is worrying you and getting you down? Pitch in and accomplish all you can today; a "bad day" passes more quickly if you are working hard.

Don't take your bad days too seriously

So this is a bad day! You feel cross and irritable and like looking for trouble. What of it? Tomorrow will be another day, and you may wake up feeling exactly the opposite. One of the good things about having lived longer than a few years is that one learns that always another day is coming and that very soon things that looked dark have a way of fading out or even changing color entirely!

The ups and downs tend to level off as we learn to organize our lives so that every day will include some work, some play, some enjoyment of both the work and the play. We learn by experience that even the best of days is seldom perfect and that the worst of days passes. And we keep our attention on where we are going and the things we have to do, rather than on just how we happen to be feeling at the moment.

Jane's doting grandmother said to her one morning, "Are you sure you're feeling well today, dear?" Jane answered, "My feelings

● The ups and downs tend to level off as we learn to organize our lives.

IF THINGS GO WRONG WHAT DO YOU DO?

Below is a list of things college students have told us that they do when things go wrong and they need to get rid of their bad feelings. Read the list and check whether these ways of expressing feeling are desirable or undesirable. Which of these do you find yourself using? Have you found some desirable ways of working off feelings that are not on this list?

	Desirable	Undesirable	I do this
1. Become quiet and moody.			
2. Argue and quarrel.			
3. Show temper.			
4. Engage in sports and games.			
5. Take a walk.			
6. Throw things or destroy things.			
7. Work or study.			
8. Talk things over with a good listener.			
9. Get sarcastic.			
10. Cry.			
11. Ride or drive.			
12. Slam doors or drawers.			
13. Play music or sing or listen to music.			
14. Watch TV or go to movie or read.			
15. Shout or scream.			
16. Blame others.			
17. Do things for others.			
18. Take out anger on pets.			
19. Sulk and show rudeness to others.			
20. Smoke or drink.			
21. Overeat.			
22. Drive recklessly.			
23. Take out anger on family.			

243

will have to take care of themselves today. I'm going to be too busy to pay any special attention to them."

In this chapter, we have been talking about health just as much as we did in the preceding chapter. In that chapter, we talked of habits of eating, sleeping, and exercise that help to build good physical health. Here we have talked of habits of meeting problems, of coping with feelings, and of handling ups and downs in life. These habits determine your mental and emotional health and are very closely related to your physical well-being.

In fact, the person who has healthy habits, mentally and emotionally, can live with physical handicaps of all degrees of seriousness and still enjoy life greatly. But the person who does not cultivate good mental health in himself can seldom enjoy good physical health.

A very old lady who had, during her lifetime, experienced almost every kind of trouble that comes to people, once said, "One reason I enjoy life so much is that I've learned that *nothing* can get me down. Some day I'll die, I suppose. But as long as I'm living, I'm going to make the troubles that come along keep in their place and I'm going to get my share of enjoyment out of every day."

She had good mental health even though she lived in a wheel chair.

In the next chapter, we shall turn to some other habitual ways of meeting problems. We need to become aware of habits that make for poor mental health just as we learn to recognize evidences of good or of poor physical health.

REVIEW QUESTIONS

1. Why is it important to have constructive ways of meeting problems in life?
2. What is the first step in attacking a problem?
3. How could running away from a problem cause more trouble than facing the problem squarely?
4. After you have defined your problem, what are some of the possible things you can do to solve the problem?

5. If a difficulty is beyond your power to change what might be the best thing to do? Give some illustrations of how this might be done.
6. Under what circumstances should one seek outside help for a problem?
7. What is meant by the statement that your feelings of anger or antagonism toward others may be from within your self?
8. How did Jack take out his feelings on others before he understood his behavior? How did he change?
9. When we take our feelings out on others, do we always feel better afterwards?
10. What things can you learn to do in order to cope better with your feelings when you feel down?
11. Can a person who does not have good mental health have good physical health?

KEY WORDS AND PHRASES

constructive
mental health

frustration
counselor
warp

antagonism
justification

PROBLEMS AND ACTIVITIES

1. If there is any problem that has been bothering you recently, try to follow the steps suggested for solving a problem.
2. *Special report.* If your school has a counseling service, have one or two students interview the counselors, asking them about the kind and extent of counseling they do. Report your findings to the class.
3. How have you learned to cope with your ups and downs? Make a list of the things you do when you feel "low." You

might also talk with some friends to see what they do when they feel low.

4. Observe some other people, either young people or adults, and make a list of the undesirable ways they seem to have for handling their bad days or their feelings of anger.

FILMS

In Chapter 9 we recommended *Control Your Emotions*. If that film were used there, you may wish to repeat it here as review; or if you did not use it with that chapter, use it here.
Snap Out of It — 14 minutes, sound, Coronet
See reading list at end of Part Five, page 282.

MENTAL HEALTH—STRAIGHT THINKING

24

This chapter will consider some of the ways in which all of us meet things that confront us in life. You will see that a type of behavior that might help you in some situations might not be so good if overdone or if used at other times. Some people meet challenges in negative ways that create problems for themselves.

Rationalization

Mary was late for school today. She told the teacher that she was late because her mother did not wake her in time. Mary was telling the truth or at least part of the truth. It is true that her mother usually took the responsibility for getting her up in time for school. But Mary had an alarm clock that she might set if she wanted to take the responsibility herself for getting up on time. And since her mother was late calling her on this day she might have hurried and taken less time to do her hair before leaving for school. Mary "rationalized" to explain her lateness.

Rationalization is a long word psychologists use for a common habit many of us have. To rationalize is to think of reasonable excuses for things we do or for ways in which we fail. A rationalization is not a lie. It may be a good and logical excuse for a failure or mistake. At least we may honestly think the excuse to be good and logical, and many of our friends would agree with us.

Tom explains, "We would have won the basketball game if the referee had not favored the other team." Perhaps the referee did make some doubtful decisions. But part of the truth might also be that Tom and several of his teammates had broken training and were not quite equal to the stiff competition against this particular team.

247

"LOOK WHAT HAPPENED WHEN WE BUMPED INTO MR. STOVER'S APPLE TREE!"

● Straight thinking?

Sue explains her failure to have dates by saying, "I would have dates like the other girls do, but I will not run after the boys the way the others do."

Perhaps it is perfectly true that she does not do some things that other girls do to attract the boys. But is that the whole story?

By rationalizing, we ease ourselves through situations. However, people who habitually rationalize may create problems for themselves because they hide from themselves facts that they ought to face. Sue, who says she does not run after the boys, contents herself with that explanation and thinks no further. It may be that she is not friendly in her ways. She may be critical and unkind in her judgments of others. When she notices that girls as well as boys seem not to care for her, she will rationalize further by saying, "The other girls don't like me because my standards are higher than theirs are. They would be friendly enough if I would do all the things that they do." Perhaps on some points she does have high standards. But as long as she thinks only of the facts that are favorable to herself and refuses to think of the whole truth about her ways and habits, she will not change. Her difficulties with both boys and girls will increase.

That is the trouble with rationalizing. It becomes a kind of self-protection against facing hard facts and growing into better ways. It may be hard to admit to yourself sometimes, "The real trouble this time was in *me*." But if you can do that and then go on to think about, "What can I do to change so that I won't make the same mistake next time?" then you will decrease instead of increase your problems.

Retreat

John has not learned social skills, and he feels self-conscious about his actions in social situations. So he avoids parties and spends more and more time working at his model airplanes. Without realizing it, he is trying to retreat to the time when he was a younger boy of whom no social skills were expected.

Almost all of us are tempted at times to try to run away from challenges because we feel doubtful or uncertain. We feel like retreating, going back to a time when we did not have to face such choices or obligations.

Peter may be no more smooth socially than John is, but Peter resists the urge to escape. He works at learning the skills he lacks. He goes out among other young people his age whenever he is

● This woman has always retreated when a problem came up. Now she's going home to Mother.

asked. Soon he realizes that almost all the rest are in the same boat with him. No one feels highly self-confident, but each one is working at learning to get along better in social groups.

While Peter is facing and overcoming his handicaps, John is making no progress and is getting left farther and farther behind the others in development. The time will come when John may have a serious problem; by retreating, he is giving himself an unnecessary handicap.

As we go through life, we constantly have to face and adjust to new stages. We cannot go back to childhood to escape them. If we could and did retreat, we would miss most of what makes life worthwhile.

Each autumn, many college freshmen "flunk out" and go back to their homes partly because they have not learned to face and handle a new stage in life. They find it easier to retreat than to adjust to new experiences and responsibilities. In the same way, some married people give up and "go home to Mother" when problems arise in marriage. They are trying to retreat to a time when life did not require so much of them.

Rationalization, if we do not let ourselves overdo it, may sometimes be a temporary help through a hard time, but retreat is almost always harmful to mental health. It creates problems and solves none.

Can you think of times when you have been tempted to retreat? What did you do? Were you glad later that you met the occasion in a better way?

Compensation

Compensation is another word psychologists use to describe a device that everyone uses at times in life. By *compensation* we mean the tendency people have to make up for a failure in one thing by shifting to a fairly satisfactory substitute. Compensation can be a useful and constructive way of meeting a defeat or a disappointment. However, it can be harmful if one makes use of the wrong kind of compensation.

Let us see just how it works. As a freshman, Harry went out for basketball. He was very much disappointed when the coach eliminated him in making the first cut in the squad. Harry felt that he

● Joe has not found good ways to compensate for his disappointments.

probably would never be very good in basketball. So he worked, instead, at his studies, and he also became active in other school organizations. He made an excellent record and at graduation he was awarded the college scholarship that he wanted. He said to a friend who congratulated him on his success, "I really always wanted to be a basketball player. I never quite got over envying the fellows who were stars in athletics. But I think, now, that perhaps I've gotten more out of my four years of high school than some boys have who didn't have enough time for studies or for activities outside of athletics. At least this college scholarship is certainly going to come in handy."

Harry had compensated in a constructive way for his disappointment. Some people in his place might not do so. Another boy might have decided to quit school if he couldn't play basketball. He might have decided it would be more fun, anyway, to work and earn money to buy a car than to stay in school. Still another might stay in school but get attention by making trouble in classes and being a bitter sidelines critic of all the boys who did make a success in sports. Such ways of trying to compensate only create problems for the person who uses them.

If we allow ourselves to compensate in negative ways, we build poor mental health by piling up disappointments and feelings of bitterness.

Mental Health — Straight Thinking　　　251

You can probably think of ways in which you have compensated; some of your compensations have been good and some perhaps not so good.

Eight-year-old Tommy, a poor reader, said, "I wish I could read better. But I'm glad I can run so fast!" Sally, who could never make school grades as good as her twin sister made, became a very fine cook and also learned to sew. Even as a freshman in high school, she made most of her own clothes. It is true that she was so content with having lovely clothes at little expense, and at being often complimented by her family on her cooking, that she gave less and less time to her studies. Her school work became more of a problem to her than it need have been. You will see that her compensation was good, but she would have had fewer problems had she not carried her compensation quite so far.

Projection

If you have small brothers or sisters who are still under school age, you know that when they make a mistake, their immediate reaction may be to try to avoid being blamed. Johnny will quickly say, "*I didn't knock over the lamp. Sally pushed me against it.*"

"WHAT HAPPENED, MOM? I HEARD A CRASH."

● Projection?

Mental Health — Straight Thinking

Some little children even go so far as to create imaginary persons who are always at hand to take the blame for anything that happens. Three-year-old Billy had an imaginary friend, "Diggy," who was always spilling food or breaking toys or getting things dirty. No matter what Billy did he was always ready with "Diggy did that. Diggy is really a good boy, but he's awfully careless," and so on. That way of trying to project blame is to be expected of little children. It is a stage that they go through and you probably find it amusing in your small brothers or sisters.

When people who are no longer small children work at pushing away from themselves, to someone or something else, the blame for things that happen or for things that they do, their behavior is called "projection." Projection is somewhat like rationalization, because it is a failure to face all the facts honestly.

A part of growing up is getting to the place where we can accept the responsibility for what we do. At fourteen, fifteen, or sixteen can you say, "Yes, I broke the lamp. I guess it isn't such a good idea to try a flying tackle in the living room!" instead of, "Why do you always keep that old lamp out there where it's so easy to trip over? I couldn't help it that it got knocked over."

People who have the habit of making alibis and blaming some one else for all mistakes or failures, will do it in situations involving far more than a broken lamp.

To blame "unfair teachers" or "too hard tests" for school failures instead of taking a careful look at one's own study habits not only delays getting at the real cause of difficulties; it also builds toward poor mental health.

As you work at overcoming undesirable ways of meeting situations, you will find that fewer problems arise. It may seem hard at first to think honestly about your own faults and failures. You might think it would be easier to rationalize, or to blame someone else for failures, than to have to take the blame in your own feelings for some of the things that happen. But that is not the way it works. Actually it is harder to fool one's self than to fool all the rest of the world. It is much more comfortable to know that you are thinking honestly and doing what you can to make progress in your ways. That contributes to healthy mental and emotional growth just as three good meals a day and plenty of sleep contribute to good physical health.

REVIEW QUESTIONS

1. Define rationalization. Give some examples of rationalization.
2. What is the difference between rationalization and lying?
3. When is rationalization good and when may it get one into trouble?
4. What is meant by retreat? Give some illustrations.
5. Is retreat ever a good solution to a problem?
6. Why are we often tempted to retreat?
7. Define compensation and give some cases to illustrate the term.
8. When is compensation good and when is it undesirable?
9. What is projection?
10. Is the tendency to project our failures on others a normal part of growing up? Explain.
11. When does projection become undesirable?

KEY WORDS AND PHRASES

negative
rationalization
psychologist

self-protection
retreat
self-conscious
projection

social situations
social skills
compensation

PROBLEMS AND ACTIVITIES

1. During the time you are studying this chapter, keep a record of the times you notice your friends or family facing problems by resorting to rationalization, compensation, retreat, projection.

2. When you come to a class, be able to give some cases of com-

Mental Health — Straight Thinking

pensation you have observed and tell whether you think compensation was being used in a way to contribute to good or to bad mental health.

3. Retreat is usually not a good solution to a problem. Can you think of a time when retreat might be a good solution?

4. After John crashed into the rear of Mr. Anthony's car at a stop light, he explained that it was not his fault, since Mr. Anthony stopped too quickly. How would you classify John's thinking?

5. Mary explains her failure to have friends by saying her mother will not let her have any attractive clothes to wear. Classify her thinking.

6. When Henry found he could not make the debating team, he decided to try out for the junior play. What was his adjustment?

See reading list at end of Part Five, page 282.

POOR MENTAL HEALTH —
ACCIDENTS, ILLNESS,
ALCOHOL, DRUGS

25

Some people have always turned away from facing unpleasant facts. Perhaps they have tried to fool themselves with excuses and have blamed other people or circumstances for all unpleasant things that have happened to them. As time passes, such people are not able really to fool themselves. They accumulate within themselves a load of unpleasant feelings from which they seek to escape.

Even after people are grown up in years, many of them could still change and begin to meet their problems in more constructive ways. They might find healthy ways to overcome their unhappy feelings. But some people of all ages try to escape by turning to illness, to drugs, or to excessive use of alcohol. Some others who know that drugs or alcohol would only increase their troubles seek an outlet through various types of recklessness. They become "accident prone" people. In this chapter, we shall look at some of the undesirable "escapes" that are attempted. It is important for you to understand how they work in people's lives and how they affect the lives of other innocent bystanders.

Emotional factors in accidents

Research studies on car accidents show that a few people have most of the accidents. Most people have no accidents. In other words a few people are *accident prone*. Accident prone people are more likely to have accidents than other people would be under the same circumstances. Statistical records of accidents show that the person who has had two accidents is more apt to have a third than the person who has never had an accident is apt to have even one accident. There are several reasons for this.

256

(1) Some people use the car as a means of getting rid of their feelings of hostility toward others. In a way, their car is a weapon they use to fight with other drivers. They sound their horns and cut in close when passing to force other cars over. They seem to find many other drivers who must be taught a lesson. People who use their cars to battle on the highway are bound to have accidents.

(2) Another group of people get a thrill out of defying the rules of society when driving. They enjoy going through stop signs and red lights, passing on curves, and exceeding the speed limit. To them driving a car is like riding on a roller coaster, a means of seeking thrills. They have not faced why they need such thrills.

(3) Another group have accidents because they use the car as a way to get rid of tension. When they have had a "bad day" they seek to get rid of their feelings of tension by driving at excessive speeds or by taking chances on the highway.

(4) A fourth and very large group who have accidents are those who have been drinking and do not realize that they are not in condition to drive.

● Some people are accident prone.

Poor Mental Health — Accidents, Illness, Alcohol, Drugs 257

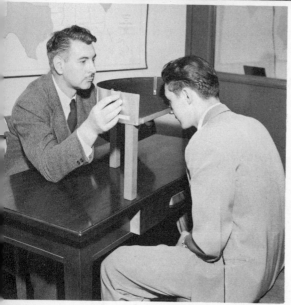

● (Above) Depth perception, measured on a special device, is important in driving a car and flying a plane. (Left) Testing field of vision on a "perimeter." Some people have accidents because they cannot see cars approaching from the side. (Below) "Glareometer test indicates ability to recover from glare. (Man and the Motor Car, *Prentice-Hall, Inc.*)

Bus Driver Retired With Perfect Record

LOS ANGELES (IP)—Here's a bus driver who's driven 1,746,441 miles in 32 years and never received a traffic ticket nor even bumped a passenger.

Dan Forbes has been on the Los Angeles-Seattle run for 21 years and eight months.

Last Excuse For Speeders

ST. LOUIS, Aug. 7 (IP)—Two motorists failed to show in City Court yesterday on charges of speeding.

City Judge Robert O. Dowd wanted to know why.

The police report:

Carl Abney, 18, charged with speeding July 1, killed July 26 in a two-car collision blamed on speeding.

Soth Reynolds, 28, charged with speeding June 19, killed July 2 in a two-car collision blamed on sideswiping.

● Two news items.

(5) Another group of accident prone people are those who are self-centered and unable to think of other people. Safe drivers are constantly putting themselves in the place of the other drivers and trying to predict what the other person will do. A careful driver knows that much of safety depends on anticipating the moves someone else may make. The safe driver knows that the driver ahead may make a left turn after signaling for a right, and he is prepared to meet the emergency. The unsafe driver speeds ahead without considering what other drivers are going to do.

(6) The accident prone person does not have a periodic checkup on his car to see that his stop light, brakes, headlights, and horn are working. He investigates after an accident instead of before.

When you learn to drive, check yourself on how you use the car. If you find that you are using it as an outlet for some of your emotions, try to find a safer outlet. You need not be a hazard on the highway.

If you have already had an accident, or if you have been involved in someone else's accident, try to figure out the whole situation. What factors were involved? Was one of the drivers "showing off"? Was someone angry or overtired? Was the car being used as a weapon on the highway? Were there physical factors such as poor eyesight involved? Did one of the drivers exhibit poor judgment?

Poor Mental Health — Accidents, Illness, Alcohol, Drugs 259

CHECK YOUR ATTITUDES *

"Pro" drivers and safety experts agree that most traffic accidents are caused by faulty driving *attitudes*. Here is a simple self-scoring quiz to reveal how "healthy" *your* driving attitudes are. Put a check in the appropriate square at the right of each question, to indicate whether you frequently, occasionally, or rarely *act* or *feel* as the question suggests.

Remember that you're not kidding anyone but yourself, so —

GIVE YOUR HONEST OPINION!

(If you live in a state that does not license drivers under the age of sixteen or older, you may not yet be driving and therefore cannot score yourself. However, there is value in studying this text on emotional factors in driving as a part of your "driver education" in preparation for driving when you can get a license. Attitudes and feelings which make good or poor drivers are developing before people begin to drive.)

	Fre-quently	Occa-sionally	Rarely
1. Do you wonder how other drivers ever manage to get operators' licenses?			
2. Do you feel that you, yourself, are the best judge of the speed at which you should be permitted to drive?			
3. Do you disregard a "No Parking" sign or fire hydrant area if you're only going to be parked for a minute?			
4. Do you disregard traffic lights at night when the streets are practically deserted?			
5. Do you bluff your way through an intersection, figuring that the other driver will stop?			

260

6. Do you let another car that's trying to pass get alongside you and then race it?

7. Do you feel that people are admiring you as you drive down the street?

8. Do you try hard to be the first one away when a red light turns green?

9. Do you want your friends to admire the way you don't have to pay attention to the road when you're driving?

10. Do you brag about the times you broke the law and didn't get caught?

11. Do you take chances in traffic "just for the fun of it"?

12. When you are at the wheel, do you insist on your "rights" as a citizen?

13. When traffic situations go wrong, do you get "sore"?

14. Do you figure there's no sense in giving the other driver an "even break" if he doesn't insist on it?

15. Do you hug the middle of the highway when another driver tries to pass you?

16. Do you resent someone being a better driver than you are?

17. In your "book," is it the other driver who is always wrong?

---

18. Do you "lean on the horn" to keep pedestrians out of your way?

---

19. In night driving, do you wait for the approaching driver to dim his headlights first?

---

20. If the driver coming toward you at night doesn't dim his headlights, do you throw yours back on the high beam?

---

21. Do you blow your horn if the driver ahead doesn't start moving the instant the light changes?

---

22. Do you speed just for the sense of power you get when your foot presses down on the gas pedal?

---

23. Do you feel that having the legal right-of-way lets you out of having to share the road?

---

24. Do you feel that traffic tickets should be "fixed" if you know the "right" people?

---

* Milton D. Kramer, *Deft Driving*, pp. 4–7. Dearborn: Ford Motor Company, 1952.

Give yourself 4 points for each check under *Frequently*, 2 points for each check under *Occasionally*, and 1 point for each check under *Rarely*, and add up your total score. The *lower* your score, the *better* your driving attitudes. If you scored 60 or more, you'd better do something about *improving* your attitudes. Sooner or later they can get you into trouble.

Unhealthy driving attitudes — irresponsibility, rudeness, inattentiveness, egotism, poor sportsmanship, uncooperativeness — result in the kind of behind-the-wheel actions that lead to highway accidents.

At the wheel, good attitudes are vital!

Sickness as an escape

Some people habitually use physical symptoms of emotional tension (like stomachaches, headaches, or tiredness) as a means of escape. They take refuge in illness and so postpone temporarily the facing of a problem or task.

When Paul was in the first grade, he found that he could get excused from school and be allowed to go home if he complained of an earache. When he appeared at home with an earache, his mother would worry over him, put warm drops into his ear, and put him to bed. He would rest for a while and then recover from the earache and go out to play. As he grew older, when he faced new tasks or difficult situations and felt butterflies in his stomach or a weakness in his knees, his mother sympathized with him and encouraged him to go to bed and take care of himself rather than to go on to meet what was ahead.

By the time Paul was in high school, he had frequent and convenient illnesses. He had never learned to judge his feelings and to know the difference between emotional symptoms and real physical illness. He always took his "symptoms" seriously and let them control him.

● "I woke up with chills and fever and headache and sore throat and earache and upset stomach—but it didn't work." (*Stan Fine and* Collier's.)

One summer he got a job working in a filling station. In some ways he liked the work, but it kept him from having time to swim and do some of the other things he liked to do. He didn't like the man in charge. The man was gruff in his ways and strict in the requirements he set for behavior on the job. After a few weeks, Paul developed a cough and began to complain that the gasoline fumes and dust from the road were getting him down, so he quit his job.

When he went to college, his roommate sometimes teased him in a good natured way. Paul also found some of his studies difficult. Whenever a hard assignment was coming up he would have a headache and have to miss class. Gradually, he got farther and farther behind in his studies. At examination time, he caught a cold and went to bed for most of a week. When he thought of how far behind he was with all of his work, and when he thought of the easy irresponsibility of life at home, he began to feel really sick.

In the end, he quit school and went home. His parents explained to friends that Paul was not well and had to drop out of college for a complete rest. Paul, himself, was so accustomed to escape through illness that he really believed illness had forced him to quit school. By his unhealthy attitudes he made real problems of circumstances that would not have been serious if he had faced them squarely and tried to do what he could about them.

All of us have to learn to find a good balance in our attitudes about health. We need to be able to decide when we really are ill and need a doctor and when to get busy and forget out symptoms or work them off in constructive action. Just as there are "accident prone" people, so there are "illness prone" people. If you are to get the most out of life, you will want to do what you can to avoid being in either of those groups.

Use of alcohol

Alcohol is often thought to be a stimulant, and that is one of the reasons why some young people begin its use. But scientists who have studied its effects know that it is an anesthetic, not a stimulant. It dulls one's awareness of what is going on. It is the kind of anesthetic that affects first the higher centers of the brain

● Alcohol affects the reaction time by slowing down the nervous system. This boy is taking a scientific test to see how alcohol affects his heart and his nervous system *(Coronet Films.)*

— the thinking processes and the ability to judge — so that a person who can still walk straight will not be able to use good judgment about his actions and choices.

Since the anesthetic effect on the judgment is a characteristic of alcohol not understood by many people, it is the thing that gets people into trouble. They think if they can "walk a straight line" they are all right, but they may do awfully foolish things without being able to judge their actions. Alcohol would be far less dangerous if it worked in an opposite way. If it affected muscles first and judgment last, one would become physically helpless to act before he became unable to think and use good sense. So he would not do dangerous and foolish things.

During the teen years, young people may start drinking because many others drink. That is probably the most frequent reason for first drinking. But those who have not found good ways of meeting situations may believe that they feel more comfortable if they take a drink before going to a dance or a party. Bill says that it is easier for him to talk to girls if he has had a drink, and that he can dance much better. He doesn't know that he dances no better and may even make a fool of himself by his talk after a few drinks — the effect of the alcohol is simply to make him less conscious of how he talks or dances. He feels less embarrassed and less self-conscious. But has he overcome any handicaps?

The important thing for Bill to do is not to drink to feel better about his awkwardness, but to work at learning better social skills so that he will not need to hide his blunders from himself by

Poor Mental Health — Accidents, Illness, Alcohol, Drugs 265

drinking. You know that a part of growing up is to feel self-conscious at times, to be embarrassed, and to wonder just what to say or do. Growing up is retarded if one uses unwise "helps" like alcohol. Moreover, early drinking may mean one is starting unhealthy habits of facing problems, habits which may result in alcoholism in middle age.

People who drink so much that they become problems to society and to themselves and their families are called "alcoholics." Young people are seldom alcoholics, for it takes a number of years to develop that form of emotional illness. A person with good mental health habits will probably never become an alcoholic. But it is important for you, while in your teens, to understand the relationship between use of alcohol at an early age, excessive use at any age, and mental ill health.

Today alcoholism is better understood than formerly. It is now known that "alcoholics" are people with poor mental health. They use alcohol as an attempt to escape from or to solve emotional problems. An earlier discussion, you will remember, pointed out that occasionally most people would like to escape problems by going back to a time when they were younger and did not have the problems. The alcoholic person uses alcohol in his attempt to retreat from life. He cannot face his bad days or his problems or the making of serious decisions; and he has found that under the influence of alcohol, he can forget about his problems for a while.

Alcoholics Anonymous is a national organization of people who understand the problem of alcoholics because they all have had serious trouble as alcoholics themselves. They believe that an alcoholic cannot be cured of the thing which causes him to wish to drink excessively, but that he can learn to find other ways of meeting his problems if he earnestly wants to.

Although young people are not alcoholics, the personality which may seek satisfaction in alcohol instead of in more constructive ways is developing in the teen years. Those who develop good mental health while young will never become alcoholics.

Using drugs as escapes

The great majority of you will never be inclined to use drugs, for the dangers in drug use have received much publicity in recent years. It is now known that people who become drug addicts do so for the same reason that others become excessive drinkers. They are sick personalities and feel a great need to escape from life's problems.

In treating the drug addict, just as in trying to cure the alcoholic, hospitals now try to understand the poor mental health that has resulted in the drug addiction. It is now known that putting the drug addict in jail will not cure him any more than jail will cure any other mentally ill person. What both need is help in developing good ways of meeting life situations.

In some communities, marijuana is sold to high-school-age young people. Marijuana is extremely dangerous to use because of its effects upon the nervous system. It has the effect of slowing down all senses so that one can be driving ninety miles an hour and feel that he is going only twenty. The user of marijuana loses all sense of right and wrong and may do many things he would never even consider doing if he were not under the influence of the drug. Marijuana is not habit forming in the way that the drugs called narcotics are, although its effects are just as dangerous.

Narcotics are habit forming in a double way. Like alcohol, they serve as a temporary escape from problems, but, also, the body develops a craving for the narcotics. The user will turn more and more to the narcotics as his troubles in life increase. At the same

● These people are learning to get along in a group and they do not feel the need for "props." (Luoma Photos.)

HOW DO YOU RATE ON YOUR
MENTAL HEALTH

	Never	Some-times	Usually	Always
	0	4	7	10

1. I know when I am rationalizing a failure.

2. When I fail in one thing, I use a desirable way to compensate for the failure.

3. I accept the blame for my failures.

4. I avoid using sickness as an escape.

5. I have developed the ability to think straight about myself.

6. I recognize bodily symptoms which result from fear or anger.

7. I have learned desirable ways to help myself overcome tension.

8. I use constructive means to overcome my feelings of self-consciousness.

9. I know when I am retreating from a difficult situation.

10. I know when I am compensating for some failure.

Total each column

Total points

time, his physical desire for the drug will become more powerful even than his craving for food.

Although marijuana is not habit forming in the same way that narcotics are, once a person has begun to seek "kicks" or release from tension through the use of any such thing as marijuana, he is already developing the kind of mental and emotional attitudes that will make him more likely to turn also to the use of narcotics.

This chapter has discussed several of the most seriously undesirable ways in which people sometimes try to avoid facing difficult things in life. All of the ways discussed here are alike in that they always build up far worse troubles than the ones that needed to be faced in the beginning.

Everyone in the world has problems either large or small. Problems can be stepping stones in growth toward better and happier ways of living. The test of the kind of person you are will come in the ways you choose for meeting your problems.

REVIEW QUESTIONS

1. What are some of the common ways of trying to escape problems that lead to poor mental health?
2. What do you understand by the term "accident prone"?
3. Give several ways in which emotions can be important factors in causing accidents.
4. How can physical sickness be an indication of poor mental health?
5. Give Paul's history to show how sickness, if used to escape problems, may create far more serious problems.
6. Why do people become alcoholics?
7. What is "Alcoholics Anonymous" and what do they believe about the alcoholic?
8. Why do some people think they have a better time if they have had a drink?
9. If one feels self-conscious and embarrassed at parties what is the best way to get over this feeling?

Poor Mental Health — Accidents, Illness, Alcohol, Drugs 269

10. What is meant by saying that the drug addict is one with a "sick" personality?

11. Why do people who are developing poor mental health find satisfaction in marijuana? In narcotics?

12. Why are problems of alcoholism and drug addiction problems in mental health?

13. People who have developed good mental health and who are happy and well adjusted do not enjoy the effects of drugs. Why?

KEY WORDS AND PHRASES

accident prone
emotional factors
refuge

irresponsibility
alcoholic
Alcoholics Anonymous
narcotics

drug addicts
sick personalities
marijuana

PROBLEMS AND ACTIVITIES

1. Review your experience either when you were behind the wheel or when others have been driving and an accident or near-accident occurred. Can you think of an illustration to fit each of the six emotional factors in accidents mentioned in the chapter?

2. Which one of the six emotional factors do you think is the most common cause of accidents among your age group?

3. Some cities have set up special schools for those who have had an auto accident. Do you think this would be a good thing for all cities to do?

4. Score yourself on the driver test "Check Your Attitudes," on page 260.

5. Did you ever use sickness as an escape when you were a child? How did it work out? Did you realize it was not a good

idea? Be ready to tell the class about it if you did. Or be ready to tell the class about an interesting case in which the person habitually uses sickness as an escape.

6. *Special report.* One or two students read up on the history, purpose, and beliefs of Alcoholics Anonymous, and report to the class.

7. What is it about the effect of alcohol that causes many people to think that alcohol is a stimulant rather than a sedative?

8. How does marijuana differ from narcotics?

FILMS

Alcohol and Tobacco: What They Do to Our Bodies — 10 minutes, sound, Coronet. (If this film was used with chapter 20, you may not wish to use it again here.)
Attitudes and Health — 10 minutes, sound, Coronet
Safe Driving Series:
Safe Driving: Fundamental Skills — 10 minutes, sound, Coronet
Streets and Highways — 10 minutes, sound, Coronet
Advanced Skills and Problems — 10 minutes, sound, Coronet

LEISURE TIME ACTIVITIES AND MENTAL HEALTH

26

During the early history of our country, play was considered wrong or, at best, useless. Any activity that did not produce income or help make a living was looked upon as almost sinful. Many of the "recreational" activities of early Americans were organized to get work done. Husking bees, log rolling contests, and barn raisings were types of social recreation, but they got the corn husked and the new barn built.

Today, attitudes have changed about leisure time use and play activities. We know now that recreation of the right kind is good for mental and physical health.

It is true that what is recreation for you might be considered hard work by someone else. If you like to use woodworking tools you may work hard at that hobby. If you enjoy sewing or cooking, you may have fun doing what others earn their living by.

So a hobby may be work that one enjoys doing in leisure time, or it may be play. In either case, as life is organized in our country today, everyone needs some special leisure-time interests or hobbies. Right now you may feel that if you just had more time, you would sleep until noon each day, and that would be all the hobby you would need. After schools closes in the spring, you may enjoy doing nothing for a while. But after a week or so you are bored, and then you have to find a job or some special activity to keep you busy.

Hobbies have many important values for you other than just filling up your time. Most of these values apply now while you are busy going to school as well as later when you will be out of school and working. Older people have found that the hobbies and interests they developed in their teens continue to be important in their lives for many years.

Hobbies as a means of building friendships

You may not think of your leisure-time activities as hobbies. You play tennis or swim, or build birdhouses or boats, or collect stamps, or make model airplanes, or tinker with motors or chemicals because you enjoy doing those things and because others you know are doing similar things.

The activity itself is what interests you at first. But very soon you find an added pleasure because your interest in any activity immediately makes you a member of a group interested in the same thing. Friendships are usually built between people who enjoy doing and talking about the same things. If you have a number of different hobbies, you will seldom be ill at ease in any social group because you will always find others who share some of your interests.

If you feel ill at ease in social situations now, you may find that developing some new interest will make it easier for you to get along with others. Skill in any line, whether it is checkers or chess or sailing a boat, will help you in associating with other people.

● In Colonial times, recreation was planned to get work done.

● Hobbies help to build friendships. *(Luoma Photos.)*

Hobbies and dating

All the boys like to date Nancy. They have not figured out exactly why. They say she has a good personality and is always fun to be with. The truth is that Nancy has many interests of her own; she is in the camera club, the dancing club, and she works on the school paper. She is also interested in athletics and in school politics. The boys never feel uneasy around her because her interest in their hobbies and activities as well as in her own draws them out. They always find plenty of things to talk about with Nancy.

In your dating as well as in your other friendships, you enjoy most being with those who share your interests.

Hobbies, interests, and marriage

Of course, marriage is a long way in the future for almost all of you. First, you want to finish your education and get ready for a vocation and for parenthood. However, it is not too soon to start thinking about certain things which will help you make a successful marriage when that time comes.

The changes in work and play activities in the last hundred years have made some differences in what marriage is like today. It used to be that when two people married, they had to work most of the time, making a living and taking care of the home

● Sharing leisure makes marriage and family life happier. *(Luoma Photos.)*

and children. After people marry today, not nearly so much of their time as formerly is taken with making the living and caring for the home and children. Whether or not husband, wife, and children enjoy the same leisure-time activities is now very important to their happiness. The happiest families are those who have more than love as a common interest.

The Hubbards are such a family. John Hubbard and Mary Jones first began dating at a lake where both families spent summer vacations. John and Mary spent their time together fishing and swimming and hiking during summer vacations. Both had enjoyed these activities before they ever met. Now that Mary and John are married, they still have these things in common. John works in a department store, and Mary is busy with the home and children. But the Hubbards all work together and enjoy planning and saving their money for the vacation times which they can enjoy at the lake.

In contrast to the Hubbards is a family like the Greys. Susan Smith and Henry Grey knew that they had entirely different interests before they were married. Henry was like John Hubbard in that he loved out-door life. Boating, hunting and fishing were his great pleasures. Susan Smith had no interest in outdoor life. She was afraid of mosquitoes, poison ivy, and deep water. She hated the smell of fish. Her hobbies were music, dancing, bridge, and reading. When Susan and Henry were dating they usually went

Leisure Time Activities and Mental Health   275

dancing. Henry did not care for dancing; but he wanted to be with Susan, so he was willing to take her dancing if that was what she wanted.

Susan thought she could get Henry to change his interests when they were married; and Henry thought that once they were married, Susan would get over her silly ideas of not liking outdoor life. They were in love with each other, and each thought the other would change after marriage.

The Greys have been married ten years, and they do not have a very happy marriage. For several years, Henry tried to change Susan, and Susan tried to change Henry. They finally gave up, and now each goes his own way as far as leisure-time activities are concerned. Henry goes fishing and hunting with his friends, and Susan spends her time alone or with some other wives who have the same problem. As a family, the Greys do not do things together. The children would like to go on camping trips with their father, but the mother is afraid they would be exposed to poison ivy or get drowned in the lake.

Today it is very important that young people find out before marriage whether they have enough interests that they can enjoy together. People do not change very much after marriage.

Hobbies and your vocation

It is not always easy to decide upon what work to do to make a living. Your leisure time activities now may help you to choose your vocation later. Some hobbies are ways of playing with real work. The boy who is interested in taking pictures and in developing the negatives may like it so well that he will specialize later in photography. The boy who is interested in taking his hot rod to pieces and putting it together again may decide to go into some line of garage work, engineering, or manufacturing.

It works the opposite way, too. The boy with the hobby of photography may discover that he does not care enough about it to make it his life work. And the boy who always thought he wanted to be an engineer may find that his interests along that line do not mean so much to him as some of his other activities. Thus, in a negative as well as positive way, your hobbies may give you guidance in choosing your life work.

● Success in any activity may give you confidence in your ability to do other kinds of work.

Hobbies and mental health

One of the greatest values of an absorbing hobby is that it is a change and a relaxation from the regular work that one does. Making a living today often requires people to work for others rather than for themselves, and many workers do not necessarily enjoy the work they are doing. Their recreation helps them keep life balanced and happy.

When people become mentally ill and are sent to hospitals for treatment, a common treatment is to encourage the people to play or to work at hobbies that they can enjoy. Mental hospitals teach ill people to dance, to crochet, to play cards, to do needlework, to do shop work, or to take part in any other kinds of physical activities that they like. An important part of the cure is to help the people get their minds off problems which are disturbing them. The same principle applies to people who are not mentally ill. In fact, mental illness is not so likely to afflict people who, from their early teens have found a variety of absorbing interests.

Hobbies as an escape

The preceding chapter discussed unhealthy ways in which people try to escape their problems. They may resort to illness, or to alcohol, or to drugs. Hobbies or recreational interests are also a form of escape, but a healthy and desirable means of escape. All of us need temporary escape from problems or responsibilities.

Leisure Time Activities and Mental Health   277

Sometimes a problem may seem so big it cannot be solved. You may simply turn away from it for a time and do something that takes all your interest and energy. Then, to your surprise, you may find when you go back to face your problem that it was not so big as it seemed. Your temporary escape into your outside interest has helped you to get a perspective so that you can solve your problem. Of course, some people overdo this type of escape. You may know of a person who neglects his job or his school work and fails to take his share of responsibility at home while he gives most of his time and energy to a hobby. He is retreating from life, through his hobby.

With leisure-time activities as with everything else in life, it is necessary to use judgment and to find a good, workable balance.

Hobbies as a way of getting recognition

Most people have a drive to get recognition in some way. It is good for your mental health to feel that you are successful in some line. A hobby often becomes an important way of winning recognition. A man may get much more recognition through his stamp collection, or his sailing, than he gets through his work at the office or in the factory.

Success in your hobby may also give you confidence in your ability to do other kinds of work.

CLASSIFICATION OF YOUNG PEOPLE'S HOBBIES BY TYPES OF ACTIVITIES

CREATIVE	COLLECTING	EDUCATIONAL	COMPETITIVE SPORTS AND GAMES	NON-COMPETITIVE SPORTS AND GAMES	SPECTATOR	SOCIAL GROUP WORK
Boat building	Autographs	Animal study	Archery	Acrobatics	Ballets	Camp leadership
Cartooning	Buttons	Bird study	Badminton	Acting	Concerts	Nursery and playground help
Cooking	China	Chemical experimentation	Baseball	Bicycling	Movies	Membership in:
Dressmaking	Coins	Clock and watch repair	Basketball	Boating	Operas	Choir
Electrical work	Guns	Music study	Boat racing	Camping	Plays	Clubs
Gardening	Insects	Reading	Bowling	Dancing	Radio	Dramatics
Greeting-card making	Ornaments	Study of stars	Boxing	Fishing	Sporting events	4-H Clubs
Knitting	Post cards		Bridge	Hiking	Television	Future Farmers of America
Leather work	Records		Checkers	Horseback riding		Future Teachers of America
Metal work	Stamps		Chess	Hunting		Girl and Boy Scouts
Model plane making	Wild flowers		Fencing	Ice skating		Girl Reserves
Photography			Football	Magic		Glee Club
Reporting			Golf	Roller skating		Hi-Y
Sketching			Hockey	Singing		Orchestra
Weaving			Shuffleboard	Swimming		Student Council
Woodworking			Soccer			Y-Teens
			Table tennis			
			Tennis			
			Track			
			Wrestling			

Choosing your interests

Most of you already have some special interests and hobbies. Make a list of all the other types of things you think you might like to do. The table on the preceding page lists many activities classified according to whether they are (1) creative activities, (2) collecting activities, (3) educational activities, (4) competitive sports and games, (5) noncompetitive sports and games, (6) spectator activities, or (7) social group work activities. Check all of the ones which you think might interest you. Do you find that they fall largely into one class? If so, would you be interested in developing more of the interests in this field?

Do all your interests lie in a field which keeps you from being with other people? If this is true, try to figure out why you take up interests which cause you to want to be alone. Perhaps you need to make a special effort to become interested in activities which include others.

REVIEW QUESTIONS

1. Why do we look upon the use of leisure time today differently from the way it was viewed in Great-grandfather's youth?

2. How did the leisure-time activities during the early history of our country differ from your leisure-time activities?

3. How can a leisure activity for one person be work for another?

4. Explain how hobbies help in building friendships.

5. How can hobbies contribute to popularity in dating?

6. How do common interests between husbands and wives contribute to happiness in marriage?

7. Contrast the marriages of the Hubbards and the Greys.

8. Is it easy for people to change leisure interests when they get older? Discuss.

9. Can hobbies help you determine what you want to choose as your vocation when you get older? Explain.

10. How do hobbies contribute to mental health?

11. How can hobbies be desirable if they are used as escapes from problems? Contrast the use of alcohol and drugs with hobbies as ways of escape.

12. Name and explain each of the seven different classifications of activities.

KEY WORDS AND PHRASES

hobby	spectator sports	educational activities
escape	creative activities	competitive sports
perspective	collective activities	noncompetitive sports

PROBLEMS AND ACTIVITIES

1. Each student list the activities or hobbies which he enjoys most. Have a class committee make a talley of these and put them on the blackboard in order of most popular to least preferred activity.

2. Think of your favorite hobby. Has it helped you in any of the following ways: in making friends? in feeling at ease in some social situation? in giving you an idea of what you wish to choose for a vocation? in escaping your problems at times? in getting recognition?

3. Study the classification of hobbies as given in the table on page 279. Put two checks by all of those you now take part in and one check by all of those you think you might like. Now study those checked. Are they largely in one area? Do you think you should try some activities in areas where you have no interest now?

4. *Class report.* Be ready to give the story of some well-known person and his hobbies, or of a well-known person whose hobby became his vocation and thus led to his fame.

5. Does your school sponsor hobby clubs? If so, what are they and how are they organized?

6. Sometimes when school boards are cutting budgets they say, "Out with the frills." Hobby clubs would probably be considered "frills" by many people. How would you defend the club program to those opposed to it?

FILM

Better Use of Leisure Time — 10 minutes, sound, Coronet

MORE ABOUT PHYSICAL AND MENTAL HEALTH

AMERICAN AUTOMOBILE ASSOCIATION, *Sportsmanlike Driving*. Washington 6, D. C., 1948.

ASSOCIATION OF CASUALTY AND SURETY COMPANIES, *Man and the Motor Car*. New York: Prentice-Hall, Inc., 1949.

BILLETT, ROY O. AND J. WENDELL YEO, *Growing Up*. Boston: D. C. Heath and Company, 1951, ch. 5.

CRAWFORD, JOHN E. AND LUTHER E. WOODWARD, *Better Ways of Growing Up*. Philadelphia: The Muhlenberg Press, 1948, chs. 11–14.

CRAWFORD, CLAUDE, E. G. COOLEY, C. C. TRILLINGHAM, EMERY STOOPS, *Living Your Life*. Boston: D. C. Heath and Company, 2nd ed., 1953, chs. 12–14.

DEARBORN, NED H. AND BILL ANDREWS, *Your Safety Handbook*. Chicago: Science Research Associates, Inc., 1952.

DIMOND, STANLEY E., *You and Your Problems*. Chicago: Science Research Associates, Inc., 1952.

ENGLISH, O. SPURGEON AND CONSTANCE J. FOSTER, *Your Behavior Problems*. Chicago: Science Research Associates, Inc., 1952.

FEDDER, RUTH, *A Girl Grows Up*. New York: McGraw-Hill Book Company, Inc., 1948, chs. 9–10.

GALLAGHER, J. ROSWELL, *You and Your Health*. Chicago: Science Research Associates, Inc., 1952.

————, *Deft Driving*. Dearborn: Ford Motor Company, 1952.

McCARTHY, RAYMOND G., *Facts About Alcohol*. Chicago: Science Research Associates, Inc., 1952.

McKOWN, HARRY C., *A Boy Grows Up*. New York: McGraw-Hill Book Company, Inc., 1949, chs. 12–15.

MENNINGER, WILLIAM C., *Enjoying Leisure Time*. Chicago: Science Research Associates, Inc., 1950.

————, *Understanding Yourself*. Chicago: Science Research Associates, Inc., 1948.

RANDOLPH, HELEN R., ERMA PIXLEY, DOROTHY D. DUGGAN AND FRED McKINNEY, *You and Your Life*. Boston: Houghton Mifflin Company, 1951, chs. 7–12; 25–34.

REMMERS, HERMANN H. AND C. G. HACKETT, *What Are Your Problems?* Chicago: Science Research Associates, Inc., 1952.

REMMERS, HERMANN H. AND ROBERT H. BAUERNFEIND, *Your Problems: How to Handle Them*. Chicago: Science Research Associates, Inc., 1953.

SEASHORE, ROBERT H. AND A. C. VAN DUSEN, *How to Solve Your Problems*. Chicago: Science Research Associates, Inc., 1952.

SHACTER, HELEN, *Understanding Ourselves*. Bloomington: McKnight & McKnight, 1945, chs. 9–17.

————, *How Personalities Grow*. Bloomington: McKnight & McKnight, 1949, chs. 10–18.

SPALDING, WILLIARD B. AND JOHN R. MONTAGUE, *Alcohol and Human Affairs*. Yonkers-on-Hudson: World Book Company, 1949.

SCHERF, C. H., *Do Your Own Thinking*. New York: McGraw-Hill Book Co., Inc., 1948.

THE TRAVELERS INSURANCE COMPANIES, *Who Me?* Hartford: Connecticut. Published annually. Free.

VOGEL, VICTOR H. AND VIRGINIA E. VOGEL, *Facts about Narcotics*. Chicago: Science Research Associates, Inc., 1952.

Part Six

GROWING UP
ECONOMICALLY

YOUR PART-TIME WORK

27

Earlier sections of this book have discussed different kinds of maturity — physical, emotional, mental, social, and chronological. This final section will consider economic maturing, your growing up in becoming able to support yourself and others.

It used to be that only boys had to think about choosing a vocation and preparing to earn a living. Girls were not concerned with the world of work outside the home. Their task was to learn to manage family income wisely, to run a household, and to contribute to the family's living through work such as canning fruits and vegetables, raising chickens or a garden, baking, and sewing.

Almost all work was clearly classified as either man's work or woman's work. Men did not do housework or care for children; women did not do office work or factory work, or drive busses, or become mechanics. But today, one-third of the total labor force in this country is made up of women. One-half of married women work at jobs outside the home during the first year of marriage, and one-fifth of all mothers work at outside jobs.

There is now no clear line drawn between man's work and woman's work. Many fathers enjoy helping to care for the babies and the small children. They accept that as a part of their responsibility. Many boys are expected to help with housework at home just as their sisters are expected to learn to do something besides housework. A boy who thinks that a man should not be seen working in the kitchen or that it is sissy to help clean house or do the family laundry — that boy is old-fashioned in his viewpoint. A girl is just as old-fashioned if she believes that because she plans to marry and have a family she needs to give no thought at all to a vocation or to preparing to support herself.

285

AMOUNT OF WORK EXPERIENCE

65%

46%

32%

40%

Reported by High School Youth

14%

3%

Full Time Work Experience
Only Part Time Work Experience
No Work Experience

From *Youth and the World of Work* (East Lansing: Michigan State College, 1949), p. 2.

Part-time jobs

Part-time jobs are your first step in developing your ability to support yourself. If you never had a job until you reached the age of twenty-one, you might have trouble holding that job. You would have so much to learn that your employer might lose patience with you. Your friends who had some job experience while they were growing up would have learned many things which you would have yet to learn about becoming a successful worker. A study of sophomores and seniors in Michigan high schools shows that most students have had firsthand experience with jobs. The jobs may differ from those they will hold after leaving school, but they provide a realistic basis for ideas about work and a possible future vocation.

Personality and work

Many studies have been made to find out what employers like in workers and which is more important in holding a job, knowledge and skills or personality. In general, such studies show that you might rate the highest in your class in bookkeeping and mathematics and yet lose a job as a bookkeeper if you could not get along with your employer or with other workers. The classmate who knows much less in the subject — but who understands other people and gets along well with others — might win an early promotion at the same job. This means that while you are working at learning and getting experience in special work skills, you must also work at increasing your understanding of other people and overcoming undesirable personality traits in yourself. Working skills are a necessity in any vocation, but also of very great importance is the ability to get along with others.

The way you work on a part-time job tells something about what kind of a worker you will be later on a full-time job. The traits you are developing now and the habits of work you are forming will be important in your later vocation.

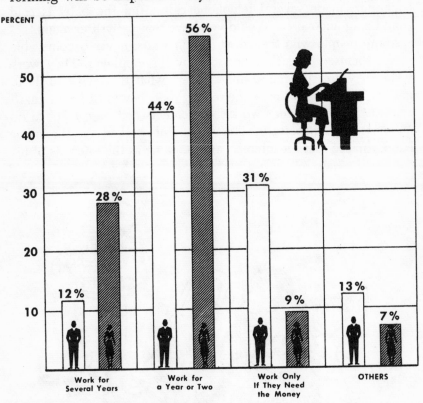

From *Youth and the World of Work*, p. 6.

● Most high school youth think girls should work before marriage; 7,000 Michigan high school students thought so. Do you agree? Why do fewer boys than girls agree? What are arguments for and against?

Your Part-Time Work   287

Suggestions for success on a job

Put yourself in the place of the employer. One of the best ways to look at yourself to see what type of a worker you are is to try to put yourself in the place of an employer. If you were hiring a boy by the hour to mow a lawn regularly, what would you want the boy to do? If he brought a friend along, and the two stood around talking, had a water fight with the hose, and wrestled on the lawn, what would you think? Or let's assume that you have hired a babysitter for your two small children. When you come home, you find your babysitter has: had three friends in for the evening; had a dance in the living room; taken food from the refrigerator; made several telephone calls. And the baby is cold from being uncovered. Would you have that babysitter again?

Many people who are grown up, in years, never become able to see themselves as they are seen by the employer. They work when they are supervised and do only what they have to do to get by. They seem to have the feeling that they must be on guard against their employer's work requirements and be careful to do no more than necessary. The successful worker, on the other hand, can see that his interests are the same as the interests of his

● Is this employer getting his money's worth?

employer: to get the job done and done right so that both can feel satisfied about their working arrangement.

If you find it easy to accept suggestions from others, your success on a job will be easier. There are many things to learn about most types of work, and you will learn more quickly if you listen for suggestions and follow them.

Do the work the way your employer wants it done. A part of your growing up is getting ideas of your own and carrying them out. If you think of a good way to do a piece of work, your way makes sense to you, and what the employer has suggested may seem silly. Nevertheless, in part-time jobs, you need first to learn to follow directions. Later, as you become a more experienced worker, you will have more opportunities to use your initiative.

If your part-time job is babysitting and the mother suggests that the baby is to be put to bed at eight, then the time to put the baby to bed is at eight and not eight-thirty or nine.

If the man wants the lawn mowed across one way and then over again the other way, that is the way to mow his lawn. You may think it unnecessary to mow the lawn twice, once lengthwise and again crosswise; it may seem that if you do a good job mowing it once one way, he will never know the difference. But in such a case you have been hired to do a piece of work as your employer wants it done; and if he gives specific directions, a good worker will follow them.

Jack was hired to work in a small neighborhood grocery store during his vacation. There were many jobs to be done around the store. Since Jack was the youngest and did not have any work experience, the store owner assigned Jack to keeping the shelves stocked and to sweeping out. Jack liked working at the store, but he did not care for the jobs assigned to him. The job Jack really liked was standing behind the check-out stand and running the cash register. At first, Jack would find excuses to fill in at the check-out stand when the other clerk was busy. But gradually he spent more and more time there, and the older clerk had to do the stock work. Jack went away for a short vacation with his parents; and when he returned, the store owner told him that he preferred to keep Bill, who had filled in during Jack's absence. The owner suggested that Jack should try working for someone else. Jack was hurt, and he could not figure out why he should not have his job

Coronet Films.

back. He was sure that he was just as good a worker as Bill.

All of us are at times selfish. Like the small child, we want our own way about things and can see only our own viewpoint. In work situations, it is necessary to overcome selfishness. There will be times when you would rather let the other fellow do the unpleasant work. And like Jack and his store job, you may tell yourself that you can do the more pleasant task better. Jack was selfish about wanting to run the cash register instead of moving stock to shelves. He lost his job to Bill, who learned to control his wishes and do what was expected. Bill watched everything that went on in the store and tried to help out where most needed. He observed when the shelves needed stocking and when the floor was dirty. He could put himself in the place of the employer and do the things that the employer wanted done. He would have preferred to stay at the counter and run the cash register, but he developed work habits that will help him in any job. Jack still has some important fundamentals to learn.

Do more than is expected. It is good practice to do more than is expected when working at a part-time job. The employer wants to feel that he is getting his money's worth. When you get older and get a full-time job, then there will probably be more of a set standard about exactly what work the job requires. But as you are beginning your work experience, it is better to develop the attitude of not being afraid that you will work too much for what you are paid. Some adult workers are always holding back in what they do, and they are often critical of other workers who do a full day's work. Their attitude of holding back actually makes their work harder for them than it would be if they pitched in and did their best. They are the workers who are always changing jobs.

Be interested in the job. When working for another person, become interested in the job and show that while you are at work your mind is on the job. The work is important to your employer, and he wants you to feel that it is important too.

Whether the job is carrying out groceries at a food market, delivering papers, babysitting, caring for a furnace, or shoveling snow, the worker is being paid for the time he is spending on the job, and he owes the work his entire attention. Even a part-time job that does not demand much skill does require attention.

The boy who is hired to carry out groceries at a market, but who spends time visiting with friends who come in instead of being at hand, ready when he is needed, will fail at his job just as much as a mechanic would fail if he knew nothing about cars.

Punctuality. A habit that is essential for success in part-time work and in your later vocation is punctuality. In some homes, the parents take all responsibility for seeing that children are on time for school even up to the time when the children are in high school. If your mother still calls you three or four times in the morning to get you up in time for school, she needs to break her bad habit. It is time you got yourself up without being called and took the responsibility for meeting all your obligations on time.

● Employers like cheerful workers.

Your Part-Time Work

291

A young man, twenty-one years old and a college senior, once missed an important final examination and telephoned the professor with this excuse, "My mother didn't get me up in time so that I could get to the campus for the examination." If that young man a few years from now gets fired from a job for failing to show up for work, will he expect his employer to accept the excuse, "My wife didn't get me up"? Will he be a successful worker?

Most of the world's work, like your school life, is organized on the basis of hours. The successful worker must learn early to pay attention to the time and to make it a habit to be on time. The punctual person is on time *always;* even a few lapses and failures to be on time mark one as an unpunctual person.

Dependability. If you agree to work on Saturday for Mr. Jones, does it mean that you will show up for work on Saturday no matter how many other attractive things to do may come up? Adults who are hiring young people for part-time work soon learn which ones are dependable. Could an employer ever say of you, "Yes, Dick is a good worker when he shows up, but you can't be sure he *will* show up," or "Mary isn't dependable; she comes late and usually has to go home early or forgets entirely about her job."

Cheerfulness. One personality trait that rates especially high in work relationships is cheerfulness. You have probably found that it is much more pleasant to work for those who are cheerful, people who show that they are enjoying life. Employers are the same. They like to have cheerful people around them. People who are moody and seem to carry all of the problems of the world on their shoulders are usually not very enjoyable to work with.

Appearance. Another important thing to watch is your personal appearance when on part-time jobs. Being neat and clean is important on all jobs. What you will wear will depend upon the job. Clean levis may be appropriate for many odd jobs. Expensive clothes are not necessary and, on many jobs, would be out of place.

Are you a good worker?

Now that you have read the discussion, how would you rate yourself as a worker? We have included a set of questions that may help you to rate your work maturity. Study these questions and then rate yourself.

HOW DO YOU RATE AS A WORKER?

	Never	Some-times	Usually	Always
	0	4	7	10
1. I accept suggestions from my employer.				
2. I am cheerful on the job.				
3. People ask me to work for them again, after they have tried me.				
4. I put myself in the place of the employer and try to do the work the way he wants it done.				
5. I work whether the employer is supervising me or not.				
6. I do more than is expected of me.				
7. I take an interest in the work I am doing.				
8. I report for work when I say I will.				
9. I am neat and clean when reporting for work.				
10. People say I am a dependable worker.				
Total each column				
Total points				

293

● Marilyn has not yet worked out a good schedule for her part-time job and her studying. *(Luoma Photos.)*

Some cautions about part-time work

Although it is good to have part-time jobs as you grow up economically, a good thing can be bad if not used properly or if over done. Let's look at some things which it is wise to guard against when you take a part-time job.

Letting your job hinder your school work. Sometimes young people become so interested in a part-time job and the money they are making that they neglect the "full-time job" they already have. Your full-time job now is your school work. It may be a thrill to earn your own money and, for the first time, to be able to buy the things you want. Or you may get great pleasure out of the work itself. Perhaps your work in a garage after school is so interesting that school work seems unimportant, and you may feel that you do not have time for school work. But getting an education is most important in the long run. Many people have become so interested in a part-time job that they quit school to work full time, only to discover later that they could not advance in their work because of a lack of education. Labor records show that most high school graduates earn as much by the time they are twenty-five years old as the average "drop-out" (the person who quit school before finishing high school) is able to earn when he is forty-five — also that high school graduates are twice as likely to earn top salaries, and their chances for steady employment improve with each year of schooling they have had.

So, no matter how much you like your part-time job, keep it in its place. Learn all you can from your part-time job, but don't let it interfere with your school work. A high school diploma will be worth more to you in the future than all the money you can earn right now.

Health and work. Avoid after-school or week-end jobs which upset your regular routine of eating and sleeping or which require you to work under unhealthful conditions. Let older workers take these jobs. In the long run, your health is going to be more important to you than any amount of money you make now and more important, also, than the job experience you might get.

In cities, many boys earn by taking morning paper routes. If you are going to take a job which requires you to miss your morning sleep, then you must get to bed early, so that you get your regular number of hours of sleep. Otherwise, your school work will suffer. If you cannot get your sleep, then it would be better to take a job which did not require early or late hours or to do less work outside of your school work.

REVIEW QUESTIONS

1. How does the division of the work of men and women differ today from the way it was in former years?

2. Why is it important to have a part-time job?

3. Why is the personality of the worker as important as knowledge and skills?

4. Why can one became a better worker by putting himself in the place of the employer?

5. Why did Jack lose his job in the grocery store? What does he still have to learn?

6. Why is it important to be interested in the job one is doing?

7. When do you develop the habit of punctuality in your life, before or after you get your first job?

8. How can you demonstrate that you are a dependable worker?

9. How may a part-time job become a hindrance?

KEY WORDS AND PHRASES

initiative   punctuality   dependability

PROBLEMS AND ACTIVITIES

1. Each class member be prepared to give his experience as a part-time worker. Pay particular attention to the things you learned about personality and success on the job.
2. Each student talk to his parents or other adults about their experience in part-time jobs when they were young and find out whether they feel that they learned things which helped them in their life work.
3. *Class survey.* What part-time jobs are available for students in your school or community? Each student be prepared to tell about at least one part-time job he knows about. Put all of your information together and make up a part-time job inventory for your community.
4. Some studies have been done which show that students who have part-time jobs also make better grades, on the average. What might be some reasons for this?
5. Interview at least one employer and ask him what traits he likes best in his workers. Be ready to report to the class.

FILMS

Helping in the Care of Younger Children — 10 minutes, sound, Coronet
Personal Qualities for Job Success — 10 minutes, sound, Coronet
How to Keep a Job — 10 minutes, sound, Coronet
Earning Money While Going to School — 10 minutes, sound, Coronet
You and Your Work — 10 minutes, sound, Coronet
See reading list at end of Part Six, page 316.

YOUR FUTURE VOCATION

28

The preceding chapter discussed part-time jobs and how the experience gained in such jobs can help you become a successful adult worker. This chapter will discuss your lifetime work, or your vocation. Your final choice of a vocation may still be far in the future, but to think about it now may help you make a wise choice when the time comes to choose.

When should you decide upon your vocation?

Since you were a small child, you have probably been asked many times by older friends and relatives, "What are you going to be when you grow up?" Even as a freshman in high school, you may have been asked to tell on a questionnaire your probable future vocation.

Many people are troubled because they cannot answer such questions. Richard, a junior in high school, said, "For years people have asked me what I'm going to do, and I don't know. My math teacher said I ought to study to be an accountant because math is easy for me. I don't think I'd like being an accountant, but I don't know what else I'd like to do. My friend, Tom, has been sure, ever since he can remember, that he would be a doctor like his father. It would be a lot easier to be sure like that and not feel undecided. I guess there's something wrong with me that I haven't made up my mind yet what vocation to study for."

There was nothing wrong with Richard's indecision. In fact, Richard, who at sixteen or seventeen does not know what he wishes to be but is thinking about it and trying to learn all he can about possible vocational choices, may eventually make a far better choice than his friend, Tom, who believes that the question was well settled years ago.

297

● "... So much for his career at college. Then, of course, he'll go on to medical school—" *(Stan Fine and the Ladies' Home Journal.)*

Many times, young people, especially boys, decide very early to follow the vocation of the father or some other relative. Parents cannot help hoping that a son will follow in his father's footsteps and carry on the family business, continue with the family skills, keep the family farm going, or carry on the family tradition in law or medicine. Therefore, whether they mean to or not, parents often put pressure upon their sons so that, from childhood, the son may accept without question the fact that his vocational choice is settled.

Often such boys (and girls) find out many years later that they are not suited to the work they are doing. In personality or in aptitudes they may be much different from the parent whose vocation they are following. The truth is, in some cases, that the person himself never really made a vocational choice. The choice was made for him by others, who perhaps did not fully understand or consider his special traits and abilities.

Sometimes it has not been parents who caused a vocational choice to be made too early. A young person may admire greatly some one in a special line of work. The work may seem glamorous

Your Future Vocation

or interesting or well paid; and without considering his own characteristics, the young person may decide to prepare for that type of work, only to find later that he is not suited to it.

Your choice of a vocation is important for your whole life. It might be more comfortable to be able to answer promptly and positively when you are asked about your future work, but it is far better in the long run not to be stampeded into too early a choice.

While you are going to school, there is much that you can learn about vocations, and about yourself, to guide you in making a wise final choice.

Jobs yesterday and today

Deciding upon a vocation is more difficult today than it used to be. In earlier days, generation after generation, the children of farmers were likely to be farmers, and the children of business or professional people were likely to follow the father's business or profession. Now, when all children go to public school, they can prepare for any one of many vocations and are not limited, as formerly, by their family background.

Today, many more occupations are open to young people than in past generations, and the number is increasing. More than 30,000 different occupations are now open to people in the United States. As new discoveries and inventions are made, more occupations develop. The discovery of radar, television, and atomic power are leading to the development of hundreds of new occupations requiring all kinds of abilities and training.

If you use your next few school years to study yourself and to learn all you can about the different vocations that people follow, then you should be able eventually to select a vocation which will bring great satisfaction to you. To drift into a vocation with little guidance or thought may mean discontent and dissatisfaction with the work, later. A recent study of factory workers in all parts of the country asked the workers whether they would choose the same work again if they could choose now with all the facts at hand. Less than a third were satisfied with their present occupation. More than half said they would choose a different occupation if they could now make a choice.

Other studies show that a large percentage of people keep shifting from one occupation to another, trying to find a vocation in which they can be satisfied. Such hapazard drifting is a wasteful and unhappy way to find a suitable vocation. People could avoid much waste of time, money, and nervous energy if they could study the facts about different vocations before a choice has to be made.

Study yourself

There are two kinds of study you must do before you are ready to choose a vocation. You need to learn all you can about the many different possible vocations, and you need to study *yourself*.

Carl may believe he would like to be a medical doctor. He has looked carefully at the profession. He knows what the educational requirements are, and he could meet them. He knows that doctors make a reasonable income and that the practice of medicine is respected as a profession. But when Carl begins to look carefully at himself and his own characteristics, he may find that he is not suited at all to the medical profession. He always feels embarrassed and uncomfortable around sick people. Nervous people upset him. He finds it hard to make quick decisions, and any loss of sleep seriously cuts down his efficiency. All of those characteristics might be of no significance in some kinds of jobs, but they would be serious handicaps for a doctor.

The first step, then, is to study yourself. What are you like? What types of experiences are especially hard for you to take? What things do you enjoy doing that some others might not enjoy? What are your special strengths and weaknesses? (Everyone has both.) Then look for a vocation that fits you. Avoid one that you would have to strain yourself into a different mold to fit, no matter how glamorous that vocation might seem.

Your mental ability and special aptitudes

The grades you make, the scores you get on intelligence tests, and the scores you get on special aptitude tests will give you some information to guide you in your vocational choice. Grade averages in school are not an absolute indication of intelligence. But they do tell something about whether or not you apply yourself

● Dick is getting help from the school counselor about vocations and about himself. Your school counselor will gladly give you information about vocations and about tests you might take to help you decide what vocations you would like to investigate. *(Coronet Films.)*

to what you have to do and how well you adjust to your school situation. With all their limitations, grades are one thing that must be considered when you plan for your future. Many vocations require a college education or at least some further education beyond high school. In order to consider any of such vocations, you must make certain grade averages in high school. If your average remains below "C," you will probably have to eliminate some vocations from your consideration. You may need to consider vocations that do not require a college education.

Tests have been constructed to measure special aptitudes in addition to general mental ability. These tests are probably given in your school. The results may be used to guide you in selecting a course of study in college or in a special school if you do not go to college. Your school guidance program attempts to help students get ready for jobs where they can use their special abilities. No one can be good in everything, but each one has some special ability. Your school record — including grades, intelligence tests, and aptitude tests — should help you know your possibilities. With 30,000 possible occupations, most people can find a place where their special abilities fit, if they have proper guidance.

● Several aptitude tests have been constructed to help measure special abilities required in different vocations. If your school provides this service in counseling, you may wish to take some of the tests. *(Coronet Films.)*

Physical factors

There are health factors which limit going into certain types of work. The person who does not have a rugged constitution would not be suited to forestry work or truck driving. The person with poor vision would not make an aeroplane pilot. The one with an extremely nervous and excitable temperament may not be suited to teaching or to other jobs that require working closely and harmoniously with people.

Are you unusually healthy and full of energy? Do you have any health conditions or factors which might handicap you in certain kinds of work but that would be of no importance in other jobs? You must evaluate yourself physically in relation to the requirements that different vocations make.

Do you have unusually good or rather poor muscular coordination? Are you quick in your movements, or are you a slow moving person? All such physical characteristics will have something to do with what work you can do best. Special aptitude tests that are given in your school will help you know yourself better on some of these points. But on some of them you can figure out for yourself what your traits are.

What do you like?

Are you happier working with other people or are you the lone-wolf type? Are you an outdoor or an indoor person? What kind of things do you like to do?

Sometimes a hobby can give a clue to one's real interests. It is said that Walt Disney was a poor student in school, that he constantly irritated his teachers because he spent all of his time drawing silly cartoons. His interest in drawing "silly" cartoons helped him get started on his life work.

Part-time jobs can also give a clue to what your interests are or are not. Warren worked in a cannery one summer. After working in the hot kitchen of the cannery, Warren decided that he was going to save his money and go to college. Before his summer work, he had thought the high factory wages were a good enough reason for giving up any idea of going to college. After his work in the cannery, he was certain he wanted to go to college and train for some type of skilled or professional work that he could do under conditions more pleasant than in the cannery.

Henry got a job working on a farm during the summer. He liked the work so much that he is considering going to the state agricultural school after high school. After trying it, he knows that he likes outdoor work.

● Bob has worked on a farm for two summers and likes farming. He plans to go to the state agricultural college. (Luoma Photos.)

Your philosophy of life and your vocation

Some thinking about what things matter most to you in life will be of help to you as you consider vocations.

Some people value financial success far above all other considerations. Others value leisure and time to relax and would be happier in a job that might bring a lower income but would allow them to live under less pressure than would be possible in a "better" job.

The person who puts special value on home life and close relationships with family would not be happy in a job that required much traveling and separation from his family.

Some people can not be satisfied in work, no matter how well paid, unless they feel that their work is useful and of service to their fellowmen. Others would consider the financial return the fundamental if not the sole consideration and would not be interested in serving others.

Those people who want to be useful in the world also have many different ideas about what is important or unimportant service. One person may believe the best service is through work fields such as teaching, nursing, the ministry, medicine, or social work. Another may believe the best service is through business or manufacturing, which produces things that add convenience or comfort to the daily lives of people.

The important thing is to know what you value as worth working for. You will be happiest in a job in which you feel your work is worth something according to your philosophy of life.

No one occupation

The many kinds of tests which have been constructed seem to show that there is not just one vocation for which a person is suited but that each with his special mental ability, personality, and interests could be successful in any one of several related vocations that require similar abilities. The people who have worked out these tests refer to related occupations as "families" of jobs.

Now that you have studied yourself and your own special make-up, you are ready to look at some of the possible vocations and sources of information about them.

REVIEW QUESTIONS

1. When should you decide upon your vocation?

2. What mistake do young people sometimes make in their vocational choice?

3. How does your deciding upon a vocation differ from the way your grandfather's generation decided upon vocations?

4. How many different occupations are open to young people today?

5. What two kinds of study should one do before deciding upon a vocation?

6. What is the difference between mental ability and special aptitudes?

7. How would mental ability guide one in looking ahead to a vocation?

8. How would physical and emotional health effect one's choice of a vocation?

9. Illustrate how hobbies or part-time jobs might guide one in his vocational choice.

10. How does one's philosophy of life affect his satisfaction and happiness in a vocation?

11. What are job "families"?

KEY WORDS AND PHRASES

aptitude tests	temperament	conception
intelligence tests	harmoniously	job families

PROBLEMS AND ACTIVITIES

1. Think of all the arguments you can for and against a boy's following the occupation of his father.

Your Future Vocation   305

2. *Special report.* One or two students in class make a study of all the vocational guidance testing and counseling available to students in your school. Report to the class.

3. Each student, after thinking about himself and his vocational interests, write a short paper discussing what type of work he thinks he might like to do and why he thinks his personality is fitted for that type of work.

4. *Special talk.* Have your vocational teacher or a vocational guidance advisor from your community talk to the class on the different vocational tests that are available.

FILMS

Choosing Your Occupation
Aptitudes and Occupations
See reading list at end of Part Six, page 316.

CONSIDERING POSSIBLE VOCATIONS

29

The statement that there are more than 30,000 different occupations open to people today may seem overwhelming. You know that you will not be able to learn about that many different occupations before you decide upon one to prepare for; however, the task is not as difficult as it appears.

The United States Employment Service lists all types of occupations in the *Dictionary of Occupational Titles*. People who have spent much time studying about occupations agree that most jobs can be classified into ten job families according to the *vocational interests* of workers. The jobs could be sorted into many other classifications, such as skills required for the job, years of education required for the job, or the income that they would bring. However, most helpful to you, first, would be to find out your vocational interests to see what general occupational job family or families might best suit you.

The table below lists ten general job families and gives some examples of the kinds of jobs that fall within each.

Many tests have been developed to help you determine in what area your vocational interests lie. One of the most commonly used is the Kuder Preference Record. If you have not taken this test, your school counselor may be able to provide it for you.

After you have found a field of interest, then it is sometimes helpful to think of yourself in terms of whether you like to work with *things*, to work with *people*, or to work with *ideas*. You may find that you like to work with things — tools or objects that can be handled. You may like agricultural or outdoor work, but within this field you wish to use tools, rather than manage people. If you are interested in clerical work, you might be most interested in the type of clerical work which keeps you in contact with people, such

THE TEN BASIC JOB FAMILIES WITH
EXAMPLES OF EACH

Job family	Job examples
Agricultural — Outdoor	forester, wheat farmer, livestock farmer, dairy worker, game warden, farm laborer
Athletic	athletic coach, professional athlete, playground director
Artistic — Musical	actor, artist, music critic, musician, designer, piano tuner, instructor in music
Clerical	file clerk, recorder, sorting, bank teller, statistician, bookkeeper
Literary	reporter, writer, poet, editor, critic, copywriter
Mechanical	toolmaker, machine operator, watchmaker, lens grinder
Personal Service	barber, cook, porter, butler, mortician, beautician, airplane hostess, taxi driver, caterer
Persuasive	politician, lawyer, salesman, auctioneer, bill collector, diplomat, advertising worker
Scientific	biologist, bacteriologist, chemist, inventor, physician, explorer
Social Service	camp counselor, social worker, minister, teacher, scout leader, farm advisor, nurse, YMCA worker

as a bank teller's job. Or it could be that your chief interest is in a research type of clerical work in which you would work with ideas more than with people or things.

Determining your interests is only the beginning. You must also match your personality and your abilities with the field of your greatest interest. You must also think of your possible chances to get an education to fit you for work in the job family that fits your interests.

In each general family of jobs there are occupations that have widely different requirements in education and training. That means that whatever your mental ability, or whether or not you can go to college, you can still find a job that suits your special traits and aptitudes. The boy who has a high mechanical interest may find work as an auto mechanic, a construction worker, toolmaker, machine operator, or an engineer in some very technical field. The jobs are different and require different years of training, but one who rates high in mechanical interests may fit into any of several jobs.

Considering specific jobs

You may find that your general interests seem to cut across several fields. It is true that many job interests overlap with interests in other job families. A study of some of the specific jobs shows that many require a combination of interests and are suited to the person with interests cutting across fields. The person in-

If I were employed by a concern I would prefer to work:

Entirely by myself   4%

Mostly by myself but with a few contacts with other employees   26%

With a small group of workers (under 25)   58%

As a member of a large group of workers   8%

No response   4%

(Opinions of 7,000 Michigan High School Students)

From *Youth and the World of Work,* p. 14.

● Are you interested in the clerical job family? *(Coronet Films.)*

terested in clerical work may also have a strong interest in social service work. Such a person might like, for example, working as a secretary in a social welfare office.

In considering specific occupations, remember what you have learned about yourself through any tests you have taken in your school guidance program. Think also what you have learned about your preferences through any part-time jobs you have had. Let us assume, for example, that you have found that your chief interest and ability lies in the general area of public contact or the persuasive job family. The next thing to do is to get all the information you can about the many different kinds of jobs that require making contacts with people. Your school will probably have pamphlets on different occupations to give you a start in your reading. The bibliographies in these pamphlets will suggest other sources where you may write for information. Possibly you can find other materials in your city or county library. If you have exhausted these sources, then you may wish to write to the following places for more information:

Occupational briefs. National Roster of Scientific and Specialized Personnel. Superintendent of Documents, U.S. Government Printing Office, Washington 25, D.C. 5¢ each. (Allow at least 3 weeks for this material.)

Occupational Abstracts. Personnel Services, Inc., Peapack, New Jersey. 25¢ each.

A study outline in considering vocations

As you consider each vocation, there are many things which you will want to think about.

Vocations which fit in with homemaking. If you are a girl and you find that your interest is in the general area of social service, and you also know that you wish to marry and have a family, then you should think of a type of social service job which would also fit in with being a wife and mother. It might appeal to you to train to be an airline hostess. But would that work fit in with being a wife and mother? You would probably have to give up the work when you married and you could not go back to it as part-time work if you found it necessary to help support your family later. In the same job family are such jobs as nursing or social work. These require some of the same skills and personality traits, yet may be continued at least part time after marriage. If you took nurses training, you would learn skills which could prepare you to help support the family if that ever became necessary. Your training would always be worthwhile to you as a mother, whether

Here are three different kinds of jobs. If I had my choice, I would pick a job which pays:

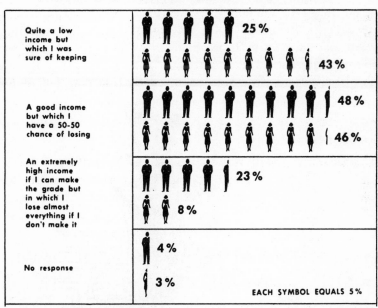

● One study of high school students revealed that they considered job security more important than high income. How do you feel on this question?

or not you had to use it as a means of support. Such considerations apply to many of the jobs you might be interested in, whether you are a boy or a girl.

Opportunities. In considering an occupation, one should also investigate the number of possible job openings. Work as an airline hostess may appeal to thousands of girls, but there may not be many openings in this type of work. On the other hand, it is said that airline hostess have opportunities to marry, so although there are relatively few jobs, there may be a rapid turnover of people in that work.

Studies of high school young people show that a much larger percentage plan to enter professional and "white-collar" jobs than there are professional and "white-collar" jobs available. Fewer plan to enter "blue-collar" jobs than are employed in "blue-collar" jobs today. The "blue-collar" and "white-collar" classification came about many years ago. Jobs in which a man could wear a white shirt without getting it dirty very quickly were called "white-collar" and those in which he worked with things or in places that put him into contact with dust, dirt, grease and such things were called "blue-collar" jobs. The classification has nothing to do with pay or even with prestige. Jobs that are extremely well-paid and require great technical knowledge and ability fall within both classifications. One study showed that 40 per cent of boys

● Fewer plan to enter blue-collar jobs than there are blue-collar jobs today.

Considering Possible Vocations

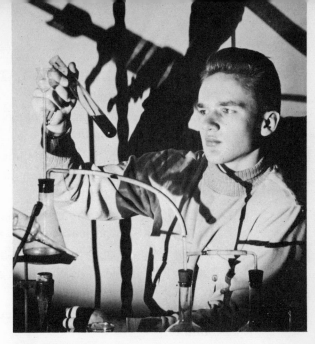

● Henry has always been interested in chemistry. He thinks he will go on with chemistry in college and train to be a research chemist. *(Luoma Photos.)*

hope to enter a profession while only 16 per cent of adult men in the section of the country where the study was made actually do work in a profession. On the other hand, only 26 per cent of the boys hoped to enter "blue-collar" jobs in factories or plants where men wear "work clothes." The study shows that many people have unrealistic or mistaken ideas about white collar and blue collar jobs.

School courses. In selecting courses next year, wherever you have a choice you might take courses that can give you greater understanding of the job family you feel you have most interest in. If you are interested in clerical work, try courses in typing, shorthand, bookkeeping, and possibly journalism.

The school courses that you take in the areas in which you think you may want to work, later, will help you to become more sure of your choices. Some people find that they do not like a type of work as well as they had thought they would like it. Others gain confidence as they study, and their eventual choice of a life work becomes easier.

From this chapter, you will have seen that it is not necessary to find your life work by trial and error, by a series of starts and stops after you are grown. While you are still in school, you can be learning many things that will help you later when the time comes to decide about your choice of a lifetime work.

REVIEW QUESTIONS

1. What different standards or choices may be used for sorting all jobs into job families?

2. What is probably the most common way of sorting jobs in job families? Name the job families in this method of classification.

3. What is the Kuder Preference Record and how is it used? Have you had experience with it, and has it been helpful?

4. Would it be possible for a person to find a job in any one of the ten job families if he could not go to college? Explain your answer.

5. Show how one's interests might cut across two or more job families.

6. What, in addition to interest in a certain vocation, is important to success in the vocation?

7. What sources might you consult for more information on specific vocations?

8. Are there questions which a girl, but not a boy, might wish to consider in selecting a vocation? Discuss.

9. What does the study of high school students show in their plans for "white-collar" and "blue-collar" jobs? How do you explain the student preferences? Does the type of community in which you live or the occupational tradition of your family influence your preference?

10. How can your high school study program help you in deciding upon your life work?

KEY WORDS AND PHRASES

vocational interests	mechanical interests	social worker
job family	social service	"white-collar"
profession	persuasive	"blue-collar"
	Kuder Preference Record	

Considering Possible Vocations

PROBLEMS AND ACTIVITIES

1. Make a list of jobs you think might interest you and then classify them within the ten different job families as given in the chapter.

2. After each of the jobs, write whether it would require working with things, people, or ideas.

3. Think of all the part-time or full-time jobs you have had. Now make a chart with the following headings and classify your job experience:

Name————————————————————

Name of jobs	What I did	Job family	I was working with things, people, ideas	I found the work interesting, not interesting.
1.				
2.				

Study your chart. Do you get any ideas of the type of work you seem to like? What job family or families suit you best?

4. Make a detailed study of one occupation and be able to give the following information:
   Job family
   Nature of work done
   Job opportunities
   Special aptitudes necessary
   Educational or special training required
   Steps one would take to enter this job
   Opportunities for advancement and other rewards, such as security, prestige, and others

5. Have one or more people from different vocations talk to your class about their work and how they happened to get into it, what its satisfactions are, etc.

6. *Interviews.* Interview people from different occupations and make a special report back to the class. You might use the outline suggested in problem 4 in your interview.

FILMS

Do I Want to be a Secretary? — 10 minutes, sound, Coronet
How to Investigate Vocations — 10 minutes, sound, Coronet
Finding the Right Job — 10 minutes, sound, Coronet

MORE ABOUT GROWING UP ECONOMICALLY

BILLET, ROY O. and J. WENDELL YEO, *Growing Up*. Boston: D. C. Heath and Company, 1951, ch. 10.

BLISS, WALTON B., *Personality and School*. Boston: Allyn and Bacon, 1951, part 4.

CHAPMAN, PAUL W., *Your Personality and Your Job*. Chicago: Science Research Associates, Inc., 1949.

CHRISTENSEN, THOMAS E., *Getting Job Experience*. Chicago: Science Research Associates, Inc., 1953.

COSGROVE, MARJORIE C., and MARY I. JOSEY, *About You*. Chicago: Science Research Associates, Inc., 1952, ch. 10.

CRAWFORD, CLAUDE C., E. G. COOLEY, C. C. TRILLINGHAM, EMERY STOOPS, *Living Your Life*, 2nd ed., Boston: D. C. Heath and Company, 1953, ch. 10.

DETJEN, MARY FORD and ERVIN WINFRED DETJEN, *Your Plans for the Future*. New York: McGraw-Hill Book Company, Inc., 1947.

DETJEN, MARY FORD and ERVIN WINFRED DETJEN, *Your High School Days*. New York: McGraw-Hill Book Company, Inc., 1947, chs. 5–6.

DREESE, MITCHELL, *How to Get the Job*. Chicago: Science Research Associates, Inc., 1953.

FEDDER, RUTH, *A Girl Grows Up*. New York: McGraw-Hill Book Company, Inc., 1948, ch. 8.

HUMPHREYS, J. ANTHONY, *Choosing Your Career*. Chicago: Science Research Associates, Inc., 1952.

KITCH, DONALD E., *Exploring the World of Jobs*. Chicago: Science Research Associates, Inc., 1952.

KUDER, G. FREDERIC and BLANCHE B. PAULSON, *Discovering Your Real Interests*. Chicago: Science Research Associates, Inc., 1953.

McKown, Harry C., *A Boy Grows Up*. New York: McGraw-Hill Book Company, Inc., 1949, chs. 16–19; 21.

Neugarten, Bernice L., Fred R. Bellmar, W. Russell Shull, Morris R. Lewenstein, William E. Henry, *Planning My Future*. Chicago: National Forum Inc., 1951, chs., 1–20.

Randolph, Helen R., Erma Pixley, Dorothy D. Duggan and Fred McKinney, *You and Your Life*. Boston: Houghton Mifflin Company, 1951, chs., 21–24.

Stoops, Emery and Lucile Rosenheim, *Planning Your Job Future*. Chicago: Science Research Associates, Inc., 1953.

United States Department of Labor, Bureau of Employment Security, *Job Guide for Young Workers*, 1953 ed. Superintendent of Documents, U.S. Printing Office, Washington 25, D.C. (20¢).

Zimand, Gertrude Folks, *Just a Minute*. New York: National Child Labor Committee, 1953. (Write for this recent study of teenagers who drop out of school. 419 Fourth Avenue, New York 16, New York.)

APPENDIX

RENTAL LIBRARIES FOR EDUCATIONAL FILMS

There are many rental libraries today in all states which will be glad to give you information on films available. Many counties and states now have free film libraries. The rental libraries listed below should have all of the films which are recommended for use with the text.

Alabama

A-V Aids Serv., U. of Ala., University

Arizona

Bureau of A-V Aids, Arizona State Coll., Tempe
Extension Div., U. of Ariz., Tucson

Arkansas

Dept. of Pub. Rel., State Teachers Coll., Conway
A-V Serv., State Dept. of Educ., Little Rock
A-V Aids Serv., State College, State College

California

Extension Div., U. of Calif., Berkeley
Ideal Pictures, 8226 Olympic Blvd., Beverly Hills
Extension Div., U. of Calif., Los Angeles
Ideal Pictures, 4247 Piedmont, Oakland 11
Photo & Sound, 116 Natoma, San Francisco

Colorado

Extension Div., U. of Colo., Boulder
Eastin Pictures, Bank Bldg., Colo. Springs
Ideal Pictures, 714 18th, Denver 2
Instr. Materials Center, State College, Greeley

Connecticut

Pix Film Service, 34 E. Putnam, Greenwich

District of Columbia

Paul L. Brand & Son, 2153 "K" St., N.W., Washington 7

Florida

Dept. of Visual Inst., Gen. Ext. Div., U. of Florida, Gainesville
Ideal Pictures, 1348 N. Miami, Miami 36
A-V Service, Florida State U., Tallahassee

Georgia

Extension Div., U. of Georgia, Athens
Ideal Pictures, 52 Auburn, N.E., Atlanta 3

Idaho

Film Library, State College, Pocatello

Illinois

Watland Inc., 13039 S. Western, Blue Island
A-V Aids Serv., Southern Ill. U., Carbondale
Visual Aids Serv., U. of Ill., Champaign
Ideal Pictures, 58 E. S. Water, Chicago 1
Selected Films, 410 Green Bay Road, Kenilworth
Lundgren's Camera Shop, 419–7th St., Rockford

Indiana

A-V Center, Indiana U., Bloomington

Iowa

Visual Inst. Serv., State Coll., Ames
Eastin Pictures, Putnam Bldg., Davenport
Ideal Pictures, 2109 Forest Ave., Box 1130, Des Moines
Extension Div., U. of Iowa, Iowa City

Kansas

Extension Div., U. of Kansas, Lawrence
Leffingwell's, 210 S. Santa Fe, Salina

Kentucky

Ideal Pictures, 422 W. Liberty, Louisville 2
Dept. of Extension, U. of Kentucky, Lexington

Louisiana

Ideal Pictures, 211½ Murray St., Alexandria

Maryland

Kunz Motion Pic. Serv., 426 N. Calvert, Baltimore
Ideal Pictures, 537 N. Howard St., Baltimore 1

Massachusetts

Ideal Pictures, 40 Melrose, Boston 16
Visual Aids Serv., Boston U., Boston
Visual Education Service, 116 Newbury St., Boston 16

Michigan

A-V Educ. Center, U. of Michigan, 4028 Adm. Bldg., Ann Arbor
Ideal Pictures, 7338 Woodward, Detroit 2
A-V Center, Michigan State College, East Lansing
Locke Films, 124 W. South, Kalamazoo

Minnesota

Ideal Pictures, 1915 Chicago, Minneapolis 4
Midwest A-V Serv., 10 West 25th St., Minneapolis
Extension Serv., U. of Minnesota, Minneapolis

Mississippi

School of Educ., U. of Mississippi, University

Missouri

Extension Div., U. of Missouri, Columbia
Ideal Pictures, 1020 Oak, Kansas City 6
Swank Motion Pics., 614 N. Skinker, St. Louis

Montana

Dept. of Vis. Educ., State Dept. of Educ., Helena

Nebraska

Extension Div., U. of Nebraska, Lincoln
Modern Sound Pictures, Inc., 1410 Howard St., Omaha 2

New Jersey

Film Library, State Museum, Trenton

New Mexico

Film Library, E. New Mexico U., Portales

New York

Museum of Science, Humboldt Park, Buffalo
Ideal Pictures, 1558 Main, Buffalo 8
Amer. Museum of Nat'l History, 79th & Central Pk. West,
    New York 24
Ideal Pictures, 233-239 W. 42nd St., New York 36
Educ. Film Library, Syracuse U., Syracuse

North Carolina

Extension Div., U. of N. Carolina, Chapel Hill
National School Supply Co., 14 Glenwood Av., Raleigh

North Dakota

Div. of Supervised Study, Agric. Coll., Fargo
The Starline Co., Box 1152, Grand Forks

Ohio

Ideal Pictures, 125 E. Sixth St., Cincinnati 2
Church School Pictures, 1118 Walnut, Cleveland 14
Sunray Films, 2108 Payne, Cleveland
Slide & Film Exch., State Dept. of Educ., Columbus
Twyman Films, 400 W. 1st, Dayton
Ideal Pictures, Farmers Bank Bldg., Mansfield
M. H. Martin Co., 1118 Lincoln Way East, Massillon

Oklahoma

Extension Div., U. of Oklahoma, Norman
Ideal Pictures, 611 W. Grand, Oklahoma City
Bureau of Film Serv., A & M Coll., Stillwater

Oregon

Visual Inst. Serv., State Coll., Corvallis
Ideal Pictures, 915 S.W. 10th, Portland 5

Pennsylvania

J. P. Lilley & Son, 928 N. 3rd, Harrisburg
B. E. George, Hawthorne
Indiana Film Library, Indiana
Millersville Film Library, Millersville
Ideal Pictures, 1733 Sansom St., Philadelphia 3
PCW Film Library, Coll. for Women, Pittsburgh
L. C. Vath, A-V Aids, P. O. Box "C", Sharpsville
A-V Aids Library, Pa. State University, State College

South Carolina

Extension Div., U. of S. Carolina, Columbia

South Dakota

Taylor Films, 79 Third St., S.E., Huron

Tennessee

Eastin Pictures, 830 Cherry, Chattanooga
Extension Div., U. of Tennessee, Knoxville
Extension Div., U. T. Jr. Coll., Martin
Ideal Pictures, 18 S. 3rd, Memphis 3
U. Extension Div., 2321 West End, Nashville
A-V Dept., Methodist Publishing House, Nashville 2

Texas

Dept. of Visual Educ., State Dept. of Educ., Austin
Extension Div., U. of Texas, Austin
Ideal Pictures, 2010 N. Lamar St., Dallas
Film Library, Baylor U., Waco

Utah

Bureau of A-V Inst., Brigham Young U., Provo
Bureau of A-V Educ., U. of Utah, Salt Lake City
Ideal Pictures, 54 Orpheum Ave., Salt Lake City

Virginia

Ideal Pictures, 219 E. Main, Richmond 19

Washington

Dept. of Visual Educ., Coll. of Educ., Ellensburg

Washington (Cont'd.)

Extension Div., State Coll., Pullman
Instr. Materials Center, U. of Wash., Seattle 5

West Virginia

Pavis Electronics & Supply Co., P.O. Box 6095, Charleston 2

Wisconsin

Fond du Lac Camera Center, 7 S. Main, Fond du Lac
Tip Top Visual Serv., 1403 Travis, La Crosse
Extension Div., U. of Wisconsin, Madison
Roa's Films, 844 N. Plankinton, Milwaukee 3

Canada

Div. of Visual Inst., U. of Alberta, Edmonto, Alberta
Benograph, 1330 Sherbrooke W., Montreal, Quebec
Benograph, 108 Peter St., Toronto, Ontario
Benograph, 269 Edmonton St., Winnipeg, Manitoba
Benograph, 577 Granville St., Vancouver, B. C.

Hawaii

Ideal Pictures, 1370 S. Beretania, Honolulu

Ireland

National Film Institute, 29 Dame St., Dublin

Philippines

Benitez and Co., Ltd., State Bldg., Manila

Puerto Rico

Commissioner of Educ., San Juan

INDEX

Cliques, 51–59
Clothes:
  choosing, 40
  conflict over (see Family), 195–200
  personality and, 40
  responsibility for, 130
Compensation, 250
Complexion worries, 36, 39
Compliments, 52
Constitution:
  Bill of Rights, 179–184
  rights in, 156
Conversation, 69–70
Cooley, E. G., 190, 223, 282, 316
Cooperation, development of, 19
Cosgrove, Marjorie, 47, 118, 316
Cosmetics, use of, 42–45
Counseling:
  help with problems, 239
  vocations and, 301
Crawford, Claude C., 190, 223, 282, 316
Crawford, John E., 47, 118, 282
Crushes, 77

D

Daly, Maureen, 118
Dating:
  advantages of steady, 95–96, 99
  age for, 86–88
  asking for dates, 88–89
  calling for date, 105, 108
  conversation and, 111
  curfew laws and, 101
  developing skills in, 85–119
  disadvantages of steady, 96–99
  eating and, 108, 110
  flowers and, 106, 109
  getting dates, 88–91
  good night kiss, 111–113
  hobbies and, 274
  how frequent, 91–92
  manners and, 105–117
  movies and, 107
  reasons for, 85
  saying good night, 108, 111–113
  saying no, 90–91
  self rating test (boys), 115
  self rating test (girls), 114
  steady, 95–100
  studies of high school students on, 87, 89, 90, 92, 101, 102, 109, 110
  transportation, 106
Dearborn, Ned H., 282
Decisions:
  choosing friends, 206

Decisions (cont.):
  moral, 168–172
  smoking, 208–212
Democracy, rights in, 179–185
  moral decisions and, 172
Dependability and jobs, 292
Depth perception, 258
Desire to be like others, 9
Detjen, Ervin, 118, 190, 223, 316
Detjen, Mary F., 118, 190, 223, 316
Dictionary of Occupational Titles, 307
Diet (see Health)
Digestion and emotions, 81
Discrimination, 156
Dreese, Mitchell, 316
Driving:
  accident proneness and, 256–259
  age for 165–166
  attitudes and, 260
  privileges and obligations of, 121–124
  tests of emotional factors in, 260–262
  tests of vision, 258
Drugs and mental health, 266–269
Duggan, Dorothy D., 119, 191, 223, 283, 317

E

Egg cell, 27–29
Emotional growth, 74–84
Emotional maturity, 74–84
Employment, part-time work and, 285–296
English, O. Spurgeon, 282
Environment:
  development of inherited ability, 31–32
  personality and, 15–26
Escapes from problems, 256–271
  (see also Mental health)
Exercise (see Health)

F

Family:
  attitudes on money, 21
  being critical of, 193
  choosing clothes, 195–200
  choosing friends, 206
  conflicts and, 195–200
  decisions and, 205–214
  development of likes and dislikes in, 18
  favorites in, 217
  jealousies and, 215–216
  perspective on, 194–195
  personality and your, 15–22